ETHIOPIA

Highlights

Philip Briggs

Edition 1

Bradt Travel Guides Ltd, UK
The Globe Pequot Press Inc, USA

Bradt

5/25/2019

About this book

One of Bradt's most popular titles since it was first published in 1995 has been its guidebook to Ethiopia, a 600-page tome that covers almost every accessible corner of the country in rigorous detail, supplemented by long lists of hotels and local eateries and overviews of public transport targeted at backpackers and independent travellers. Written by the same author as our established Ethiopia guidebook, *Ethiopia Highlights* is a more selective book aimed mainly at visitors who plan to join an organised tour covering the country's main highlights. As such, it has two main aims: first, to help those considering a trip to Ethiopia to decide what they'd like to see and do, and therefore to construct their itinerary or liaise with tour operators in an informed way; and, second, to provide an entertaining, colourful and informative guide to carry on the trip itself. With that in mind, the book provides overviews of every town, reserve and city that ranks as a possible highlight, a quick summary of practicalities and a short list of recommended accommodation. The selections are made by Philip Briggs, who is one of the world's most renowned guidebook writers on Africa. In addition, we have called upon the expertise of both local and international tour operators – those that know best what the country has to offer – to recommend their favourite itineraries and activities.

These tour operators were invited to contribute on the basis of their reputations for excellence; they also made a payment towards the production costs of the book.

These pages are unique in bringing together the selections of a top writer and experienced operators, ensuring this is a useful guidebook for those planning an organised tour to Ethiopia.

You can read a description of each of these tour operators on pages 68–9.

Feedback request

If you have any comments about this guide (good or bad), we would welcome your feedback. Please email us on ℮ info@ bradtguides.com. Go to http://updates.bradtguides.com/ethiopia for updated news and information.

Author

Born in the UK and raised in South Africa, Philip Briggs has been exploring the highways, byways and backwaters of Africa since 1986, when he backpacked from Nairobi to Cape Town. In 1991, he wrote the Bradt guide to South Africa, the first to be published internationally after the release of Nelson Mandela. Throughout the 1990s, Philip wrote a series of pioneering Bradt guides to destinations that were then – and in some cases still are – otherwise practically uncharted by the travel publishing industry. These include the first dedicated guidebook to Ethiopia, now in its sixth edition. He still spends at least four months on the road every year, usually accompanied by his wife, the travel photographer Ariadne Van Zandbergen, and spends the rest of his time battering away at a keyboard in the sleepy village of Bergville, South Africa.

Author's story

My first contact with things Ethiopian came at a Nairobi restaurant run by Ethiopian refugees. The food was extraordinary – a fiery orange stew called *kai wat*, splattered on what looked like a piece of foam rubber with the lateral dimensions of a bicycle tyre. But even that didn't prepare me for what was to follow, as a troupe of white-robed musicians approached our table, and erupted into smirking discord. Then, signalled by an alarming vibrato shriek, all hell burst loose in the form of a solitary Ethiopian dancer, mouth contorted into a psychotically rapturous grimace, eyes aglow, shoulders jerking and twitching in a manic, dislocating rhythm. I left that room with one overwhelming impression: Ethiopians are completely bonkers. I knew, too, that I had to visit their country.

A year later, in July 1994, I found myself flying to Addis Ababa to research the first edition of Bradt's *Ethiopia*. And over the four months that followed, I discovered Ethiopia to be every bit as fantastic as I had hoped: culturally, historically and scenically, the most extraordinary country I have ever visited. Since then, I have returned several times, both as a tour leader and to research subsequent editions of that guidebook. On every visit, I am struck afresh at how very, very different it is to the rest of Africa. Be warned: Ethiopia can be a frustrating country to travel in, and though its tourist industry has come a long way since the early 1990s, it still lacks the slickness associated with the likes of, say Kenya or Tanzania. But it is also an immensely rewarding country, and never, ever dull!

Contents

(AZ)

Introduction	**vii**
Introducing Ethiopia	1

1 Background — 3
History	5
Economy	23
People and culture	25

2 The Natural World — 35
Geography and climate	36
Habitats and vegetation	41
Wildlife	46

3 Planning a Trip — 63
When to visit	64
Itinerary planning	65
Red tape	80
Getting there	80
Health and safety	81
What to bring	84
Organising your finances	86

4 On the Ground — 89
Health and safety in Ethiopia	90
Banking and foreign exchange	93
Food and drink	94
Shopping	99
Media and communications	101
Business and time	102
Cultural etiquette	103

5 Addis Ababa and Surrounds 107
Addis Ababa 108
Around Addis Ababa: short trips 120

6 Lake Tana Region 131
Bahir Dar and surrounds 132
Gondar and the Simiens 144

7 Tigrai 155
Axum and surrounds 156
Eastern Tigrai 169

8 Lalibela and the Northeast Highlands 185
Lalibela and surrounds 187
Northeast Highlands 202

9 Eastern Ethiopia 215
Harar and the far east 216
The northern Rift Valley 228

10 Southern Ethiopia 239
Southern Rift Valley 241
Bale Mountains and surrounds 251
South Omo 260

Language 272

Selected Further Reading 276

Index 280

(EL)

List of maps

Addis Ababa	108
Around Addis Ababa	120
Axum	160
Bahir Dar	136
Eastern Ethiopia	216
Eastern Tigrai	169
Ethiopia	inside front cover
Gondar	146
Harar	220
Lake Tana region	132
Lalibela and surrounds	192
Northeast Highlands	186
South Omo	260
Southern Rift Valley	240
Tigrai	156

Transcription of Ethiopian names

Ethiopians use a unique script to transcribe Amharigna and several other languages. This has led to a wide divergence in English spellings of Ethiopian place names and other Amharigna words, as well as the inconsistent use of double characters. Even a straightforward place name like Matu is spelt variously as Metu, Mattuu, etc, while names like Zikwala can become virtually unrecognisable (Zouquela). When consulting different books and maps, it's advisable to keep an eye open for varied spellings and to use your imagination. My policy in this book has been to go for the simplest spelling, or the one that to me sounds closest to the local pronunciation. I have stuck with Ethiopian versions of names: for instance Tewodros (Theodore), Yohannis (John), Maryam (Mary) and Giyorgis (George). The exception is that if hotels or restaurants are signposted in English, then I have normally (but not infallibly) followed the signposted spelling exactly.

Introduction

The priest Francisco Alvarez, chronicler of a pioneering 1520 Portuguese expedition to the imperial court of Ethiopia, was the first outsider to lay eyes on the celebrated cluster of subterranean churches carved into the rocks of Lalibela. Years later, his memorable narrative *A True Relation of the Lands of Prester John of the Indies* cut short his description of these fantastic rock-hewn edifices with the defensive assertion: 'It wearied me to write more of these works, because it seemed to me that [my readers] would accuse me of untruth'.

Penned almost 500 years ago, Alvarez's sentiment is one with which I can empathise. Ethiopia is a country of enviable cultural wealth, historical depth, natural abundance and geographic diversity. It is the only country that survived the so-called scramble for Africa uncolonised, thanks to the military and diplomatic prowess of an imperial dynasty whose founder was reputedly the bastard son of King Solomon and the Queen of Sheba. Yet in the 15-plus years since I first visited Ethiopia, the questions I'm asked about this diverse and fascinating country almost always relate to the widespread misperception of it as the Land of the Famine, a barren wasteland where – in the influential words of the Live Aid anthem 'Do they know it's Christmas?' – 'nothing ever grows, no rain or rivers flow'.

It can indeed sometimes be difficult to discuss Ethiopia without slipping into a tone of defensive weariness. 'Nothing ever grows'?

The city of Gondar is best known for the 17th-century castle in its Royal Enclosure. (AZ)

Actually, Ethiopia has a greater proportion of arable land than any other country in the eastern half of Africa, and its agricultural sector feeds a population two-thirds larger than that of similarly sized South Africa. 'No rain'? Not exactly: roughly half of Ethiopia receives an average annual rainfall higher than that of London. As for 'no rivers'?, well that certainly puts the Nile in its place – as it does the three other less-celebrated cross-border river systems that originate in the Ethiopian Highlands, which also house about a dozen lakes with an extent greater than 100km^2.

So why does popular perception diverge so greatly from reality? At the risk of being grossly simplistic, Ethiopia is a country of two climatic halves: the dry lowlands of the thinly populated south and east, and the more fertile and densely inhabited highlands to the north and west. Without wishing to trivialise the suffering they caused, all modern famines in Ethiopia have been avoidable localised affairs, triggered by cyclic rainfall failures where the two climatic zones converge, and elevated to tragic proportions by a combination of rickety infrastructure, inadvertent economic mismanagement and/or overt political cynicism. Indeed, the two most notorious famines in recent Ethiopian history were greatly exacerbated by denialism and ineptness under Emperor Haile Selassie's doomed feudal regime in 1974, and then by his successor President Mengistu's malicious refusal to allow aid to reach drought-stricken areas that opposed his dictatorial rule in 1985.

Fortunately, since Mengistu was forced into exile in 1991, Ethiopia has enjoyed a relatively high level of political stability and economic growth, allowing it to nurture a more positive international image – at least among the travel cognoscenti, for whom it has become one of Africa's most popular emerging destinations. Make no mistake: almost everything about Ethiopia is, in a nutshell, quirky and idiosyncratic.

One of the few countries in sub-Saharan Africa whose tourist industry revolves around culture and history, Ethiopia is where Africa and the Judaeo-Christian world meet. In several respects, it is unique. There's the fiery food, the singular Arabic-looking script, the eerie pentatonic music, and the indescribably bizarre shoulder-twitching dancing. And, pivotally, there is the Ethiopian Orthodox Church, which was founded in the 4th century and subsequently evolved – or stagnated – in virtual isolation from other denominations to inform one of the most unusual and self-contained cultures on this planet.

Ethiopia's most celebrated historical attraction is Lalibela, the apex of a Christian chiselling tradition that has resulted in more than 300 rock-hewn churches scattered around the country, most still in use today. In addition, there are the pre-Christian stelae and other monuments

Far from a barren wasteland, Ethiopia's landscapes are rich and diverse. Here in the Omo Valley canoes are still the main form of transport in the more remote areas. (EL)

The Hamer still wear traditional clothes and indulge in ancient practices such as body scarification. (EL)

surrounding the ancient capital of Axum, the 17th-century castles at Gondar, the walled Islamic city of Harer, the Lake Tana island monasteries and Blue Nile Falls near Bahir Dar.

Ethiopia also has much to offer natural history enthusiasts. In addition to the consistently dramatic scenery, it boasts more endemic bird species than any African country except for South Africa. There are also several endemic large mammals – the mountain nyala, Ethiopian wolf, gelada monkey and Walia ibex – best seen in the Bale and Simien mountains, which also offer excellent, inexpensive hiking possibilities.

In short, Ethiopia is a sure-fire contender for the title of the world's most misunderstood country. And if what you know about it derives from television coverage in time of conflict and famine, then the reality will be a true revelation. Dervla Murphy said in 1968 that 'travelling in Ethiopia gives one the Orlando-like illusion of living through different centuries'. Despite many subsequent concessions to modernisation, this isolated highland country still feels the same today.

Introducing Ethiopia

Chapter 1	Background	3
Chapter 2	The Natural World	35
Chapter 3	Planning a Trip	63
Chapter 4	On the Ground	89

History

History   **5**

Prehistory   5
Traditional history   7
The Axumite Empire (1st to 7th centuries AD)   8
Medieval Ethiopia (8th to 16th centuries AD)   9
The Muslim-Christian War (1528-60)   11
The Gondar period (1635-1855)   13
Emperor Tewodros II and Yohannis IV
    (1855-89)   14
Emperor Menelik II and his successors
    (1889-1930)   15
Haile Selassie (1930-74)   17
The Derg (1974-91)   20
Modern Ethiopia   21

Economy   **23**

People and culture   **25**

People of South Omo   29

1 Background

Ethiopia is in many respects a unique and contradictory land. Its claim to be the cradle of humankind is possibly the best of any country on earth, thanks to the wealth of early hominine fossils unearthed in the Afar region. In the classical era, it hosted one of the world's most economically influential and technologically advanced trade empires, one that spread from Yemen to the Sudanese Nile, and was capable of erecting monuments as inspired as the pre-Christian temple of Yeha and the monolithic stelae of Axum. More recently, it is the site of ancient Christian and Islamic civilisations, respectively founded in the 4th and 7th centuries, and responsible for some of Africa's most compelling religious shrines, most notably the legendary rock-hewn churches of Lalibela and Tigrai. While the north of the country is dominated by Judaic influences, the south - inhabited by the likes of the Oromo and myriad tribes of South Omo - is emphatically African in mood, with closer cultural links to the Maasai or Turkana of Kenya than to any of their northern compatriots.

Ethiopia at a glance

Location A land-locked republic in the 'horn' of northeast Africa, lying between 3.5 and 15°N and 33 and 48°E, Ethiopia shares its longest border with Somalia (including the unrecognised state of Somaliland) to the east, and it is also bounded by Eritrea and Djibouti to the northeast, Kenya to the south, and Sudan and new state of South Sudan to the west.

Area 1,104,300km² (27th largest in the world and tenth largest in Africa)

Climate Varies by region, from temperate highlands to hot lowland desert

Status Federal Republic

Head of State President Girma Wolde-Giorgis and Prime Minister Meles Zenawi

Capital Addis Ababa (population 3.5 million)

Other main towns Dire Dawa, Adama (Nazret), Gondar, Dessie, Mekele, Bahir Dar, Jimma, Bishoftu (Debre Zeyit), Hawassa, Harar

Economy Subsistence agriculture, coffee, *khat*, mining, tourism

GDP US$900 per capita (purchase power parity [PPP] estimate)

Currency Birr

Rate of exchange US$1 = birr 17, €1 = birr 23, £1 = birr 28 (April 2012)

Population 82.5 million (14th in the world and second in Africa)

Life expectancy 55 years (2008 estimate, CIA World Factbook)

Languages/Official language Amharigna (Amharic), Oromigna and English are most widely spoken.

Religion Main religions are Ethiopian Orthodox Christianity, Islam and Protestant Christianity.

National airline/airport Ethiopian Airlines/Bole International Airport

International telephone code +251

Time GMT +3

Electric voltage 220V current alternating at 50Hz. Plug standards vary; most common are the Type C (European two-pin) and Type L (Italian three-pin).

Weights and measures Metric

Flag Vertical bands of green at the top, yellow in the centre and red at the base. In the middle of this is a symbol representing the sun – a yellow pentagram from which emanate several yellow rays.

National anthem 'March Forward, Dear Mother Ethiopia'

Public Holidays 7 January, 19 January, 2 March, 1 May, 5 May, 28 May, 11 September, 27 September, plus the moveable holidays Ramadan, Moulid, Ethiopian Good Friday and Ethiopian Easter.

History

Ethiopia is the only country in sub-Saharan Africa with tangible archaeological relics stretching back to the classical era, and a basic grasp of the country's history is integral to getting the most from a visit. It should be noted, however, that the traditional accounts familiar to Ethiopians and the orthodoxies of Western historians often diverge greatly and sometimes come across as parallel narrative universes. Furthermore, historical writings about Ethiopia are riddled with contradictory dates and hypotheses, while archaeological research of major sites remains fragmentary, so that many aspects of the country's rich past are open to interpretation. Fortunately, it is not my job to resolve these contradictions here, and what follows draws both on the unverifiable Ethiopian traditions and on more conservative academic research.

Prehistory

The East African Rift Valley is almost certainly where modern human beings and their hominine ancestors evolved, and Ethiopia has as strong claims as any African country in this respect. Indeed, the Afar region, in the northern Rift Valley of Ethiopia, has yielded the world's oldest undisputed **hominine remains**, thought to be around 5.5 million years old (when the lowland regions of the Horn of Africa were far moister and better wooded than they are today) and ascribed to the species *Ardipithecus kadabba*. In addition, several fossils of *A. ramidus*, a probable descendent of *A. kadabba* that lived at least 4.4 million years ago, have been located in the region. It was also in Afar that the famous 3.2-million-year-old *Australopithecus afarensis* skeleton named **Lucy** was uncovered in 1972.

At 3.2-million-years-old, Lucy was the oldest known hominid fossil at the time of discovery. (AZ)

The world's oldest known **stone tools**, dating back more than 2.5 million years and manufactured by an unknown hominine species, have been excavated at Gona, along an extinct riverbed used by an earlier incarnation of the Awash River, also in the Afar region. Exactly where *Homo s. sapiens* – modern humans – took their first steps is an open question (as, for that matter, is the classification of and relationship between the numerous *Homo* taxa that have lived within the past million years). However, a pair of **human skulls** uncovered in 1967 in southern Ethiopia, alongside the

Biblical Ethiopia

There is no getting around the strong presence of Ethiopia (or Cush, as it was known to the Hebrews) in the Bible. Genesis, for instance, talks of the Ghion River that 'compasseth the whole land of Ethiopia', a fairly unambiguous reference to the Blue Nile, which forms a sweeping arc beneath the area on which pre-Axumite civilisation was centred. Elsewhere, Isaiah talks of 'the country ... beyond the rivers of Cush, who send ambassadors by sea, in papyrus skiffs over the waters ... a people tall and bronzed', while the Book of Zephaniah's reference to 'the daughter of my dispersed ... from beyond the rivers of Ethiopia' implies some sort of Jewish dispersal to Ethiopia.

These passages have also been cited to support the tenuous claim that the sacred Ark of the Covenant has been stashed away at various Ethiopian sites ever since it vanished from Israel circa 587BC, and is currently locked away in an outbuilding of the Church of Maryam Tsion in Axum (a claim investigated further in Graham Hancock's controversial but readable and surprisingly plausible book *The Sign and the Seal*).

Omo River, and originally thought to be around 130,000 years old but re-dated to be 195,000 years old in 2005, is now frequently cited as the oldest known fossil of anatomically modern humans, placing Ethiopia at centre stage not only of early hominine evolution, but also of more modern developments in the emergence of our species.

Archaeological evidence suggests that **pastoralism** was practised in northern Ethiopia circa 4000BC, and conclusive evidence of millet cultivation dating from around 3000BC has been found near Axum, alongside indigenous pottery of a similar vintage. A combination of archaeological and written sources leave no doubt that by 1000BC northern Ethiopia supported an urbanised agricultural society of some magnitude, sometimes referred to as the **pre-Axumite civilisation**. The most important surviving pre-Axumite site is **Yeha**, which houses a well-preserved 2,500-year-old stone temple, as well as the remains of stone dwellings and catacombs. Other sites in the region have yielded impressive sculptures and free-standing altars (many on display in the Addis Ababa National Museum) that show strong religious and cultural links with the Sabaean Kingdom of modern-day Yemen. Isolated discoveries of Egyptian and other foreign artefacts, as well as the implied Greek influences on indigenous pre-Axumite pottery, suggest that pre-Axumite Ethiopia was in contact and probably traded with several other classical civilisations.

Traditional history

Ethiopia has a strong oral historic tradition, one that stretches back over several millennia and is almost impossible to verify. According to this tradition, the country was first settled by a great-grandson of Noah called Ethiopic, whose son Aksumai established his capital at Axum and founded a ruling dynasty that endured for more than 50 generations. The last of these monarchs, and many say the greatest, was **Queen Makeda**, who Ethiopians believe was the so-called Queen of Sheba of Biblical fame. It is claimed that Makeda ruled Ethiopia and Yemen for 31 years over the cusp of the 11th and 10th centuries BC, and that she owned a fleet of 73 ships and a caravan of 520 camels that traded with places as far afield as Palestine and India.

Early in her rule, tradition has it, Makeda travelled to Jerusalem with gifts of gold, ivory and spices for King Solomon, who converted her to Judaism and impregnated her. On her return home, Makeda gave birth to their son, who she called **Menelik** (a bastardisation of Ibn-al-Malik, literally 'Son of the King'). Menelik returned to Jerusalem aged 22 to learn the Law of Moses and as Solomon's eldest son, he was invited to be the formal heir to the Jewish throne. He, however, declined the offer in favour of returning home to Ethiopia. Following this decision, Solomon ordered all his high commissioners to send their eldest sons to Ethiopia with Menelik, and each of the 12 tribes of Israel to send 1,000 people.

A mural in St George's Cathedral, Addis Ababa depicts King Solomon with the Queen of Sheba. (SS)

7

Accompanying Menelik on his journey home was Azariah, the first-born son of the high priest of the temple of Jerusalem. Azariah was told in a dream that he should take with him the holiest of all Judaic artefacts, the **Ark of the Covenant**. When Menelik was first told about this, he was angry, but then he dreamt that it was God's will. King Solomon discovered the Ark's absence and led his soldiers after Menelik's enormous entourage, but he too dreamt that it was right for his first-born son to have the Ark, though he insisted on keeping its disappearance a secret. The Ark has remained in Ethiopia ever since, and is now locked away in the Church of Maryam Tsion in Axum. Following his mother's abdication, Menelik took the Axumite throne and established the so-called Solomonic Dynasty that ruled Ethiopia (with a few interruptions) until the 237th monarch Haile Selassie was overthrown in the 1974 revolution.

Although most Ethiopians accept this version of events as gospel, it has never been taken seriously by Western historians. The oldest written account of Makeda and Menelik is in the 14th-century *Kebre Negest*, which purports to be a Ge'ez translation of a lost 4th-century Coptic document, but was more likely fabricated by the so-called Solomonic Dynasty when it reclaimed the Ethiopian throne after several centuries of Zagwe rule.

The Axumite Empire (1st to 7th centuries AD)

The earliest independent reference to the Axumite Kingdom is in the ***Periplus of the Erythraean Sea***, a Greek document that describes the trade route along the African coast of the Red Sea and Gulf of Aden in the 1st century AD. The *Periplus* suggests that the kingdom stretched along the coast from modern-day Port Sudan south to the Somali port of Berbera, and into the interior almost as far as the Nile. According to the *Periplus*, it traded with India, Arabia, Persia and Rome from the port of Adulis, which now lies in ruins 50km from Massawa (Eritrea). The kingdom's namesake capital, ruled by a king called Zoscales, was eight days travel inland.

A stone tablet from Yeha written in ancient Sabaean and Ge'ez script. (SS)

King Ezana

The most influential Axumite king was Ezana, who ruled in the early 4th-century along with his twin brother Saizana. A strong military leader whose exploits are recorded on several inscribed stelae dotted around Axum, Ezana led at least two successful military campaigns, one across the Red Sea to conquer Yemen, and the other inland to the confluence of the Nile and Atbara rivers. However, the most enduringly influential of his actions, following his conversion by two shipwrecked Christians from Syria, was the instatement of Christianity as the official state religion, an event recorded by the Roman writer Rufinus, as well as on contemporary Axumite coins (the older sun and moon symbols were replaced by a cross on mints subsequent to AD341). Ezana and Saizana were almost certainly synonymous with the legendary twins Abreha and Atsbeha, who reputedly initiated the excavation of many Tigraian rock-hewn churches.

The Axumites were a literate people who developed a unique language called **Ge'ez** and used a script based on the Sabaean alphabet. They were skilled masons and builders, but their most impressive (and baffling) technological achievement was the erection of several solid granite **stelae** – the largest, now collapsed, some 33m high – at Axum.

Christianity only made serious inroads into the Axumite Empire in the 5th century, under the ministry of the nine so-called '**Syrian monks**' (in fact, refugees from all corners of the Roman Empire) who were later canonised by the Ethiopian Church. Meanwhile, the empire's prosperity continued to grow and peaked under **King Kaleb**, who took the throne in the early 6th century and ruled for at least 30 years. Kaleb's palace, on a hill above Axum, was visited circa AD525 by the Byzantine traveller Cosmos, who marvelled at its many statues, and at the tame elephants and giraffes that roamed the grounds. Kaleb's son, Gebre Meskel was the patron of Abba Yared, the saint credited with inventing the notation and form of Ethiopian religious music, and with writing many songs and chants still in use today.

Medieval Ethiopia (8th to 16th centuries AD)

Many reasons have been put forward for Axum's economic collapse between the late 6th and early 7th century, but the main factor was almost certainly the **rise of Islam** and subsequent Arabian usurpation of the Red Sea trade routes once ruled by Axum. By AD750, Adulis had become a ghost town, and Axum itself fell into global obscurity, though it remained – as it still does today – the effective headquarters of the Ethiopian Orthodox Church. Domestically, however, the old ruling dynasty of Axum started to expand its influence to include the Jewish communities of the Lalibela and Lake Tana region all the way south to the vicinity of present-day Addis Ababa. Indeed, it could be argued that it was between AD750 and 1270 that the Axumite Kingdom was territorially transformed into the Abyssinian Empire, and the Ethiopian Church evolved into the cohesive and idiosyncratic institution it is today (most of Ethiopia's 300 rock-hewn churches, for instance, date from this period).

Ethiopian traditions relating to the end of the 1st millennium AD are dominated by the memory of **Queen Yodit**, also known as Esat or Gudit, both names meaning 'the monster'. The daughter of a Falasha king called Gideon, Yodit was born in Lasta at a time of great religious tension. The Christian expansion southwards had led to the repression of the Falasha Jews, who refused to pay taxes to the Axumite monarchy and suffered regular punitive raids as a result. Yodit is credited with uniting the Falasha into a cohesive unit, and with leading a march

The Solomonic Dynasty

Haile Selassie claimed to be the last emperor in the Solomonic line. (SS)

According to tradition, the Solomonic Dynasty ruled Ethiopia for 3,000 years, a practically unbroken lineage of 237 emperors stretching from Menelik I, son of King Solomon and the Queen of Sheba (see page 7), to Haile Selassie, who was executed in 1974. Like so much else that passes for Ethiopian history, however, this tradition is also something of a myth. For one, even the most imperialistic of Ethiopians accepts that the Solomonic chain was broken by several centuries of Zagwe rule prior to the late 13th century, when it was restored by Emperor Yakuno Amlak. Furthermore, there is no known historical basis for Yakuno Amlak's claim to Solomonic ancestry: on the contrary, academic opinion is that the Solomonic link was invented by his spin doctors to substantiate his claim to the throne. And one needn't delve that deep into Ethiopia's past to debunk the Solomonic myth: even within historic times, Yohannis IV, crowned the last ruler of Gondar in 1872, was related neither to his predecessor Tewodros I nor to his successor Menelik II, and none of these emperors was related to the last in the so-called Solomonic line, Haile Selassie.

Queen Yodit

There is little doubt that Yodit was a genuine historical figure. Exactly when she lived is another matter. Ethiopian tradition dates her rise to AD852, and claims that her onslaught precipitated the move of the Axumite monarchy south to Showa. However, contemporary Arab writings suggest the Axumite rulers maintained sporadic contact with Yemen well into the 10th century, while documents written in AD980 state unambiguously that Ethiopia was plagued by a hostile queen at this time. It seems more likely, then, that Yodit's reign of terror was in the late 10th century. In which case her legendary destructiveness might explain why Kubar, mentioned in certain Arabic documents as the 9th- and 10th-century capital of Ethiopia, has never been found.

on Axum with the intention of removing Christianity from Ethiopia altogether. The holy city was reduced to rubble by her army, and dozens of other churches and Christian settlements were burnt to the ground.

It is said that Yodit died when a whirlwind swept her up near Wukro. Once news of her death filtered to Showa, the Solomonic heir Anbessa Wudim returned to Axum and defeated the Falasha in battle to reclaim his right to the throne. Axum remained unstable, however, and King D'il Nead was overthrown by one of his generals, Tekle Haymanot, who took the regal name of Zagwe and founded the dynasty of the same name. It is also possible that the **Zagwe Dynasty** was founded by Jews who later converted to Christianity, and that it followed directly from Yodit's rule. Either way, the Zagwe leaders appear to have introduced a new stability and unity in Ethiopia. It was under the most renowned Zagwe king, **Lalibela**, that Ethiopian Christianity reached the pinnacle of its physical expression in the form of the cluster of **rock-hewn churches** carved at the Zagwe capital of Roha (which later became known as Lalibela in honour of the king). The Zagwe period of rule ended when Yakuno Amlak, supposedly a distant descendant of King Solomon (see box, *The Solomonic dynasty*, opposite), took the throne in 1270.

The Muslim–Christian War (1528–60)

Islamic presence in Ethiopia dates back to the lifetime of the **prophet Muhammad**. In AD615, several of Muhammad's followers, his wife among them, fled to Axum where they were offered protection by the king and allowed to settle at Negash. Muhammad himself held Ethiopians in great esteem and warned his followers never to harm them. For several centuries, an uneasy peace existed between Christian Ethiopia and the

Islamic world, even as an increasing amount of Islamic settlement took place along the eastern fringes of the Christian kingdom. By the end of the Zagwe era, the Muslim faith had spread throughout the Somali and Afar territories and to the southern highlands around Harar, Bale and Arsi, while small bands of Muslims had dispersed into areas that were traditionally part of the Christian empire. Sensing a threat to their sovereignty, and to trade routes to the Red Sea, the Ethiopian Christians launched an attack against the Muslims of Adal in around 1290, which led to a series of skirmishes and wars, and, ultimately, in the mid-14th century, to the expansion of the Christian empire deep into southern Ethiopia. In its attempts to retain its sovereignty, Ethiopia made great efforts to convert pagan highlanders and Falasha to the Christian faith, and also sent envoys abroad to strengthen its links with Christian communities in the Sudan, Egypt, Alexandria and Armenia.

In 1528, the Somali Muslim leader known as **Ahmed Gragn** (Ahmed the left-handed) took control of the Harar in the eastern highlands. From Harar, Gragn led his army of Afar and Somali Muslims on an annual raid on the Christian highlands, timed every year to exploit the weakness of Christians during the Lent fast. Gragn's destructiveness can be compared to that of Yodit several centuries earlier. Many rock-hewn churches throughout Ethiopia still bear the scars of his campaign; of less permanent structures, such as the church at Axum, which was rebuilt after Yodit's reign, no trace remains. The Ethiopian emperor of the time, Lebna Dengal, was chased around his kingdom by Gragn, eventually to die a fugitive in 1540. By 1535, Gragn held Showa, Lasta, Amhara and Tigrai – in other words most of Christian Ethiopia.

Gragn's campaign more or less coincided with the first contact between Europe and Ethiopia. This occurred in 1493, with the arrival – via Egypt, India and the Persian Gulf – of **Pero de Covilhão**, a 'spy' sent by King John of Portugal in search of Prester John (who, according to European legend, ruled over a wealthy 'lost' Christian kingdom located somewhere in Africa or Asia). Instead of fulfilling the second part of his mission by returning home, however, Covilhão stayed on to serve as an adviser to a succession of emperors and regents. He was still there in 1520, when the first full Portuguese expedition to Ethiopia, as documented by the priest Francisco Alvarez in *A True Relation of the Lands of Prester John of the Indies*, was received at the Monastery of Debre Libanos by Emperor Lebna Dengal. Shortly before his death in exile, Lebna Dengal wrote to Portugal asking for help in restoring his kingdom. Were it not for the intervention of the Portuguese, it is quite likely that Ethiopian Christianity would have been buried under the Muslim onslaught.

In 1543, **Emperor Galawdewos**'s army, propped up by the Portuguese, killed Gragn and defeated his army in a battle near Lake Tana. Galawdewos's attempts to rebuild the shattered Christian empire were frequently frustrated by raids led by Gragn's wife and nephew. In 1559, the emperor was killed and his severed head displayed in Harar. But the long years of war had drained the resources of Christians and Muslims alike; the real winners were the **pagan Galla** (now known as the Oromo) who expanded out of the Rift Valley into areas laid waste by the fighting. By 1560, the Galla had virtually surrounded Harar and had overrun much of Showa, providing not only a buffer zone between the exhausted Christians and Muslims, but also a new threat to both of the established groups.

The Gondar period (1635–1855)

The Christians were faced with a new disaster as Portuguese ex-soldiers settled around the temporary capital on Lake Tana. In 1622, **Emperor Susneyos** made a full conversion to **Catholicism** under the influence of his close friend and regular travelling companion, the Spanish-born Jesuit priest **Pedro Páez**. He then outlawed the Orthodox Church, suspended traditional church officials, and encouraged the persecution of many thousands of Orthodox Christians for pursuing their centuries-old faith. Increasingly isolated from his subjects, the emperor was forced to abdicate in favour of his son **Fasil** in 1632. The new emperor reinstated the Orthodox Church and banned foreigners from his empire. From the 1640s until James Bruce's journey in 1770, only one European, a French doctor, was permitted to enter Ethiopia.

Gondar was named capital of Ethiopia in 1636 and remained so for 200 years. (AC)

Ethiopia had lacked a permanent capital since 1270. In order to help reunite church and state, Fasil broke with this tradition by settling at the small town of Gondar, north of Lake Tana. Gondar was named the permanent capital of Ethiopia in 1636, a title it kept for more than 200 years. This move to Gondar signalled an era of relative peace under a succession of strong, popular emperors, most notably Fasil himself and **Iyasu I**. Then, under Iyasu II (1730–55), the throne was gradually undermined by Ras (Prince) Mikael of Tigrai, who assumed an increasing backstage importance, twice assassinating emperors and replacing them with others of his choice. By 1779, when Takla Giyorgis took power, the king's role was little more than ornamental. The period between 1784 and 1855 is generally referred to as the '**era of the princes**'; the Gondar-based rulers of this period are remembered as the 'shadow emperors'.

Emperor Tewodros II and Yohannis IV (1855–89)

By the mid 19th century, Ethiopia was not so much a unified state as a loose alliance of squabbling fiefdoms run by wealthy local dynasties, which were in turn reigned over by an ineffectual emperor. The empire was threatened not merely by internal power struggles, but also by the external threat posed by Egypt, who wanted to control the Nile from its source at Lake Tana. Indeed, Ethiopia could well have collapsed altogether were it not for the vision of **Kasa Hayla**, a local leader who gradually accumulated a powerful army until he was able to defeat the heir to the Gondarine throne, and have himself crowned **Emperor Tewodros II**, in 1855.

History has cast Tewodros as the instigator of Ethiopian unity, and he is now among the country's most revered historical figures. That he never achieved much popularity in his lifetime is due to the brutality and ruthless fanaticism with which he pursued these goals. He managed to reunite the country under a strong central government, and to partially modernise the national army. He also had strong anti-feudal instincts, which led to his abolition of the slave trade and his expropriation of large tracts of fallow church-owned land for the use of peasant farmers – socialist efforts that won him many enemies among the clergy and the nobility.

Tewodros's frustration was cemented by his failure to enlist Britain's support for his modernising efforts and his quest for absolute Ethiopian sovereignty. In 1867, he retreated embittered to his fortified arsenal atop Makdala Hill, taking with him several British prisoners in a final desperate bid to lever European support. It was a fatal misjudgement.

In 1869, Sir Robert Napier led a force of 32,000 British soldiers to capture Tewodros at Makdala. Instead of fighting, the emperor wrote a long letter to Napier listing his failed ambitions and castigating his countrymen for their backwardness. Then he took his own life.

A bloody succession battle was won by Kasa Mercha, the deeply religious ruler of Tigrai, who was crowned as **Emperor Yohannis IV** in 1872. Yohannis attempted to forge national unity through diplomacy rather than military means, an ambition undermined by the combination of British duplicity, Egyptian ambitions

El Mundo en La Maso depicts Tewodros's suicide. (ss)

and infighting instigated by the rival Sahle Maryam, Prince of Showa. Yohannis led successful campaigns against Egypt over 1875–76, but had less luck when it came to outside recognition of Ethiopian sovereignty. In 1884, he signed a treaty allowing British dominion over the port of Massawa, but despite Ethiopia's substantial support in rescuing British troops from the Mahdist forces in neighbouring Sudan, Britain reneged a year later by handing Massawa to Italy.

A newcomer to Africa, Italy, with the tacit support of Britain, proved a major threat to Ethiopian sovereignty, occupying several of its Red Sea ports in 1886. In March 1888, Yohannis led an 80,000-man attack on the Italian garrison at Saati, but he was forced to withdraw to deal with the more immediate news of a successful Mahdist attack on Gondar (still the official capital of Ethiopia) and of Sahle Maryam's plans to rise against him. In March 1889, Yohannis was fatally wounded in a victorious attack on the Mahdist stronghold at Matema. Six months later, Sahle Maryam was crowned Emperor Menelik II of Ethiopia.

Emperor Menelik II and his successors (1889–1930)

Between 1882 and 1888, while Yohannis was engaged in fighting external foes, **Menelik** vastly expanded Showan territory by capturing Harar, Arsi, most of the fiefdoms of the southwest, and large tracts of Galla land. In doing so, he paved the way for modern Ethiopian unity, even if his major motives were entirely self-serving. This period of military conquest was halted by the Kefu Qan ('Evil Days') of 1888–92, the most severe famine in Ethiopia's recorded history. A direct result of a rinderpest epidemic triggered by the importation of cattle by the Italians, exacerbated by drought and locust plagues, this famine cannot be seen in isolation from the ongoing wars of the 19th century, nor can it be dissociated from the greed of the feuding princes, which had stretched peasant resources to the limit.

In May 1889, Menelik signed the Treaty of Wechale, granting Italy the part of Ethiopia which was to become Eritrea in exchange for recognition of Ethiopian sovereignty over the rest of the country. What he didn't realise was that the Italians had inserted a clause in the Italian version of the document, but not in the Amharigna equivalent, which demanded that Ethiopia make all its foreign contacts through Italy, in effect reducing Ethiopia to an Italian protectorate. Menelik refused to recognise this new status, and so Italy responded by occupying Adigrat, on the Tigraian side of the border, in October 1895. Menelik led a force of 100,000 men to Tigrai and, after a couple of inconsequential skirmishes, the two armies met in the hills around Adwa. The memory of the **Battle of Adwa**, which took place on 1 March 1896, remains one of the proudest moments in Ethiopian history, as the first time that a European power was defeated by Africans in a battle of lasting consequence. As a result, Ethiopia was the only part of Africa to enter the 20th century as an independent state.

Menelik at the Battle of Adwa (I/A)

Menelik died of old age in 1913. His chosen successor, **Iyasu**, though potentially the leader Ethiopia needed to drag it out of feudalism, embarked on a series of relatively progressive reforms that antagonised the slave-owning nobility, the clergy and the political status quo. He was overthrown in 1916, while visiting Jijiga in an attempt to improve relations with Ethiopia's Somali population, to be succeeded by **Empress Zawditu**, Menelik's sheltered daughter, who was favoured by the Showan nobility and church leaders for her political naivety and evident potential for ineffectuality. Meanwhile, her main rival, **Ras**

Menelik's achievements

In many senses, Menelik completed the process of unification and modernisation that had been started by Tewodros and Yohannis. His period of rule saw the introduction of electricity, telephones, schools and hospitals, and also the building of the Addis Ababa-Djibouti railway. It also saw a re-intensification of the slave trade which, although it had been present in Ethiopia since time immemorial, had been curbed if not halted by Tewodros. Slavery was the pretext used by Europe to block Ethiopia's entry to the League of Nations and to sanction against the import of arms and ammunition to Ethiopia. The slave raids, in which many thousands of Ethiopians died, were the major blemish on a rule that was one of the longest periods of sustained peace Ethiopia had known for a long time.

Statue of Menelik, Addis Ababa (AC)

Tefari, the ambitious son of the Harari governor Ras Mekonnen, was appointed official heir to the throne, and allowed to assume a regent like role, effectively governing in tandem with Zawditu. This ambiguous relationship was resolved in 1930, when the empress died of heartbreak two days after her husband was killed in rather murky circumstances in a civil battle. Ras Tefari was crowned as emperor under the name **Haile Selassie** (meaning 'Power of the Trinity') in November 1930.

Haile Selassie (1930–74)

The first serious challenge to Haile Selassie's rule came not from within the country but from Italy, whose defeat at Adwa still rankled, particularly in the nationalistic fervour that accompanied Mussolini's rise to power in 1922. The first harbinger of war was the **Walwal Incident** of December 1934, wherein a remote Ethiopian military post on the disputed Italian Somaliland border region was attacked by Italian troops. The skirmish was initiated by Italy, and Italy suffered considerably less loss of life than Ethiopia. Nevertheless, the political climate in Europe was such that countries like Britain and France were more than willing to sacrifice Ethiopian interests to the cause of frustrating an alliance between Mussolini and Hitler. Italy made absurd demands for reparations. Ethiopia took these to the League of Nations (it had become a member state in 1925) for arbitration, but its perfectly valid arguments were ignored; Italy was in effect given a free hand in Ethiopia.

The Italian army crossed from Eritrea to Tigrai in October 1935, and within a month it had captured Adigrat, Mekele and Adwa. In January 1936, the Ethiopian army entered Tigrai, where Italy's superior air power and use of prohibited mustard gas proved decisive. Following the **Battle of Maychew** of 31 March 1936, Ethiopia was effectively under Italian occupation, and Haile Selassie fled into exile. Over the next five years, the Ethiopian nobility combined time-buying diplomacy and well-organised guerrilla warfare to undermine the regime. The fascists' response was characteristically brutal. In 1937, for instance, following an unsuccessful assassination attempt on the Italian viceroy, the Blackshirts ran riot in the capital, burning down houses and decapitating and disembowelling Ethiopians, mostly at random, though the intelligentsia was particularly targeted and few survived the rampage. Despite the Ethiopian resistance winning few battles of note, its role in demoralising the occupiers laid the foundation for an easy British victory over the Italian troops in the **Allied liberation campaign** of January 1941. Immediately afterwards, Haile Selassie was returned to his throne.

After the war, prompted largely by US and British regional interests, as well as pressure exerted by Haile Selassie, the UN forced Eritrea into a highly ambiguous federation with Ethiopia. As the oil-rich Middle East came to play an increasingly important role in international affairs, so too did the Red Sea harbours now effectively controlled by Haile Selassie. In exchange for using Asmara as their Red Sea base, the US developed a military training and armoury programme for Ethiopia which, by 1970, absorbed more than half the US budget for military aid to Africa. Little wonder, then, that the world barely noticed when Ethiopia formally annexed Eritrea in 1962, and then proceeded to dissolve the Eritrean Assembly and placed the territory under military rule. The terms of federation gave Eritrea no recourse to argue its case before the UN. So began a war for self-determination that lasted almost 30 years, cost the lives of more than 100,000 Eritreans, and never once figured on the UN agenda.

Despite the mystique that surrounded Haile Selassie, he did very little to develop his country. Indeed, a few cosmetic constitutional overhauls notwithstanding, Ethiopia in 1960 wasn't substantially less feudal than it had been in 1930. As a result, the wave of colonial resistance that swept through Africa after World War II was mirrored by a rising tide of imperial resistance in post-occupation Ethiopia. In December 1960, while Haile Selassie was away in Brazil, the Imperial Bodyguard led a failed coup that changed the complexion of Ethiopian politics forever. True, on the pan-African front the figurehead status of Ethiopia's septuagenarian head of state was further entrenched when Addis Ababa was made the headquarters of the Organisation of African Unity (OAU) in 1963. On the domestic front, by contrast, the attempted coup prompted widespread calls for reform, as well as a more militarised approach from the Eritrean Liberation Front (ELF) and Eritrean People's Liberation Front (EPLF).

Matters came to a head over the tragic **1973 famine** in Wolo and Tigrai. As the BBC aired heartbreaking footage of starving Ethiopians, the imperial government at first refused to acknowledge the famine's existence, and then – having retracted its initial denials – failed to respond to the crisis with any action meaningful enough to prevent the estimated 200,000 deaths that ensued. On 12 September 1974, following months of strikes, demonstrations, peasant revolts and military mutinies, the emperor was arrested in his palace, and – in mockery of a grandiose imperial motorcade – driven to a prison cell in the back of a Volkswagen Beetle, while his embittered subjects yelled out '*Leba!*' ('Thief!'). The imperial imprisonment ended on 27 August 1975, when the deposed emperor succumbed not to a heart attack, as the official line stated at the time, but to a smothering pillow held in place by his successor Colonel Mengistu Haile Maryam.

Haile Selassie is now buried alongside his wife in the Church of Kiddist Selassie in Addis Ababa. (AZ)

The Derg (1974–91)

The socialist-inspired **Military Co-ordinating Committee**, better known as the Derg, took power, but soon proved to be even more ruthless and brutal than its predecessor. A series of radical policies was implemented, most crucially a Land Reform Bill that outlawed private land ownership and allowed for the formation of collective land use under local councils. However, these and other early attempts at collectivisation, villagisation and resettlement met neither with popular support nor with significant success. Vice-Chairman **Mengistu Haile Maryam** responded to this dissent with mass arrests and executions, and an internal purge of the Derg, which culminated in the execution of seven party leaders, and propelled him to an unopposed position of leadership in the provisional government.

Opposition groups mushroomed in the climate of oppression. By 1977, large parts of Eritrea were under rebel rule. Also in the north, the Tigraian People's Liberation Front (TPLF) allied itself to the Eritrean self-determination movements, whilst also demanding a truly democratic government for Ethiopia itself. There were rumblings from the newly founded Oromo Liberation Front (OLF), which represented Ethiopia's largest ethnic group. Aided by troops from Somalia, the Somali-populated far east rose against the government army, precipitating Russian and Cuban withdrawal from Somalia and support

Skulls displayed in the Red Terror Museum are a reminder of the massacres committed under the Mengistu regime. (AZ)

for Ethiopia, and initiating a bloody war in which some 10,000 troops on each side died in 1978 alone. Unrest spread to the capital, where street conflict resulted in several hundreds of deaths. Mengistu responded by arresting and killing opposition leaders, and orchestrating purges in which untold thousands of civilians were killed.

In 1985, Ethiopia experienced the worst **famine** in living memory, following three successive years of rainfall failure in Tigrai, Wolo and the eastern lowlands. The drought was a natural phenomenon, but the tragic proportions of the famine were largely attributable to Mengistu, and his unwillingness to allow food aid to reach the troublesome province of Tigrai. A million Ethiopians died as a result.

In September 1987, Ethiopia technically returned to civilian rule, when Mengistu won a contrived election in which all candidates were nominated by the Derg. In the same year, the Ethiopian People's Revolutionary Democratic Front (EPRDF), allied to the TPLF and supported by the EPLF, was formed with the major aim of initiating a true national democracy as opposed to regional secession. In May 1988, the government declared a state of emergency in Tigrai and Eritrea as an increasing number of major towns fell under rebel rule. The Derg was further weakened by the collapse of European socialism in 1990, which resulted in a cutback in military aid. In early 1991, the EPRDF finally drove the weakened army out of Tigrai and Eritrea, and in May of the same year it had also captured Addis Ababa. Before he could be arrested, Mengistu jetted to safety in Zimbabwe, where he still resides to this day, despite repeated requests for extradition.

Modern Ethiopia

The only African country that had avoided long-term colonialism was also one of the last to enjoy a semblance of democratic rule. This changed after 1991, however, when the EPRDF established a transitional government, headed up by **President Meles Zenawi**, and abandoned Mengistu's failed socialist policies and autocratic approach. In December 1994, the transitional government implemented a **federal constitution** that divided the country into 11 federal regions with borders delineated along established ethno-linguistic lines. Comprising three city-states and eight larger regions, these federal entities were each guaranteed political autonomy on domestic matters, and proportional representation in central government. This move paved the way for the country's **first democratic election** in May 1995, which saw Zenawi voted in as prime minster alongside **President Nagasso Gidada**, a coupling that was returned to power in the election of 2000.

Eritrea was granted full independence in April 1993, following a referendum in which Eritreans voted overwhelmingly in favour of secession. Relations with Ethiopia soon soured, however, and within five years the two countries found themselves on the brink of a war catalysed in May 1998 by a failed Eritrean attempt to capture the disputed border town of Badme, in the otherwise insignificant 400km^2 of barely arable earth known as the Yirga Triangle. Hostilities escalated on 5 June, when an unprovoked Eritrean cluster-bombing of residential parts of Mekele left 55 civilians dead and 136 wounded. Further attacks followed on both sides of the border, and by the end of the month at least 20,000 Ethiopians and a similar number of Eritreans had been killed in the conflict. Over the next 18 months, repeated attempts at

Ethiopian names

Ethiopian personal names follow a system normal in the Islamic world but not in most Western countries. All Ethiopians have a given name, but their second name is simply the father's given name, not a surname as we know it. In other words, an Ethiopian man called Belai Tadese is not Belai of the Tadese family, but Belai, the son of Tadese, and he would be addressed as Ato (Mister) Belai. If Ato Belai has a daughter named Guenet, she will be known as Guenet Belai, and would be addressed formally as Waziro (Madam) Guenet, irrespective of whether or not she is married. Because of this, officials will often ask for your father's name when they want to know your surname. Even in formal situations, Ethiopians usually address Westerners according to their custom rather than ours – if your name is Joe Bloggs, you'll be addressed as Ato or Mister Joe, never as Mr Bloggs.

reaching a diplomatic solution, generally initiated by Ethiopia, were followed by fresh outbursts of fighting. Over the course of 2000, however, Ethiopia recaptured most of the Yirga Triangle, and its reoccupation was formalised in a peace agreement signed on 12 December 2000. Nevertheless, the financial toll of the war – money that could so easily have been pumped into the road infrastructure, education, you name it really – was immeasurable, as was the loss of the economic momentum and international confidence that had characterised Ethiopia's immediate post-Derg years.

Partially as a result of this long and wasteful war, Ethiopia's third general election, held in May 2005, demonstrated a mass retraction of urban support for Zenawi and the EPRDF, which won its third term gaining 327 of the 547 available parliamentary seats, a dramatic swing from the 2000 election when it had gained all but 12 of those seats. In the tense post-election climate, around 200 rioters were killed and many thousands were arrested, leading to widespread fears that Ethiopia's short-lived democracy would collapse. Stability was soon restored, however, and the swing was reversed in the 2010 election, when a 90% turnout of eligible voters gave the EPRDF a convincing majority, comprising 499 of the 547 seats. Although some irregularities were noted in this election, it was substantially free and fair, and the swing back towards Zenawi and the EPRDF probably reflects the enormous infrastructure expansions, and steady double-digit economic growth, of the previous decade.

Following **rainfall failures** in 2009 and 2010, the far east of Ethiopia has been afflicted by the crippling drought that led the UN to declare parts of neighbouring Somalia a famine zone on 20 July 2011. The direct impact on Ethiopia is unlikely to take on the proportions it has in earlier droughts, since the government is now open about its food aid needs, and distribution channels are in place to minimise famine within the country. However, this is far from being the case in Somalia, the epicentre of the famine, where Western food aid and humanitarian support has been blocked by Al-Shabaab (an insurgency group with alleged ties to Al Qaeda), forcing an estimated one million Somalis across the border into overcrowded and disease-ridden refugee camps in Ethiopia and northern Kenya.

Ethiopia's relations with some of its neighbours remain tense. All overland crossings into Eritrea remain closed, and the border conflict between these countries has the potential to erupt at any time – with Eritrea now being involved in an additional border dispute with Djibouti. Another concerning development has been conflict in the eastern Ogaden region, where Ethiopian Somali separatists, organised as the Ogaden National Liberation Front (ONLF), attacked a Chinese oil operation in the town of Abole in April 2007, killing 74. Tensions also exist with Somalia itself, since Ethiopia is the only country in the world to share diplomatic links with breakaway Somaliland, effectively treating this largely peaceful and democratic entity as a legitimate state, to the chagrin of the (unelected) government in Mogadishu. Nevertheless, in direct contrast to the naked oppression that characterised the autocratic Imperial and Derg eras, Ethiopia in 2011 ranks among the most well-governed and politically stable countries in Africa, with tourism playing an increasingly important role in the fast growing economy.

Economy

Ethiopia is one of the world's poorest nations. In the late 1980s, the per capita income was US$120 per annum, and it remained at that level until recently. Due to rapid growth in the post-Derg era, the current per capita estimate has tripled to around US$250 per annum. (This is the nominal figure in terms of purchasing power parity (PPP) GDP per capita is US$900.) This rise, however, largely represents the emergence of a wealthy middle class and does not reflect an improved quality of life for all. The average life expectancy previously dropped from 47 to 45, primarily due to AIDS-related deaths, but has recently rebounded to 55 years.

Most salt tablets mined by the Afar in the Danakil find their way to shops in Mekele. (RS/X/R/C)

The Ethiopian economy is dominated by **subsistence agriculture**. The Ethiopian Highlands are very fertile, and are criss-crossed by large rivers with enormous untapped potential for irrigation projects, but many parts of the country, particularly in the east and northeast, are prone to periodic rain failures and locust plagues, so there is a constant threat of local famines. The **growing of coffee** occupies 25% of the population and coffee accounts for 35% of Ethiopia's exports. The main crop grown for local consumption is *tef*, the grain used to make the staple *injera*.

Ethiopia is rich in mineral deposits, and ores such as **gold** and **iron** have been mined since ancient times. There has been little commercial exploitation of Ethiopia's minerals, largely due to inaccessibility, but a new network of Chinese-built roads may change this in the near future. The main product mined is **salt**.

Manufacture in Ethiopia is limited almost entirely to the processing of agricultural products, although Ethiopia did recently celebrate its first domestically built automobile courtesy of a joint Dutch venture.

The war with Eritrea forced the government to throw a large proportion of their scarce reserves at military investment, and to increase taxes. Development of services and infrastructure suffered as a result of the war which also precipitated a sharp decline in foreign investment. Both foreign investment and large, foreign-backed infrastructure projects have rebounded, but government services continue to suffer, with water and power shortages still common.

People and culture

Northern Ethiopia has a cultural, historical and linguistic identity quite distinct from that of the rest of Africa, largely because it has spent long periods of its history in virtual isolation. It is fair, if rather simplistic, to say that it is where the ancient world and Africa meet. **Northern Ethiopia**, or more specifically the ancient Axumite Kingdom, which centred on the modern province of Tigrai, had strong links with ancient Egypt, the Judaic civilisations of the Middle East, and Greece, evidenced by much of the ancient art and architecture that has been unearthed in the region. Pre-Christian civilisation in Tigrai is divided by historians into several eras, but stripping away the technicalities it can be said that Axum was an urbanised culture of blended classical and African influences from at least 600BC and quite possibly earlier. **Christianity** arrived in Ethiopia in the 4th century AD, when the Ethiopian Orthodox Church was founded in Axum. **Islam**, too, arrived in Ethiopia in its formative years, and it is still the dominant religion in eastern Ethiopia south of Tigrai.

The dominant religion in most other parts of the country is the **Ethiopian Orthodox Church**, a decidedly singular denomination that has developed in virtual isolation since the 4th century AD. An offshoot of Alexandria's Coptic Church, which broke away from Rome and Constantinople in AD451 after a doctrinal dispute, the Ethiopian Orthodox Church is infused with all sorts of archaic **Jewish rituals**, ranging from customary male circumcision a few days after birth and a variety of menstruation taboos to religious dances considered blasphemous by other Christian denominations. At the heart of the church lies an unfathomable relationship with the **Ark of the Covenant**, the very core of Judaism until its apparent disappearance from

An Orthodox priest (AZ)

Ethiopian music

The music of Ethiopia, in common with so many other aspects of this insular highland country, sounds like nothing you've ever heard before. And while the trademark lurching three-four signature, twitchy cross-rhythms, brassy instrumentation, taut pentatonic melodies and nail-on-blackboard vocal affectations can be somewhat impenetrable on initial contact, Ethiopia's diverse blend of the traditional and the contemporary, of exotic and indigenous styles must rank as one of Africa's greatest undiscovered musical legacies, reaching its apex with the ceaselessly inventive and hypnotically funky horn-splattered sides of 'Ethiopian swing' – splattered with hints of influence as diverse as James Brown, Motown, psychedelic blues and ska – recorded for a handful of independent labels in Addis Ababa between 1969 and 1978.

An excellent introduction to the genre is the ever-expanding series of *Ethiopiques* CDs compiled by Francis Falceto for the Buda label (Ⓦ www.budamusique.com) and available through online retailers such as Ⓦ www.amazon.com or Ⓦ www.emusic.com. Highlights of the series – there aren't really any lowlights – include *Ethiopiques 1* and *Ethiopiques 3*, which anthologise some of the most popular tracks released by Amha Records over 1969–75, providing an excellent overall introduction to the era's leading artists, including the legendary **Mahmoud Ahmed**. Also highly recommended, not least for its greater focus on female artists such as the sublime **Bizunesh Bekele** (the uncrowned 'First Lady' of Swinging Addis) and **Hirut Bekele**, is *Ethiopiques 13: Ethiopian Groove*, a re-release of an early 1990s collection of Kaifa Records 1976-78 output. *Ethiopiques 5* performs a similar round-up of the more traditional, drum-based Tigrigna recordings made by the era's most prominent Eritrean artists, including the irresistibly nicknamed **Tebereh 'Doris Day' Tesfa-Hunegn.** Another good entry-level compilation is the *Rough Guide to Ethiopian Music*, which was released in 2004 and includes tracks by artists including Aster Aweke, Mahmoud Ahmed and Alemayehu Eshete.

A boy in Mekele plays a handmade instrument. (SS)

A music shop in the northern town of Debark (SS)

Probably the most consistently popular Ethiopian recording artist since she first appeared on the scene in the late 1970s is Gondar-born, California-based **Aster Aweke**, who still enjoys such a high profile among her compatriots that it is remarkable to go a full day in any Ethiopian city without hearing what the *Rough Guide to World Music* describes as 'a voice that kills'. It is certainly one of the most thrilling and vocal instruments ever to have emerged from Africa, pitched somewhere between Aretha Franklin (a stated influence), Kate Bush and Björk, with a fractured but raunchy quality that can be utterly heartbreaking. Aster has 20 albums to her credit, and while her earliest – and some say best – material for Kaifa is available only on hard-to-track-down cassettes in Addis Ababa (and long overdue the attention of *Ethiopiques*), the likes of *Aster*, with its standout acoustic rendition of the chestnut 'Tizita', and *Ebo* are both worth investing in. The heir apparent to Aster's long-standing international status as Ethiopia's best-known singer is **Ejigayehu Shibabaw**, who embarked on a solo career under her more concise nickname of **Gigi**, and whose second eponymous CD, released in 2001, is a stunner.

The Timkat celebration (Ethiopian epiphany) is a colourful and flamboyant event in the Ethiopian calendar. (PJ/A)

Jerusalem led to the reforms of Josiah in around 650BC. Ethiopians believe that the original Ark was brought to Axum in the 1st millennium BC, and that it rests there to this day. What's more, the most holy item in every Ethiopian church is the *tabot* – a supposed replica of the Ark of the Covenant that is removed from the Holy of Holies only on important religious days, and it is at all times obscured from view by a cover of draped sheets.

In this torrent of well-attested Judaic influences, it is often forgotten that much of what is now **southern Ethiopia** has few ancient links to the Judaic world. The **Oromo** (referred to as the Galla prior to the 20th century) are Ethiopia's largest linguistic group. They were pagan when they first swept up the Rift Valley into Ethiopia in the 15th century, but are now predominantly Christian, with imported Catholic and Protestant denominations more influential than they are in northern Ethiopia. The society and culture of southern Ethiopia are more typically African in nature than those of the north.

People of South Omo

In the **Omo Valley** and the **far western lowlands** near Sudan is a variety of peoples whose modern lifestyle is still deeply African in every sense – in fact, you would struggle to find people anywhere in east Africa so cut off from the mainstream of modern life. Some of the different tribes likely to be encountered by visitors to South Omo are as follows:

Tsemai

The dominant people of Weita, on the Konso–Jinka road, are this group of around 5,000 subsistence farmers who practise flood cultivation of sorghum and maize, but also rear cattle and keep beehives. The Tsemai speak an east Cushitic language closely related to Konso, which is from where their founding chief hailed some 200 years ago. Tsemai society is structured around four fixed age-sets, which graduate in seniority once a decade, when a new generation of boys aged 11–22 is initiated.

Ari

Occupying the largest territory of any group in South Omo, extending from the northern border of Mago National Park into the highlands around Jinka, the Ari numbered 100,000 souls in the 1984 census, and the population is much larger today. They speak an Omotic language, and are mixed farmers who grow grains, coffee and enset, keep livestock and produce excellent honey. In rural areas, Ari women might still wear a traditional *gori* (a dress made with leaves), and decorate their waist and arms with colourful beads and bracelets.

The Ari are mixed farmers who supplement livestock with agriculture. (AZ)

Women of the Hamer tribe (EL)

Hamer

Numbering about 35,000 and occupying a large territory running east from the Omo River to Lake Chew Bahir, these are archetypal people of South Omo. Not only do they speak one of the Omotic tongues unique to this small area of southern Ethiopia, but their elaborate selection of body decorations embraces the full gamut of Omo specialities (excepting for lip plates). The women have thickly plaited and ochred hair hanging down in a heavy fringe, leather skirts decorated with cowries, a dozen or more copper bracelets fixed tightly around their arms, and thick welts on their body created by cutting themselves and treating the wound with ash and charcoal. The men, though also given to body scarring, are more plainly adorned, though some have clay hair buns fashioned on their heads – indicating that they killed a person or a dangerous animal within the last year. The most important event in Hamer society is the Bull Jumping Ceremony, the culmination of a three-day-long initiation rite held between late February and early April.

Dasanech

Originally pure pastoralists who lived a nomadic lifestyle, the Dasanech are migrants from the Turkana region of Kenya, and the abundant water frontage and fertile soil of their present territory has subsequently pushed them towards a more diverse economy, based around fishing and agriculture as well as livestock. The nomadic roots of the Dasanech are most clearly seen today in their flimsy traditional domed huts, which are strongly reminiscent of the impermanent structures built by other African desert pastoralists.

Bumi

A tribe of around 6,000 pastoralists who live on the western side of the Omo River, the Bumi speak an eastern Nilotic language, and their affiliations with the Turkana people of northern Kenya are immediately evident in the tentacle-like tangle of leather necklaces and side-cropped hairstyles worn by the women. The men share with the Turkana a reputation for aggression and ferocity, and they are often involved in fatal inter-tribal cattle raiding altercations with their neighbours.

Karo

This small tribe, which inhabits the east side of the Omo River, is best known for the elaborate body painting indulged in by the men, who daub their torsos with white chalk paint, in imitation of the plumage of

Members of the Karo tribe (EL)

a guinea fowl, and complement this with colourful facemasks prepared with a combination of chalk, charcoal, powdered yellow rock and iron-ore pastes. The hairstyle favoured by the women is also striking: tightly cropped at the side, and tied into bulbous knots and dyed ochre on top, it looks as if they have rushed out of the bathroom without removing their shower cap.

Mursi

The most celebrated residents of South Omo, the Mursi – the subject of several television documentaries and books – are best known for the lip plates worn by the women. The custom is that when a Mursi

The fierce stick fight of the Mursi people (EL)

woman reaches the age of about 20, a slit is cut beneath her lower lip, creating a small hole between the lip and the tissue below. Over the next year, this gap is progressively stretched, forming a 'lip loop' large enough for a small circular clay plate, indented like a pulley, to be inserted between the lip and the mouth. As the lip stretches, so the plate is replaced with a larger one, a process repeated until eventually she can hold a clay plate of perhaps 15cm (6 inches) in diameter. The larger the lip plate a woman can wear, the greater her value when she is married, but the path to matrimony is no smoother for Mursi men, with rival suitors traditionally partaking in a violent stick fight that frequently goes to the death.

Geography and climate 36

Habitats and vegetation 41

Desert and semi-desert 41
Savanna 42
Forest 43
Aquatic 45
Mountains 46

Wildlife 46

Predators 47
Primates 49
Antelope 50
Other large mammals 54
Reptiles 56
Birds 58

2 The Natural World

Far from being the monotonous thirstland of myth, Ethiopia is characterised by immense ecological contrasts and a rich biodiversity. Altitudinally, it embraces the lowest point in Africa, dipping to 130m below sea level, yet it is also dominated by the continent's largest contiguous highlands, studded with dozens of peaks that top the 4,000m mark. While the eastern lowlands do conform to arid stereotypes, the fertile highlands support everything from rolling grasslands to lush rainforests, along with vast swathes of cultivation. For casual visitors, Ethiopia's outstanding natural asset is the compelling scenery. But while it supports a less impressive fauna than, say, Kenya or Tanzania, its transitional ecology - essentially African but with strong links to Eurasia - has resulted in high levels of endemism, as manifested by the presence of such unique creatures as the Ethiopian wolf, Walia ibex and gelada monkey, along with perhaps 50 endemic or near-endemic bird species.

Geography and climate

Ethiopia's landscape is dominated by the **Ethiopian or Abyssinian Highlands**, a region often but somewhat misleadingly referred to as a plateau, since it is in fact dramatically mountainous. Isolated to the north, east and south by lower-lying desert or semi-desert, and the west by the relatively moist Nile Valley, these highlands comprise a massive block of ancient Archaean rock, formed about three billion years ago. Most of it lies above the 2,000m contour, and it is studded with dormant volcanic cones and more extensive mountain ranges that rise to above 3,500m, and in some cases occasionally receive snow. The most impressive massif in the north is the **Simien Mountains**, where Ras Dashen rises to 4,620m, making it the fifth-tallest peak in Africa, while the highest and most extensive range in the south is the **Bale Mountains**, whose highest peak Tullu Demtu reaches an altitude of 4,377m.

The Ethiopian Highlands are incised with a number of immense canyons and fissures, formed over time by the erosive action of rivers. Most spectacular among these is the **Blue Nile Gorge**, which runs for hundreds of kilometres between Lake Tana – the country's largest lake, contained within a volcanically dammed basin in the northwest highlands – and the Sudanese border northwest of Addis Ababa. Other important riverine gorges include the Muga, Jemma and Tekezé, all of

The Blue Nile falls (AZ)

Climate chart

ADDIS ABABA

(2,400M)	Jan	Feb	Mar	Apr	May	Jun	Jul	Aug	Sep	Oct	Nov	Dec
Ave temp (°C)	16	17	18	18	18	17	16	16	15	15	15	15
Rainfall (mm)	30	40	45	70	90	110	210	280	160	30	10	15

GONDAR

(2,120M)	Jan	Feb	Mar	Apr	May	Jun	Jul	Aug	Sep	Oct	Nov	Dec
Ave temp (°C)	19	20	21	22	21	19	18	18	19	19	18	18
Rainfall (mm)	10	10	25	40	90	170	310	300	160	30	20	15

HARAR

(1,850M)	Jan	Feb	Mar	Apr	May	Jun	Jul	Aug	Sep	Oct	Nov	Dec
Ave temp (°C)	18	20	20	20	19	18	18	18	18	19	18	18
Rainfall (mm)	10	20	30	100	50	50	80	150	75	30	10	10

which form part of the Nile drainage system, and the Wabe Shebelle in the south.

A far greater chasm than any of the above, however, is the **Rift Valley**, which is the largest single geographical feature on earth, stretching for 5,500km from the Red Sea to Mozambique. Following a fault line associated with tectonic plate activity (the phenomenon that caused the monolithic landmass of Gondwanaland to start breaking up into its present-day constituent parts some 200 million years ago), the Rift Valley was created about 30 million years ago, when the Arabian and African tectonic plates first started to slide apart. Within Ethiopia, it flanks the eastern edge of the northern highlands, forming the near-uninhabitable Danakil Depression (a highly volcanic region that mostly lies below sea level) and slightly more hospitable Awash Valley. Further south, a moister and more fertile stretch of the Rift Valley, studded with more than half-a-dozen large lakes, divides the southern highlands into its ecologically distinct eastern and western components.

Ethiopia displays a high level of **climatic variation** reflecting its topography. At one extreme, the upper reaches of the Bale Mountains receive periodic **snowfall**. At the other, the Danakil Desert, officially listed as the **hottest place on earth**, regularly experiences daytime temperatures in excess of 50°C. As a rule, however, the Ethiopian Highlands have a temperate climate, with an average daytime temperature of 16°C belying their proximity to the Equator, while the

Climatic zones

Ethiopians traditionally recognise five climatic zones, each of which has distinctive features linked to altitude, rainfall and temperature. These are as follows:

Bereha
Hot and arid desert lowlands that typically lie below 500m and receive significantly less than 500mm of precipitation annually. Not generally cultivatable so mostly inhabited by pastoralists. Includes most of the Somali border area and much of the Rift Valley north of Addis Ababa.

The Danakil Depression is largely desert and its Afar inhabitants are dependent on deep wells for water. (AZ)

Kolla
Warm to hot mid-altitude locations that receive sufficient rainfall for cultivation without relying on irrigation, such as the Rift Valley between Addis Ababa and Hawassa, or the Gambella region.

Weyna Dega
Warm to cool, medium- to high-altitude locations typically receiving more than 1,500mm of rainfall annually, often naturally forested though much of this has been cleared over the centuries. Excellent for cultivation of grains (especially *tef*; see page 94) and coffee. Areas include Addis Ababa, Gondar, Goba and most other highlands below the 2,600m contour.

Dega

Cool to cold, medium-to-high rainfall, high-altitude locations that would naturally support grassland or coniferous forest and now are mostly used to cultivate grains such as barley and wheat. Dinsho, Debre Birhan, Ankober and other highland areas with an altitude in the range 2,600–3,200m.

Worch

Chilly, medium-to-low rainfall Afro-alpine regions supporting a cover of heath-like vegetation

Mountain scenery, Ankober (AZ)

that isn't generally conducive to cultivation, such as Sanetti Plateau (Bale Mountains National Park), the eastern peaks of the Simiens and other plateaux or peaks above 3,200–3,500m.

The Sanetti Plateau supports heath-like vegetation which is typical of Afro-alpine habitat on Africa's tallest mountains. (AZ)

The extraordinary landscapes of the Danakil Depression (DS/DT)

southern Rift Valley, much of which lies at around 1,500m, is temperate to hot and seasonally moist. The hottest parts of the country, aside from the searing Danakil, are the Somali border area and the humid western lowlands bordering South Sudan.

Possibly the most widespread misconception about Ethiopia is that it is uniformly arid. In reality, most of the highlands and the southern Rift Valley receive a very high level of **precipitation**: parts of the far west have an annual average rainfall of 2,000mm, the Addis Ababa area gets around 1,300mm (almost double the figure for London), and other highland and mid-altitude areas typically fall in the range of 700–1,200mm. Rainfall is very seasonal, however, with most rain in the north falling between July and September, give or take a week or two. The rains usually start and end a few weeks earlier south of Addis Ababa, while most of the rain in South Omo falls between March and May. The northeast highlands are much drier, and have a less reliable rainy season than other highland parts of Ethiopia, hence their vulnerability to periodic droughts and famines. (See also the *Climate chart*, page 37, and *Climatic zones*, pages 38–9).

Habitats and vegetation

Just as climate is directly influenced by topography and altitude, so are the varied habitats of Ethiopia largely a product of climate, influenced to some extent by soil types, slopes, the presence of standing water and other factors. Likewise, for visitors with a strong interest in wildlife, it is useful to recognise that most creatures are adapted to very specific habitats – a term that in this context might refer to something quite local and contained such as a lily-covered pool or isolated hill, or to a more generic landscape like the open savanna of the southern Rift Valley or grassy meadows typical of uncultivated parts of the highlands. An overview of the most important habitats follows.

Desert and semi-desert
Within Ethiopia, true **deserts** – typically receiving a rainfall of below 250mm per annum – are confined to the little-visited Afar and Somali Federal regions. However, much of the far south, including the Rift Valley south of Dilla and South Omo region, might be characterised as **semi-desert**, receiving an annual rainfall of below 500mm, or seasonally arid, making it too dry to support cultivation or commercial ranchland. These arid and semi-arid areas vary greatly in soil type, from the red earthy

plains of South Omo to the black stony expanses of the Danakil, but generally they are either practically bereft of vegetation, or they support a cover of scrubby acacia thicket that transforms into a short-lived blanket of greenery after good rains. Wildlife tends to be thinly distributed, and it is comprised mainly of desert-adapted creatures, though the semi-arid plains of the south are productive for birds, notably dry-country specials such as spectacular vulturine guineafowl, Somali ostrich, golden pipit, golden-breasted starling, and a few very localised or endemic larks.

Savanna

Savanna is a loosely defined term sometimes used to describe any area of wooded grassland or open canopy woodland, but in this part of Africa it most often refers to low- or medium-altitude grassland habitats studded with fire-resistant trees. Within Ethiopia, this habitat is widespread in the south, particularly in the Rift Valley, South Omo and the drier areas bordering Kenya and Somalia. Characteristic of the Africa savanna are thorn-trees of the genus *Acacia*, which include the tall flat-topped *A. tortilis* and *A. abyssinica*, the more shrub-like three-thorned acacia *A. Senegal* and hook-thorn *A. mellitero*, and the scraggly whistling thorn *A. drepanolobrium* – the latter so named for the low whistling sound created by the wind passing through ant galls fashioned around its

Savanna is the favoured habitat of most large African antelope, including Swayne's hartebeest. (AZ)

twinned thorns. Elsewhere in Africa, savanna habitats often support immense herds of grazing ungulates, but this is no longer the case anywhere in Ethiopia. However, the savanna of the Rift Valley does host a wonderfully rich avifauna, including conspicuous perching birds such as rollers, shrikes, bee-eaters and raptors along with the more active sunbirds, lovebirds, parrots, hornbills, starlings and helmet-shrikes, and the relatively secretive bush-shrikes, owls, woodpeckers, cuckoos and batises.

Forest

Forest differs from woodland in having a closed canopy and it typically comprises several tall vertically layered sub-canopies that cast a

permanent shadow over a tangle of undergrowth, epiphytes and vines. It will come as a surprise to many that some 35% of Ethiopia naturally supports a cover of indigenous forest, though much of this has been lost to cultivation in recent centuries, the natural forest cover is still estimated at around 3– 5%, concentrated mostly in the western and far-southern highlands. Two broad forest types dominate: moist **broad-leafed jungle-like tracts** with a similar species composition to montane rainforests elsewhere in East Africa occur widely in the south (for instance Harenna Forest on the southern footslopes of Bale) and west, while **coniferous forest**, usually dominated by fragrant juniper and hagenia trees, is associated with the northern slopes of Bale and copses in the northern highlands. Typical forest creatures in Ethiopia include the striking colobus monkey and a plethora of birds, including several endemics. The western forests in particular remain very poorly known in scientific terms, and are almost certain to harbour many undescribed species.

Flamingoes are an impressive sight at Lake Abiata. (AZ)

Aquatic

Looking at any map of Ethiopia, the surprising amount of blue infills and blue lines pays testament to the moist climate of the highlands. The country's largest body of water is Lake Tana, which extends over some 3,500 km² in the northeast, and forms the main source of the Blue Nile, supplying most of the water that flows into Egypt's Nile Valley. Other important **lakes** include Hayk and Ashenge in the northwest, and the string of eight lakes that lines the Rift Valley floor south of Addis Ababa, while lesser ones include the crater lakes around Debre Zeyit and elsewhere in the central highlands. Equally, the Blue Nile is but one of many significant **river systems** in Ethiopia, the others being the Baro and Tekezé, both of which feed the White Nile (the river that flows out of Lake Victoria in Uganda to join the Blue Nile at Khartoum in Sudan); the Wabe Shebelle, which rises in the Bale area and courses through the southeast of the country through Somalia and into the Indian Ocean; the Omo River, which rises in the western highlands to

drain into Lake Turkana on the Kenyan border; and the Awash, which rises near Addis Ababa and then follows the course of the Rift Valley northwards before being swallowed by the series of desert lakes near the Djibouti border. In addition to these large rivers and lakes, the country also supports numerous **marshes** and other **wetland** habitats. The most characteristic large mammal of these aquatic habitats is the hippo, but many wetlands also support ferocious Nile crocodiles along with more than 100 species of water-associated bird.

Mountains

Red-hot pokers, Sanetti Plateau (AZ)

The upper slopes of Ethiopia's taller mountains, including Bale and the Simiens, support a rarefied, almost ethereal cover of pastel-shaded Afro-alpine moorland and grassland. These **montane grasslands** often host a wealth of flowering perennials such as orchids, proteas, geraniums, lilies, aster daisies, spike-leafed aloes and marsh-loving red-hot pokers, attracting prodigious numbers of colourful nectar-eating sunbirds, while the **higher moorland belt** is characterised by grey-pink heathers studded with otherworldly giant forms of lobelia and senecio. The Sanetti Plateau, in the Bale, is the most accessible such habitat in Africa, traversed as it is by the continent's highest motorable road, and it supports a wide range of unusual creatures, most famously the endemic Ethiopian wolf. Also reasonably accessible by road, the Simien Mountains form the last stronghold for the endangered Walia ibex, and they support the word's largest concentrations of the grass-eating gelada monkey, which nest on the cliffs at night.

Wildlife

Much of Ethiopia's once prolific plains game has been hunted out, and even those parks that do protect typical African savanna habitats – Nechisar, Mago, Omo and Awash – support low wildlife volumes compared to their counterparts elsewhere in eastern and southern Africa. However, the forests of the highlands still harbour significant mammal populations, and the country is of great interest to specialised wildlife enthusiasts for the presence of several alluring endemics (species unique to the country) including Ethiopian wolf, gelada monkey, mountain nyala, Walia ibex and Somali wild ass. Ethiopia is also one of the most popular and rewarding birding destinations in Africa, in large part due to the unusually high proportion of national and regional endemics on the checklist of 850-odd species.

Predators

The most-common large predator is the **spotted hyena**, which is reasonably visible in most national parks and reserves and also frequents the outskirts of several towns, in particular Harar, where a so-called hyena man uses raw meat to attract a few semi-habituated individuals every evening (see page 221).

Africa's three large feline species – **lion**, **leopard** and **cheetah** – are all present, but they are thinly distributed, with the possible exception of the leopard, and tend to be notoriously secretive, so sightings are very unusual. The one place you can be certain of seeing a lion – the local Abyssinian race, which is distinguished by the male's impressive black mane – is at the zoo at Siddist Kilo in Addis Ababa!

Aside from the **Ethiopian wolf** (see box, page 48), the country also supports all three African **jackal** species, with black-backed jackal commonest in the south and Eurasian jackal in the north. The endangered **African hunting dog** has been recorded in southern Ethiopia, but is probably now verging on extinction there. The **bat-eared fox** is common in parts of South Omo, while widespread but very rarely seen nocturnal predators include civet, genet, serval, caracal and aardvark.

The bat-eared fox is a common sight in South Omo. (AZ)

The Ethiopian wolf

IUCN listed as Critically Endangered, the Ethiopian wolf (*Canis simensis*) is the rarest of the world's 37 canid species, and until recently it was also the most taxonomically enigmatic, as reflected by such misleading common names as Simien fox or *kai kebero* ('red jackal') in Amharigna. Recent DNA tests have determined that it is neither fox nor jackal, but the descendant of an extinct ally of the European grey wolf that colonised the area in the late Pleistocene era.

The Ethiopian wolf stands about 60cm high, has a long muzzle similar to that of a coyote, and a rufous coat with a black tail and a white throat and flanks. Unlike most dogs, it is a courser rather than a hunter, feeding diurnally on the endemic giant mole-rat and other rodents in Afro-alpine moorland and grassland. Two distinct races are recognised, distinguished by slight differences in coloration and skull shape, with the Rift Valley forming the natural divide between them.

As recently as the mid-19th century, the Ethiopian wolf was widespread and common in the Ethiopian Highlands. Numbers have since dwindled dramatically, largely due to introduced diseases such as canine distemper and rabies, but also through hunting and interbreeding with domestic dogs. Around 500 Ethiopian wolves survive today in seven isolated populations. The main stronghold, **Bale National Park**, hosts around 200 wolves – a major decline from Chris Hillman's 1976 estimate of 700 – and is centred on the open Sanetti Plateau, where sightings are virtually guaranteed.

Another 80 to 150 Ethiopian wolves live in the **Arsi Highlands**, immediately east of Bale, most likely as part of a shared gene pool with its Bale neighbours. The northern race may number fewer than 100 in the wild, and is divided evenly between the **Simien Mountains** and the **Guassa Plateau**, though a few other packs survive in remote moorland locations such as **Mount Guna** and **Mount Abuna Yoseph**. See Ⓦ www.ethiopianwolf.org for more information.

(AZ)

Black-and-white colobus monkey (AZ)

Primates

The most commonly observed group of large mammals in Ethiopia is the monkeys. In the south and west, the handsome **black-and-white colobus** (guereza monkey), easily distinguished by its white beard and flowing white tail, is abundant in forested habitats, and often smaller stands of moist woodland, most notably on the shore of Lake Awasa and at Wondo Genet. Also common in wooded habitats, but associated more with savanna than true forest, where it often spends time on the ground, the **grivet** (sometimes regarded as conspecific with the east African vervet) is a highly sociable grey monkey with prominent white cheek marks.

In addition to the rather baboon-like **gelada monkey** (see box, page 50), at least one primate species is endemic to Ethiopia. This is the **Bale monkey**, which was first described in 1902 and has long been treated as a probable subspecies of the grivet monkey. However, a 2008 scientific expedition to study Bale monkeys in the remote Obobullu Forest, to the east of the Bale Mountains, determined that it is a distinct species that relies upon bamboo for around three-quarters of its diet (more than any primate other than the bamboo lemurs of Madagascar) and is also a lot more arboreal than a typical grivet and vervet. Dark grey-brown with bold white cheeks and chest markings, this very secretive species is confined to bamboo stands in the Bale Massif and a few other mountains in southeast Ethiopia.

Two species of baboon – distinguished from other monkeys by their large size, dog-like face and crook-like tail – occur in Ethiopia. Most common is the **Anubis baboon**, a dark olive-brown creature whose wide habitat tolerance means it is common in most national parks, as well as in rocky areas and cliffs, in the south and west. Endemic to the Horn of Africa and the southern Arabian Peninsula, the **Hamadryas baboon,** paler and more lightly built but with a distinctive mane in the case of the male, occurs in Awash National Park and more northerly parts of the Rift Valley.

Hamadryas baboon
(PRG/MP/FLPA)

(JK)

Gelada monkeys

The least vulnerable of the large mammal species endemic to Ethiopia, with a population estimated to be at least 200,000, the unmistakable gelada monkey (*Thercopithecus gelada*) is unique among primates in that it feeds predominantly on grasses. Though the female gelada is rather nondescript, the male is spectacularly handsome, with an imposing golden mane and a heart-shaped red chest patch that serves the same purpose as the colourful buttocks or testicles of less sedentary monkeys. Distributed throughout the **northern highlands**, it is generally associated with cliffs and ravines, and is most common in the Simien Mountains, but also quite numerous on the Guassa Plateau, and in the vicinity of Ankober and Debre Libanos.

In evolutionary terms, the gelada is something of a living fossil, being the only surviving representative of a genus of grazing monkeys that once ranged far more broadly across Africa, and is ancestral not only to modern baboons, but also to the drills and to the smaller and more arboreal mangabeys, both of which have re-adapted to rainforest habitats. The gelada is probably the most sociable of African monkeys, with conglomerations of 500 or more regularly recorded in one field, and its harem-based social structure is regarded to be the most complex of any animal other than humans.

Antelope

The world's most-diverse group of bovids, the antelopes are an unwavering feature of the African landscape, naturally thriving in every habitat from rainforest to desert – except where they have been eliminated by human activity, which is sadly the case in much of

Ethiopia. So, while a large number of antelope species are present in Ethiopia, many have a very limited distribution, partially because so many different habitats converge around the Ethiopian Highlands, but also largely as a result of persecution.

The *Tragelaphus* family, a group of antelopes that is notable for its spiralled horns and striking markings, is one of the best represented antelope genus in Ethiopia, and it includes the endemic **mountain nyala** (see box, page 53). The most widespread Tragelaphine, however, is the **bushbuck**, a slightly hunchbacked forest and woodland inhabitant. The handsome **Menelik's bushbuck**, a jet black highland race commonly seen in Bale National Park and in forests near Addis Ababa, is of particular interest. In addition, the **greater kudu**, the second tallest of all African antelopes, notable for the male's magnificent 1.5m spiralling horns, is common in drier climates alongside the similar but less-striking **lesser kudu**. The only antelope larger than the greater kudu, the **eland**, a Tragelaphine with a rather bovine appearance, is seasonally abundant in parts of South Omo but absent elsewhere.

Associated more with arid habitats, gazelles are medium-sized antelopes with gently curved small to medium-sized horns, a tan coat with white underparts and in some species a black side-stripe. **Grant's gazelle**, a long-horned unstriped species that will be familiar to anybody who has visited east Africa's reserves, reaches the northern extent of its range in the southern Rift Valley of Ethiopia, and is often seen in Nechisar National Park and along the Moyale road south of Dilla. Its range doesn't overlap with that of **Soemmerring's gazelle**, an unstriped species with a black face and white cheek stripes that is quite common on the plains around Awash National Park and the roads to Harar and Assab. The paler **Dorcas gazelle** is a Saharan species quite common in the Djibouti border area of Ethiopia. The most commonly seen large antelope in the South Omo region is the **gerenuk**, an atypical and unmistakable gazelle with a red-brown coat, a very long neck, and a habit of browsing on the higher branches of acacia trees in a goat-like manner, up on its hind legs with neck outstretched.

Soemmerring's gazelle (NB/FLPA)

51

Relatives of the wildebeest, hartebeests are tan and rather ungainly antelopes of which several distinct forms exist, but are usually regarded as races rather than full species. The **Lelwel hartebeest** is quite common in parts of South Omo, while the **tora hartebeest** is present in unknown numbers in the northwest lowlands, and the endangered **Swayne's hartebeest**, effectively endemic to Ethiopia following extinction in Somalia, is thinly distributed in the southern Rift Valley, where the total population of around 500 is split between Senkele Game Reserve and Nechisar National Park. The closely related **tiang**, similar in gait and shape to the hartebeest, but much darker, occurs widely in the Omo Valley and the Gambella region.

With its unmistakable scimitar-like horns, the **Beisa oryx** is a large handsome dry-country antelope that occurs in dwindling numbers in and around Awash National Park, as well as in the South Omo region. Two plain tan and virtually indistinguishable reedbuck species are found in Ethiopia: the **Bohor reedbuck** is common in Bale National Park, while the **mountain reedbuck** occurs throughout the country and is regularly seen at Fantelle Volcano in Awash National Park. Related to the reedbuck, the **waterbuck** is a large antelope with a shaggy brown coat and sizeable lyre-shaped horns found at a few scattered localities in southern Ethiopia. The related **Nile lechwe** and **white-eared kob** are both near-endemic to marshy ground and floodplains in the Sudanese Nile Valley, but their range extends to the Gambella area in the far western lowlands of Ethiopia.

Dik-diks are small, brown antelopes with tan legs, white eye-rings, and distinctive extended snouts. Four species are recognised, two of which are found in Ethiopia. **Guenther's dik-dik** is found throughout the southern lowlands and is often seen from the roadside in South Omo, while **Salt's dik-dik**, endemic to the Horn of Africa, is widespread in the dry east. The **klipspringer**, a slightly built antelope with a stiff-looking grey-brown coat, is associated with rocky hills and cliffs throughout Ethiopia, and is common in Bale National Park.

Guenther's dik-dik (IY/FLPA)

(AZ)

Mountain nyala

The mountain nyala (*Tragelaphus buxtoni*) has the distinction of being the most recently discovered of African antelopes; the first documented specimen was shot by one Major Buxton in 1908, and described formally two years later. However, it is not, as its name suggests, a particularly close relative of the nyala of southern Africa, but more probably evolved from a race of greater kudu, which it resembles in size and shape, though it is much shaggier and has smaller (though by no means insignificant) horns, with only one twist as opposed to the greater kudu's two or three.

The mountain nyala lives in herds of five to ten animals in juniper and hagenia forests in the **southeast highlands**, and it has always had a somewhat restricted range, though numbers outside of national parks have declined greatly in recent decades, and it is now IUCN listed as Endangered, with the total population estimated at around 2,500 individuals. The main protected stronghold is **Bale National Park**, where large numbers are present around the park headquarters at Dinsho and nearby Mount Gaysay. Elsewhere, a small population is protected in the **Kuni Muktar Sanctuary**, in the highlands southeast of Awash National Park. Substantial populations still cling on in forested parts of the **Arsi Highlands** such as Dodola, though numbers are unknown.

Walia ibex

(IY/FLPA)

Ethiopia's rarest endemic mammal, the Walia ibex (*Capra walie*) was once widespread in the mountains of the north, but is now restricted to the **Simien Mountains**, where it is uncommon but quite often seen by hikers. A type of goat that lives on narrow mountain ledges, it can easily be recognised by the fearsome decurved horns that adorn adults of both sexes – growing up to 1m long in the case of some males. The presence of carved ibex on many pre-Christian religious shrines in Axum indicates that it was once considerably more prevalent than it is today. By the 19th century, however, its range was restricted to the Simiens, which supported a population of several thousand before the Italian occupation. By 1963, only 200 ibexes remained in Ethiopia, largely as a result of indiscriminate hunting, but this has increased to slightly more than 500 today, and it is hoped that within a few decades the park will have realised its potential of supporting 2,000–3,000 individuals.

The duiker family comprises 15 species of small antelope, most of which live in forest undergrowth, though the **common duiker**, the species confirmed for Ethiopia, is also the only member of the family associated with more open country. In 1986, a small red duiker was reliably observed in the Harenna Forest within Bale National Park, while in 1996 a similar duiker was observed in Omo National Park. The geographical probability is that the former is **Harvey's red duiker** and the latter **Weyn's red duiker**, but this is far from certain, and an endemic race or species is not out of the question.

Other large mammals

Within Ethiopia, many of Africa's most distinctive large mammals are practically restricted to South Omo, among them **elephant**, **giraffe**, **buffalo** and **black rhinoceros**, the last almost certainly now exterminated. Another small elephant population occurs in Babile Elephant Sanctuary to the south of Harar, and small numbers of giraffe and buffalo occur elsewhere in the little-visited Kenyan and Sudanese border areas.

The **hippopotamus** is widely distributed in the lakes and larger rivers of Ethiopia. It is common in Lake Tana and in most of the Rift Valley lakes, though current details of status are not available. The best places to see hippos are Nechisar National Park, at the source of the Nile near Bahir Dar on Lake Tana, at Lake Boye near Jimma, and at Koko Dam near Adama.

Two swine species are found in Ethiopia. The **desert warthog**, a species more-or-less endemic to the Horn of Africa, occurs in wooded savanna and is frequently seen near water. It is found in most national parks and is especially common around Dinsho in Bale. The **bushpig** is a larger, darker and hairier beast found in forests or dense woodland. It is probably common in all Ethiopian forests but its nocturnal habits and chosen habitats make it difficult to see. I was very lucky to see a pair in the Harenna Forest in Bale.

Burchell's zebra – also called the common or plains zebra – is the common equine of sub-Saharan Africa. It is found throughout the south of Ethiopia and is the most numerous large mammal species in Nechisar National Park. The larger and more densely striped **Grevy's zebra** is restricted to southern Ethiopia and northern Kenya. In Ethiopia, it is thinly distributed in the Kenyan border area east of the Omo Valley, and in the Rift Valley north of Awash National Park. Ethiopia's Yangudi Rassa National Park, bisected by the Assaita road to the north of Awash National Park, supports a few hundred of the Critically Endangered **African wild ass**, the ancestor of the domestic donkey. The wild ass is not a true Ethiopian endemic – Somalia alone supported a population of around 10,000, and it still occurs in parts of India – but Yangudi Rassa now hosts the only remaining confirmed African population.

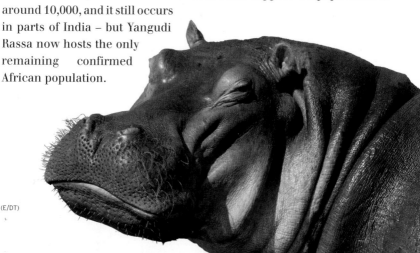

Reptiles

The **Nile crocodile**, the largest living reptile, regularly grows to lengths of up to 6m and is remarkably unchanged from fossil crocodilians that lived contemporaneously with dinosaurs. Once common in most large Ethiopian rivers and lakes, it has been wiped out in many areas since the early 20th century, hunted professionally for its skin as well as by vengeful local villagers. Today, large specimens are mostly confined to protected areas. The gargantuan specimens that lurk around the so-called 'Crocodile Market' in Nechisar National Park are a truly primeval sight. Other possible sites for croc sightings are the southern Omo River, the Baro River downstream of Gambella, the Awash River near Awash National Park and Nazret, and other large bodies of water at lower to medium altitudes.

A wide variety of snakes is found in Ethiopia, though – fortunately, most would agree – they are typically very shy and unlikely to be seen unless actively sought. Africa's largest species is the non-venomous **rock python**, which has gold-on-black mottled skin and regularly grows to lengths exceeding 5m. Most other snakes are also non-venomous, and these smaller species aren't potentially harmful to any living creature much bigger than a rat. Of the venomous snakes, one of the most dangerous is the **puff adder**, a thickset resident of savanna and rocky habitats, with a notoriously sluggish disposition that means it is more often disturbed than other snakes. Several **cobra** species, including the spitting cobra, are present in Ethiopia, most with characteristic hoods that they raise when about to strike.

All African lizards are harmless humans, with the arguable exception of **giant monitor lizards**, which grow up to 2.2m long – hence they are sometimes mistaken for a small crocodile – and could theoretically inflict a nasty bite if cornered. Visitors to tropical Africa soon become familiar with the **common house gecko**, an endearing bug-eyed, translucent white lizard which, as its name suggests, reliably inhabits most houses as well as lodge rooms, scampering up walls and upside down on the ceiling in pursuit of pesky insects attracted to the lights. The **agamas** are distinguished from other common lizards by their relatively large size (typically 20–25cm), basking habits and almost plastic-looking scaling – depending on the species, a combination of blue, purple, orange or red, with the flattened head generally a different colour from the torso. Another common family is the **skinks**: small, long-tailed lizards, most of which are quite dark and have a few thin black stripes running from head to tail.

Giant monitor lizard (NB/FLPA)

The most common shelled reptile in the region is the **leopard tortoise**, which is named after its gold-and-black mottled shell, and has been known to live for more than 50 years in captivity. The form present in Ethiopia is the giant leopard tortoise (often designated as the race *S. p. somalica*), which can weigh over 50kg. Four species of terrapin – essentially the freshwater equivalent of turtles – are resident. The largest is the **Nile soft-shelled terrapin**, which has a wide, flat shell and in rare instances might reach a length of almost 1m.

Nile crocodiles on Lake Chamo (GA/DT)

Birds

Ethiopia's proximity to the Equator and great habitat diversity mean its avifauna is one of the richest in Africa, with around 850 species recorded, including a high proportion of species endemic to Ethiopia or the Horn of Africa. For a first-time visitor to Africa with a passing interest in birds, it will be the most colourful and largest species that capture the eye: rollers,

An Abyssinian longclaw – for the dedicated birder this is a must-see. (NB/FLPA)

bee-eaters, cranes, storks, hornbills and such. By contrast, for any dedicated birdwatcher planning a once-in-a-lifetime trip to Ethiopia, a primary goal will be to identify most of the 50 species whose range is actually – or practically – confined to Ethiopia.

These 'must-see' birds fall into several categories. Most importantly, there are the true endemics, which are not known to occur outside of Ethiopia, a category that includes at least 14 species, possibly more, depending on several unresolved taxonomic uncertainties. A similar number of species might be described as former Ethiopian endemics, since their range extends into a small part of Eritrea, which became an independent state in 1993, but would seldom be visited in its own right as a birding destination. A third category constitutes at least 25 Horn of Africa endemics or other near-endemics whose range extends into contiguous but little visited (and in some cases, unsafe to visit) parts of northern Kenya, Somalia and/or eastern Sudan.

A full list of these national endemics, near-endemics and other 'key' species follows, with names and sequence following Redman, Stevenson and Fanshawe's *Birds of the Horn of Africa*, the most useful field guide for Ethiopia.

The Abyssinian roller is a colourful inhabitant of Awash National Park. (NB/FLPA)

Birds endemic to Ethiopia

Abyssinian catbird
Parophasma galinieri

Prince Ruspoli's turaco
Tauraco ruspolii

Abyssinian longclaw
Macronyx flavicollis

Salvadori's serin
Serinus xantholaemus

Ankober serin
Serinus ankobernis

Spot-breasted plover
Vanellus melanocephalus

Black-headed
siskin *Serinus nigriceps*

Streseman's bush crow
Zavattariornis stresemanni

Blue-winged goose
Cyanochen cyanopterus

White-tailed swallow
Hirundo megaensis

Harwood's francolin
Pternistes harwoodi

Yellow-fronted parrot
Poicephalus flavifrons

Nechisar nightjar
Caprimulgus solala

Yellow-throated seedeater
Serinus flavigula

Note: In addition to the species listed above, the following controversial or undescribed species are possible endemics: Bale parisoma *Parisoma griseaventris*, Brown saw-wing *Psalidoprocne antinorii*, Erlanger's lark *Calandrella erlangeri*, Ethiopian cliff swallow *Hirundo spp*, Gillett's lark *Mirafra gilletti* and Sidamo lark *Heteromirafra sidamoensis*.

Blue-winged geese (NB/FLPA)

Birds endemic to Ethiopia and Eritrea

Abyssinian (golden-backed) woodpecker
Dendropicus abyssinicus

Abyssinian oriole
Oriolus monacha

Abyssinian slaty flycatcher
Melaenornis chocolatina

Banded barbet
Lybius undatus

Black-winged lovebird
Agapornis swinderiana

Rouget's rail
Rougetius rougetii

Rüppell's (black) chat
Myrmecocichla melaena

Thick-billed raven
Corvus crassirostris

Wattled ibis
Bostrychia carunculata

White-backed (black) tit
Parus leuconotus

White-billed starling
Onychognathus albirostris

White-collared pigeon
Columba albitorques

White-throated seedeater
Serinus xanthopygius

White-winged cliff-chat
Myrmecocichla semirufa

A thick-billed raven in a stand off with a bearded vulture. (I/FLPA)

Near-endemics or 'Horn of Africa' endemics

(Abyssinian) long-eared owl
Asio abyssinicus

African citril
Serinus citrinelloides

African white-winged dove
Streptopelia semitorquata

Brown-rumped seedeater (serin)
Serinus tristriatis

Chestnut-naped francolin
Francolinus castaneicollis

Dwarf raven
Corvus edithae

Erckell's francolin
Pternistes erckelii

Ethiopian boubou
Laniarius aethiopicus

Hemprich's hornbill
Tockus hemprichii

Heuglin's bustard
Neotis heuglinii

Juba weaver
Ploceus dischrocephalus

Orange River francolin
Scleroptila gutturalis

Red-billed pytilia
Pytilia lineata

Rüppell's weaver
Ploceus galbula

Shining sunbird
Cinnyrus hebessinica

Somali bulbul
Pycnonotus somaliensis

Somali starling
Onychognathus blythii

Somali wheatear
Oenanthe phillipsi

Sombre rock chat
Cercomela dubia

Swainson's sparrow
Passer swainsonii

White-cheeked turaco
Tauraco leucolophus

White-rumped babbler
Turdoides leucopygia

Moorland francolin
Scleroptila psilolaemus

Note: Of the species listed above, (Abyssinian) long-eared owl, red-billed pytilia, sombre rock chat and moorland francolin are as good as endemic to Ethiopia, a status denied them on the basis of, at most, a handful of records in one site outside the country.

When to visit — 64

Public holidays — 65

Itinerary planning — 65

Booking — 67

Your itinerary: 20 top attractions — 70

Living Christian shrines — 70
Other cultural sites — 72
Other historical sites — 75
Scenery — 76
Wildlife and birds — 78

Red tape — 80

Getting there — 80

Health and safety — 81

Inoculations — 81
Deep-vein thrombosis — 81
Malaria — 82
Women travellers — 82
Disabled travellers — 83

What to take — 84

Clothing — 84
Photographic gear — 85
Binoculars — 85
Other essentials — 86

Organising your finances — 86

3 Planning a Trip

Although Ethiopia can be a challenging travel destination, especially for independent travellers using public transport, planning an organised trip with a specialist operator - several are recommended in this chapter - is pretty straightforward. However, there are a number of factors that you might want to consider as you investigate your itinerary options, and (as the trip draws closer) pack and prepare your paperwork. There are seasonal considerations, inoculations and malaria prophylaxis, and deciding what to pack. Most important in the early stages of your planning is deciding which parts of this vast and varied country most pique your interest, a question addressed in our selection of Ethiopia's 20 top attractions, which showcase the best of this varied country's cultural, historical, scenic and wildlife highlights.

When to visit

Tourism to Ethiopia is focused on the highlands, which – because their proximity to the Equator is tempered by the altitude – have an equable climate throughout the year, seldom becoming uncomfortably hot or cold. Most of Ethiopia can thus be visited at any time of year, the one exception being the South Omo region, whose rough roads often become temporarily impassable in the local rainy season, which typically runs between April and May, but may extend a month either side of that.

To witness Meskel, visit towards the end of September. (AZ)

In the days when the likes of Lalibela had dry-season-only airstrips, and most roads were unsurfaced, there was a strong case for avoiding the northern historical circuit rainy season, which runs from July to early October. Contrary to what you might hear elsewhere, this is no longer the case. Indeed, in certain respects, the rainy season is the nicest time to be in Ethiopia, partially because there are fewer people at the more popular tourist sites, but also because the scenery is so much more impressive when it is green and well watered.

A lovely time of year to travel in northern Ethiopia is September through to early October, when the rains are usually winding down, and the countryside is a riot of yellow Meskel wildflowers. Alternatively, many travellers try to schedule their trip to coincide with important festivals such as Ethiopian New Year, Ethiopian Christmas, Timkat

Timkat

RAINBOW TOURS

Our small group departures enable people to witness the spectacularly colourful processions of the Ethiopian Epiphany/Timkat. The processions are at their most impressive in Addis Ababa which is the perfect springboard for Timkat groups to go on to enjoy the popular historical circuit. Be warned: January might climatically be one of the best times to visit, but Timkat places high demand on an already fragile tourism infrastructure and services can start to suffer.

or Meskel. The European winter – November to April – is the best time for birdwatching tours, as resident species are supplemented by large flocks of Palaearctic migrants.

For more information on average temperatures and rainfall, see *Chapter 2*, page 37.

Public holidays

The most significant practical consequence of public holidays in Ethiopia is that banks will be closed. This is something you may need to plan around, especially if you are travelling between March and May, when most of the holidays are concentrated. Public holidays that are also religious festivals generally involve colourful celebrations and processions, so it is worth trying to get to one of the main religious sites – Lalibela, Gondar or Axum – for the occasion. Check the moveable dates before you travel.

7 January	Ethiopian Christmas	**1 May**	International Labour Day
19 January	Ethiopian Epiphany	**5 May**	Patriots' Victory Day
2 March	Adwa Day	**28 May**	Downfall of the Derg
Moveable	Ramadan	**Moveable**	Moulid
Moveable	Ethiopian Good Friday	**11 September**	Ethiopian New Year
Moveable	Ethiopian Easter	**27 September**	Meskel

Itinerary planning

Ethiopia's main tourist focus is the well-defined '**northern historical circuit**', which is usually covered as a road or air loop out of Addis

Ababa, taking in the region's four main established tourist centres, Bahir Dar (the base for visiting the Lake Tana monasteries and Blue Nile Falls), Gondar, Axum and Lalibela. Travelling **by air**, set aside at least two nights at each of these stops, since domestic flights don't always run at times that allow for any significant sightseeing on the day you fly, and delays aren't unknown, which means that you ideally need eight nights out of Addis. **Travelling overland**, the above loop entails a minimum driving distance of around 2,500km, and while roads are a lot better than they used to be, allow at least two weeks, ideally longer, to avoid a scenario where you spend more days on the road than you do sightseeing.

Flight-based northern itineraries could easily be extended to 12–14 days by adding on visits to the two other main regional highlights, Simien Mountains National Park and the rock-hewn churches of Tigrai, as well as a stand-alone two-night trip out of Addis Ababa to Harar in the eastern highlands. Likewise, it would be easy to extend a road trip through northern Ethiopia over three or four weeks by adding on the same sites, as well as a few off-the-beaten-track excursions.

Ethiopia's second-most important tourist circuit runs through the **southern Rift Valley to the wild South Omo region**, a trip that can only realistically be undertaken **by road**, ideally in a private 4x4. At the very minimum, you'll need to set aside a week to tour this area, and ten days would be better, extending to two weeks if you also want to

High-clearance vehicles, ideally 4x4, are needed in many remote parts of Ethiopia. (SS)

visit the underrated Bale Mountains National Park. The south is also the most important part of the country for ornithological tours, and visitors with this interest are advised to book through an operator with specialist experience of setting up birding itineraries.

Booking

A choice that you will need to make when planning your trip is whether to book through a local ground operator or a tour agency at home. By using an agent in your home country, you can plan an itinerary face-to-face, you may well get a cheaper flight, payment is more straightforward, and (assuming the agent is bonded) you will have a significantly higher level of financial protection. Booking a package through an unbonded Ethiopian operator will usually be cheaper, but you will be less well protected in the event that something goes wrong and you will almost certainly need to buy additional travel insurance.

See pages 68–9 for details of our recommended tour operators.

UK-based operators

Exodus ⓦ www.exodus.co.uk. Activity and adventure holidays.

Footloose Adventure Travel ⓦ www.footlooseadventure.co.uk. Small group and activity group adventure tours.

Gane & Marshall ⓦ www.ganeandmarshall.com. Long-established Africa and wildlife-travel company.

Journeys by Design ⓦ www.journeysbydesign.com. Tailor-made luxury tours.

Onyx Travel ⓦ www.onyxafrica.co.uk. Family run, organises tailor-made tours.

Silk Steps ⓦ www.silksteps.co.uk. Bespoke personal service.

Steppes Travel ⓦ www.steppesdiscovery.co.uk. Specialists in off-the-beaten track destinations.

The Zambezi Travel & Safari Company ⓦ www.zambezi.com/countries/ethiopia. Africa specialists. UK and US offices.

Undiscovered Destinations ⓦ www.undiscovered-destinations.com. Adventure holiday specialist.

Wild Frontiers Adventure Travel ⓦ www.wildfrontiers.co.uk. Adventure travel.

US-based operators

Adventure Center ⓦ www.adventurecenter.com. Hiking, biking, culture and more.

Africa Adventure Company ⓦ www.africa-adventure.com. Africa specialist.

Journeys by Design ⓦ journeysbydesign.com. US office. See above.

Kensington Tours ⓦ www.kensingtontours.com. Private, flexible itineraries.

Palace Travel ⓦ www.palacetravel.com. Has offices in some African countries.

Recommended tour operators

Abeba Tours Ethiopia

ⓣ 011 515 9530/31 ⓔ info@abebatoursethiopia.com
ⓦ www.abebatoursethiopia.com

Abeba Tours Ethiopia is a full-service tour operator based in Addis Ababa serving individual, group, business and incentive travellers. They specialise in tailor-made trips, and are a front-runner in offering sustainable and community-based programmes.

Amazing Ethiopia

ⓣ 091 142 7728/011 618 6499
ⓔ info@amazingethiopia.com ⓦ www.amazingethiopia.com

Founded in 2004 and based in Ethiopia, Amazing Ethiopia offers a unique range of trips to popular routes, including historic and religious tours, the Omo Valley cultural route and nature trips in the Danakil Depression. We make every effort to customise itineraries according to personal interest.

Awaze Tours

ⓣ 011 663 4439
ⓔ info@awazetours.com ⓦ www.awazetours.com

Awaze Tours operates exclusively in Ethiopia and offers both custom and scheduled tours. Whether its historical trips to the north; guided treks in the national parks; or adventures to the remote tribal areas of the south, you're assured a lasting memory of this fascinating and hospitable country. Based in Ethiopia.

Local operators

Dinknesh Ethiopia Tours ⓦ www.dinkneshethiopiatour.com. Trips are client-oriented.
Inspiration Tour Operator ⓦ www.ethiopianinspiration.com. Focus on cultural trips.

BJ Tours & Trekking

℡ 058 111 5073 Ⓜ 911 831 629

Ⓔ bjtours@ethionet.et Ⓦ www.bjtoursandtrekking.com

A wide variety of tours appealing to a wide range of interests: from history and culture, trekking and climbing, to birdwatching, horseriding, fishing and safaris in the Omo and Mago national parks. BJ Tours & Trekking offers all-inclusive tours on all our customised packages.

Ethiopian Quadrants

Ethiopian Quadrants PLC
To the four corners of the country

℡ 011 515 7990 Ⓔ ethiopianquadrants@ethionet.et

Ⓔ ethiopianquadrants@gmail.com Ⓦ www.ethiopianquadrants.com

Based in Addis Ababa, Ethiopian Quadrants runs tours for those travellers who want that little bit more – not simply good service but also insights into the culture and customs of the countries they visit. History and culture, trekking, photo safaris, birdwatching, specialist and study tours – let's plan together your perfect trip.

Paradise Ethiopia Travel

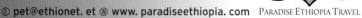

℡ 011 662 6623 or 011 551 3494

Ⓔ pet@ethionet. et Ⓦ www. paradiseethiopia. com   PARADISE ETHIOPIA TRAVEL

We have been offering high-quality tours in Ethiopia for 15 years and have excellent relationships with local communities and organisations. We cater for all tastes and abilities with over 200 itineraries on offer; our customers are our top priority and we pride ourselves on our professionalism and commitment to superior service.

Rainbow Tours

RAINBOW TOURS

℡ 0207 666 1250

Ⓔ info@rainbowtours.co.uk Ⓦ www.rainbowtours.co.uk

From small group tours to privately guided trips, we can take you to Ethiopia's iconic highlights as well as its hidden corners. Our honesty, enthusiasm and extensive firsthand experience has been recognised with four Best Tour Operator awards. With a decade of working collaboratively with our recommended lodges, local knowledge, service and value are our hallmarks.

Timeless Ethiopia Ⓦ www.timelessethiopia.com. Wide-range of tours.
Vast Ethiopia Tours Ⓦ www.vastethiopiatours.com. Covers popular routes and custom packages.
Village Ethiopia Ⓦ www.villageethiopiatour.com. Popular routes plus more specialised tours.

Your itinerary: 20 top attractions

An important first step in planning an itinerary to any country is deciding which sites you absolutely *must* visit, and Ethiopia is no exception, even though it does have a more standardised tourist circuit than many African countries. Having identified those must-sees, you might want to tailor the rest of your itinerary around them, focusing on places of interest that don't require you to divert too far from your main route. In order to help you with this decision, a brief synopsis of our 20 top attractions in Ethiopia is listed below, divided thematically into (active) Christian shrines, other (active) cultural sites, and other (non-active) historical or archaeological sites, as well as scenic attractions, and wildlife and birding highlights.

Living Christian shrines

1 Lalibela

Frequently listed as the Eighth Wonder of the Ancient World (though in fact they are medieval rather than ancient), the complex of rock-hewn churches at Lalibela is the most remarkable of all Ethiopia's living Christian shrines, both for its aura of brooding spirituality and for the sheer craftsmanship of monoliths such as Bet Giyorgis and Bet Medhane Alem.

(SS)

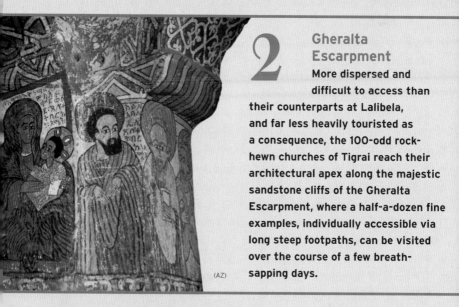

2 Gheralta Escarpment

More dispersed and difficult to access than their counterparts at Lalibela, and far less heavily touristed as a consequence, the 100-odd rock-hewn churches of Tigrai reach their architectural apex along the majestic sandstone cliffs of the Gheralta Escarpment, where a half-a-dozen fine examples, individually accessible via long steep footpaths, can be visited over the course of a few breath-sapping days. (AZ)

3 Lake Tana monasteries

Less architecturally impressive than the rock-hewn churches to their northeast, the monastic churches that scatter the islands of Lake Tana rank among the oldest in Ethiopia, and are notable for their fine ecclesiastical paintings and jam-packed treasuries. The boat trip to the islands from Bahir Dar is great fun too.

(AC)

4 Debre Damo

Boasting an impregnable clifftop position atop a 3,000m-high *amba* (flat-topped hill) north of the Axum-Adigrat Road, this male-only monastery houses the oldest non-rock-hewn church in the country, a classic Axumite construction reputedly built under the tutelage of its 6th-century founder Abba Aregawi. The 15m-high ascent, to the top on a leather rope hauled by the monks, is not recommended for altophobics.

(SS)

Other cultural sites

5 Harar

The spiritual heart of Ethiopia's ancient Islamic culture, the walled city of Harar is notable for its densely clustered alleys, busy markets and wealth of religious shrines. Set in the verdant eastern highlands, it is also an important centre of *khat* and coffee production, and home to the legendary Hyena Men of Harar.

(EL)

6 Karat-Konso

The animist Konso of the far southern highlands have a complex society based on generational age-sets, and their picturesque walled hilltop villages - which bear an unexpected (though purely coincidental) resemblance to the Dogon settlements of Mali - are surrounded by ceremonial victory stones, generation poles and *waga* grave markers.

(EL)

7 South Omo

Inhabited by two dozen different tribes, representing four of Africa's major linguistic groups, this fascinating enclave of traditional animist cultures is almost uniquely untouched by outside influences - as manifested by the ongoing use of quirky adornments from pie-sized lip plates and ochre-dyed plaits to ritual body scarification and body painting.

(AZ)

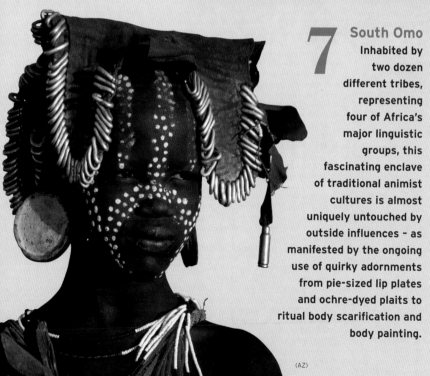

8 Addis Ababa

An altogether more modern face of Ethiopia is reflected in the bustling streets of the capital, highlights of which include the vast and lively Mercato, the early 20th-century architecture of the Piazza, some superb traditional restaurants (complete with wild-eyed Amhara and Tigraian dancers) and the excellent National Museum.

(SS)

Other historical sites

(AZ)

9 **Axum**
Formerly the epicentre of a trade empire of global importance, dusty Axum may be past its prime today, but the giant stelae field on its outskirts remains a striking monument to its glory days, as do the numerous multi-lingual tablets and ruined palaces recently unearthed by archaeologists.

10 **Gondar**
Capital of Ethiopia from the mid-16th to late 19th century, the city of Gondar, in the highlands north of Lake Tana, is mainly of interest for the impressive castles that stud the central royal compound. The church of Debre Birhan Selassie, on its northern outskirts, boasts some of the finest ecclesiastic murals anywhere in the country.

(AZ)

(SS)

11 Yeha

Often visited as a day trip out of Axum, Yeha is the site of the country's most important pre-Axumite structure, a remarkably well-preserved temple that stands 12m high, comprises 52 layers of masonry, and was constructed more than 2,500 years ago.

12 Tiya

The most accessible of the fields of engraved stelae that mark a series of mysterious medieval cemeteries in the southern highlands, Tiya makes for an easy day trip out of Addis Ababa, ideally combined with the isolated rock-hewn church Adadi Maryam, and the prehistoric site at Melka Kunture.

Scenery

13 Simien Mountains National Park

The altitudinal and scenic apex of the dramatically mountainous northern highlands, the Simien Mountains, though accessible by all-weather road, are seen to best advantage by hikers and trekkers. The park is also the best place to see the endemic gelada monkey and Walia ibex, and it hosts the world's densest population of lammergeyer.

(AC)

14 Blue Nile Falls

When it isn't reduced to a trickle by a recently installed hydroelectric plant, this magnificent waterfall, a short drive away from the Nile's source at Lake Tana, is one of the most spectacular in Africa, ranking second only to the peerless Victoria Falls.

15 Danakil Depression

Officially the hottest place in the world, and the lowest point on the African continent, this volcanically hyperactive stretch of the northern Rift Valley doesn't conform to conventional notions of chocolate-box prettiness, but its stark scenic highlights include live lava lakes, sulphurous multi-hued geysers, and remote salt pans that have been mined for centuries by the hardy Afar people.

(AZ)

16 Bishoftu crater lakes

An easy short excursion from the capital, the lively highland town of Bishoftu is surrounded by one of Africa's most accessible crater-lake fields, several of which now house upmarket spa resorts and cheaper hotels. (AZ)

Wildlife and birds

17 Bale Mountains National Park

The top wildlife destination in Ethiopia, Bale is also a fabulous destination for hikers and trekkers, though somewhat more remote from other popular attractions on the tourist circuit. It's the best place to see the endemic Ethiopian wolf, mountain nyala and Menelik's bushbuck, along with around half of the bird species endemic to Ethiopia and Eritrea. (AZ)

18 Rift Valley lakes

The string of gem-like lakes that runs through the Rift Valley offers superb birding opportunities, from the flamingos that congregate on Lake Abiata to the storks and pelicans that forage alongside Lake Ziway. The lakes protected within Nechisar National Park are home to large numbers of crocs, hippos and plains wildlife, while surrounding bands of riparian woodland support enchanting grivet and colobus monkeys.

(AZ)

(AZ)

19 Awash National Park

Though wildlife isn't as plentiful as it used to be, this scenic park bisected by the main road between Addis Ababa and Harar is the best place to see dry-country specials such as Hamadryas baboon, Beisa oryx and greater kudu. The phenomenal birdlife includes several localised bustard species and the spectacular carmine bee-eater.

20 The Goba-Yabello Road

One of the most remote roads in the country, this is a fixture on birding tours to Ethiopia, as it offers access to the restricted ranges of some the country's most localised birds, including the lovely Prince Ruspoli's turaco and bizarre Stresemann's bush crow. Dry-country mammals such as kudu and dik-dik are also plentiful.

Tourist information

The best sources of information outside Ethiopia are guidebooks and specialist tour operators, as well as Ethiopian Airlines offices and Ethiopian embassies. In Ethiopia **The Ministry of Culture and Tourism** (ⓔ info@tourismethiopia.org ⓦ www.tourismethiopia.org) operates a tourist office on Meskel Square in Addis Ababa, a good place to pick up illustrated free booklets about Bale, Simien and Lalibela when they are in stock, but not much use when it comes to practical advice. There is also a regional tourist office in every regional capital, the most useful being the Tigrai tourist office in Mekele, which stocks some great booklets about nearby rock-hewn churches and other regional attractions, and can also give detailed advice about the more obscure churches.

Red tape

All visitors require a **passport**, with at least two full pages empty, valid for at least six months after the end of their stay. A **visa** is also required. For several years, it has been possible to buy a one-month single-entry visa for US$30 upon arrival at Bole International Airport. Shortly before going to print, however, the government indicated that it is rethinking the 'visa on arrival' policy for security reasons relating to a perceived terrorist threat from neighbouring Somalia and Eritrea. The situation remains unclear at the time of writing, but we will be monitoring it closely and recommend that readers check our update website ⓦ http://updates.bradtguides.com/ethiopia for news.

Getting there

All international flights arrive and depart from **Bole International Airport** in Addis Ababa. The national carrier **Ethiopian Airlines** (ⓦ www.flyethiopian.com) is Africa's oldest airline, and it has an excellent safety record, as well as the most extensive intra-African flight network of any carrier, and links to several major European and North American cities. Other major airlines that fly to Addis Ababa are **Air France** (ⓦ www.airfrance.com), **Alitalia** (ⓦ www.alitalia.com), **British Airways** (ⓦ www.britishairways.com), **Emirates** (ⓦ www.emirates. com), **KLM** (ⓦ www.klm.com) and **Lufthansa** (ⓦ www.lufthansa.com).

Health and safety
with Dr Felicity Nicholson

Inoculations

You may be advised to have **yellow fever** vaccine on health grounds as a large part of western and central Ethiopia has the disease. Either way, you will be required to show a **vaccination certificate for yellow fever** upon arrival if you are coming from a yellow fever-endemic area. This may also include a transit in an airport of another African country, as immigration officers won't make a distinction. It is also important to be up-to-date on **tetanus, polio** and **diphtheria**, and you would be advised to be immunised against **hepatitis A** and **typhoid**. **Other vaccines** that may be recommended include hepatitis B, rabies, meningitis, cholera, and tuberculosis.

Deep-vein thrombosis (DVT)

Prolonged immobility on long-haul flights can result in deep-vein thrombosis (DVT), which can be dangerous if the clot travels to the lungs to cause pulmonary embolus. The risk increases with age, and is higher in obese or pregnant travellers, heavy smokers, those taller than

Personal first-aid kit

Depending on where and how you travel, and for how long, a minimal kit might contain the following:

• A good drying antiseptic, eg: iodine or potassium permanganate
• A few small dressings (Band-Aids)
• Suncream
• Insect repellent
• Antihistamine tablets/cream
• Antimalarial tablets
• Aspirin or paracetamol
• Antifungal cream (eg: Canesten)
• Ciprofloxacin or norfloxacin, for severe diarrhoea
• Antibiotic eye drops
• A pair of fine-pointed tweezers
• Alcohol-based hand rub or a bar of soap in a plastic box
• Thermometer

6ft/1.8m or shorter than 5ft/1.5m, and anybody with a history of clots, recent major operation or varicose veins surgery, cancer, a stroke or heart disease. If in doubt, consult a doctor before you travel.

Malaria

This mosquito-borne disease is the biggest single medical threat to visitors to many African countries. Within Ethiopia, however, it is a localised concern: visitors are most unlikely to be exposed to malaria in Addis Ababa or anywhere along the northern circuit (though isolated outbreaks do occur in the vicinity of Bahir Dar and Lake Tana) but it is seasonally prolifi. lower lying areas such as the Rift Valley and South Omo, particularly during the rains, and travellers visiting these areas are strongly urged to take precautions.

There is no vaccine for malaria, but several types of oral prophylactics are available, with Malarone (proguanil and atovaquone) being widely recommended for short trips, as it is very effective and has few side effects (though it is relatively expensive). Other possibilities include mefloquine and doxycycline, so visit a travel clinic for up-to-date advice about the most suitable option.

For on-the-ground advice on preventing malaria, plus other health issues to consider whilst in Ethiopia, see *Chapter 4*, page 90.

Women travellers

Ethiopia is a relatively safe country for single women travellers. The risk of being raped or subjected to genuinely threatening harassment is probably lower than in many Westernised countries. That said, some women travellers complain about regular low-grade harassment, for instance teenage boys yelling obscenities or making lewd propositions from across the street, and this can start to feel slightly threatening after a while. The junction town of Shashemene in southern Ethiopia has a particularly bad reputation for this sort of thing, as does the Mercato

Dress code

Female travellers should be conscious that Ethiopians tend to be modest dressers. It is advisable to follow suit (except perhaps in Addis Ababa), particularly in areas that are predominantly Muslim. Never expose knees or shoulders in public, which means that shorts and sleeveless tops are out. It isn't normal for local women to wear trousers, but neither will it cause serious offence.

in Addis Ababa. Single women are urged to avoid shoestring hotels, many of which have a brothel-cum-bar room vibe. Be aware, too, that outside of Addis Ababa, no respectable Ethiopian woman visits a bar, as it carries such a strong association with prostitution.

One final point is that when Ethiopians ask you to play with them, they are not suggesting a quick grope but that you make conversation – the Amharic phrase *techawot* means both 'to talk' and 'to play'.

Disabled travellers

with Gordon Rattray (Ⓦ www.able-travel.com)

A country famed for steep, soaring mountains and sunken rock-hewn monuments does not sound like the ideal destination for people with disabilities. However, with some planning, almost anyone can enjoy Ethiopia's unique landscapes, culture and history without too much hardship.

Accommodation

Only top-end hotels in Addis Ababa have facilities designed with access in mind. That said, more budget accommodation is often ground floor and it is never difficult to find willing hands to help lift you over and around obstacles.

Road travel

Taxis and public vehicles in general can be old and in bad repair, and road conditions may also contribute to a bumpy ride. Therefore, if you use a pressure-relieving cushion in your wheelchair it may be wise to use it in vehicles too. Drivers are usually very happy to help with transfers, but do give good guidance as enthusiasm alone can be less than helpful.

Air travel

Ethiopian Airlines's website has 'special' guidelines for travellers from the USA, but these are aimed at making your flight as comfortable as possible. A MEDIF form may also be required. During internal flights in Ethiopia I found that a letter from my doctor stating that I am fit to fly (despite being unable to walk) was very useful. Detailed information about flying with a disability can be found in Bradt's *Access Africa* (see below).

Tour operators

As yet, there are no disability-specialised tourist services in Ethiopia, but most mainstream agents and operators will listen to and try to cater to your needs. One such company I would recommend is **Village Ethiopia** (page 69) – they were also able to provide me with a very reliable personal assistant.

Health and insurance

Doctors will know about 'everyday' illnesses, but you must understand and be able to explain your own particular medical requirements. Ethiopian hospitals and pharmacies are often basic, so it is wise to take as much essential medication and equipment as possible with you, and it is advisable to pack this in your hand luggage during flights in case your main luggage gets delayed. Ethiopia can be hot; if this is a problem for you then try to book accommodation with fans or air conditioning, and a useful cooling aid is a plant-spray bottle.

Travel insurance can be purchased in the UK from **Age UK** (① 0845 600 3348 ⓦ www.ageuk.org.uk), who have no upper age limit, and **Free Spirit** (① 0845 230 5000 ⓦ www.free-spirit.com), who cater for people with pre-existing medical conditions. Most insurance companies will insure disabled travellers, but it is essential that they are made aware of your disability.

Further information

Although Bradt's *Access Africa: Safaris for People with Limited Mobility* does not cover Ethiopia directly, it is packed with useful advice and resources about all of the above for disabled and senior adventure travellers. The Ethiopian Center for Disability and Development have produced a detailed guide entitled 'Accessible Addis Ababa'. It is available in PDF format from ⓔ info@eccdd-ethiopia.org (ⓦ www.ecdd-ethiopia.org).

What to take

Clothing

This will probably constitute the bulk of your luggage, so give some thought to what you bring. A good mix of comfortable light clothing is advisable, similar to what you might wear on a warm summer's day in Europe (though not so scanty as to offend local sensibilities; see *Women travellers*, above) and best carry enough items to last at least a week without doing laundry. Be warned, however, that highland nights can be chilly, so bring a couple of sweatshirts or similar, and possibly some sort of waterproof jacket. Heavier clothing might be required if you intend to hike or trek in the Bale or Simien Mountains, parts of which lie at altitudes above 4,000m. In lower lying areas such as South Omo, it's advisable to wear closed shoes, socks and long trousers after dusk, to protect against mosquito bites. Decent walking shoes or boots are essential for hiking and will be useful when exploring the rock-hewn churches of Lalibela and other outdoor sites.

Photographic gear

Few people would consider travelling without a camera and/or video recorder. For decent results, however, an SLR camera is preferable to a 'point and shoot', and a pair of good zoom lenses (eg: 28–70mm for scenic shots and 70–300mm for portraits and wildlife) allows for greater compositional flexibility. If you use a digital camera, make sure you have all the batteries, plugs, connectors and storage devices you need, as well as a universal adaptor. If you use film, be aware that this may not be readily available, so bring as many rolls as you're likely to need. Make sure your camera bag is well insulated against the insidious dust associated with many parts of Ethiopia.

Say cheese! A photographer gets up close to wildlife in the Simien Mountains National Park. (IY/FLPA)

Binoculars

These are essential for distant wildlife and obtaining close-up views of birds. For dedicated birdwatchers, 8x magnification is the minimal requirement, but 10x, 12x or (only for the steady of hand) 16x is even better. The trade-off between full-size binoculars (such as 8x40 and 10x50) and their compact counterparts (8x25 or 10x30) is that the former have a wider field of vision and tend to show colours more brightly as a result of capturing more light, while the latter are considerably more portable and steady to hold, and tend to be cheaper. If your budget runs to it, it's worth paying for a recognised brand. Avoid gimmicky binoculars (such as those with features like zoom or universal focus) at all costs.

Other essentials

Don't forget to bring sunscreen, a hat and sunglasses, a day pack to carry binoculars and field guides et al, a toilet bag containing razors, deodorant, tampons, lip salve and whatever other accessories you might need, a basic medical kit (see page 81 for suggestions on what this should include), a penknife, torch and possibly an alarm clock. Contact-lens users with sensitive eyes might be glad of a pair of glasses in the dusty conditions that often prevail on road trips through Ethiopia. Travel guides and field guides are also best bought in advance, as they may be difficult to locate within the country.

Finally, don't leave home without adequate **travel insurance**. This should include both medical insurance (specifically one that will fly you home in the event of an emergency) and a travel protection plan which would cover non-reimbursed travel expenses if an emergency occurs before or during your trip causing it to be cancelled, interrupted or delayed. Check out ⓦ www.worldtravelcenter.com and ⓦ www.globaltravelinsurance.com for more information.

Organising your finances

People who visit Ethiopia on a pre-paid tour generally won't need to carry a great deal of money on their person, as most costs will be built into the package, including airport and other transfers, ground transport, services of a driver and/or guide as specified, pre-booked domestic flights, entrance fees and accommodation. Hotels may or may not be booked on a full-board basis, so check this in advance with your operator. Either way, additional **day-to-day expenses** such as drinks, tips and curios are unlikely to tally up to more than US$500, which you can bring in the form of hard currency cash (ideally US dollars or to a lesser extent British pounds or euros), which can be converted to local currency at any bank or foreign exchange office. Note that US dollar bills printed before 2002 may be refused.

Without being overly dependent on a **credit or debit card**, it is definitely worth carrying one as a backup. These days, Addis Ababa has numerous 24-hour ATMs, notably at the airport and at the Hilton and Sheraton hotels, where local currency can be drawn against an international credit card. However, there is always a risk of the machine being out of commission or temperamental, and this could enforce unwanted delays. Visa is far and away the most widely recognised brand of card, with the likes of Maestro, MasterCard and American Express simply not being recognised at most ATMs and other outlets.

Entrance fees

These are charged at most museums, national parks, historical sites and churches, but they will generally be included in the price of an organised tour. If you need to pay yourself, fees are generally quite moderate by international standards, though the church fees can add up over the course of a trip to somewhere such as Tigrai. To give an example or two, the entrance fee to the Royal Compound at Gondar is now birr 100 (equivalent to US$6), the blanket fee for all the churches at Lalibela is birr 350 (around US$20), and most stand-alone churches of historical note charge around birr 30–50 (US$2-3), as do museums in Addis Ababa. Entrance fees to national parks also stand at birr 50 per 24 hours.

The National Museum of Ethiopia, Addis Ababa (AZ)

Health and safety in Ethiopia 90

Malaria 90
Sunstroke and dehydration 90
Travellers' diarrhoea 90
Bilharzia 91
HIV/AIDs 92
Skin infections 92
Wild animals 92
Rabies 93
Snake and other bites 93

Banking and foreign exchange 93

Food and drink 94

Eating out 94
Drinks 97

Shopping 99

Media and communications 101

Television 101
Telephone 101
Internet and email 102

Business and time 102

Time 102

Cultural etiquette 103

4 On the Ground

On an organised tour, the ground operator and/or their appointed guide will handle most day-to-day practicalities, whether it be checking into a hotel, paying entrance fees for archaeological sites and churches, locating a suitable place to eat, or finding somewhere to exchange money or draw it against a credit card. Professional guides in Ethiopia are generally very helpful and should be able to assist in dealing with anything that requires local savvy; nevertheless, some advance knowledge about how things work locally can be useful, and this chapter deals with a few important points, from foreign exchange and telecommunications to tipping and shopping. It also includes an overview of health and safety issues within Ethiopia.

Health and safety in Ethiopia
with Dr Felicity Nicholson

Malaria
Malaria is not as widespread in Ethiopia as it is in most other African countries. It is largely absent from the northern historical circuit (the main exception for tourists being around Bahir Dar) and even where it is present in southern Ethiopia, it generally manifests in seasonal outbreaks rather than being a permanent year-round health risk. Nevertheless, visitors are advised to visit a doctor or health clinic for advice about prophylactic pills, several types of which are available. See page 82 for more information.

No malaria prophylactic is 100% effective, so take all reasonable precautions against being bitten by the nocturnal *Anopheles* mosquito that transmits the disease. These including donning a long-sleeved shirt, trousers and socks in the evening, and applying a DEET-based insect repellent (ideally 50–55% concentration) to any exposed flesh, and sleeping under a net – or failing that in an air-conditioned room, under a fan, or with a mosquito coil burning. Malaria normally manifests within two weeks of being bitten, but it can be as short as seven days and as long as a year. So if you display possible symptoms after you get home, go to a doctor immediately, and ask to be tested.

Sunstroke and dehydration
Overexposure to the sun can lead to short-term sunburn or sunstroke, and increases the long-risk of skin cancer. Wear a T-shirt and waterproof sunscreen when swimming. When walking in the direct sun, cover up with long, loose clothes, wear a hat, and use sunscreen. The glare and the dust can be hard on the eyes, so bring UV-protecting sunglasses. A less direct effect of the tropical heat is dehydration, so drink more fluids than you would at home.

Travellers' diarrhoea
Many visitors to unfamiliar destinations suffer a dose of travellers' diarrhoea, and Ethiopia is certainly no exception. By taking precautions against travellers' diarrhoea you will also avoid rarer but more serious sanitation-related diseases such as typhoid, cholera, hepatitis, dysentery, worms, etc. The maxim to remind you what you can safely eat is:

PEEL IT, BOIL IT, COOK IT OR FORGET IT.

Tickbite fever and quick tick removal

Ticks in Africa are not the rampant disease transmitters that they are in the Americas, but they may spread tickbite fever along with a few dangerous rarities. Tickbite fever is a flu-like illness that can easily be treated with doxycycline, but as there can be some serious complications it is very important that you visit a doctor.

Ticks should ideally be removed as soon as possible because leaving them on the body increases the chance of infection. They should be removed with special tick tweezers that can be bought in good travel shops. Failing that, you can use your finger nails: grasp the tick as close to your body as possible and pull steadily and firmly away at right angles to your skin. The tick will then come away complete, as long as you do not jerk or twist. If possible douse the wound with alcohol (any spirit will do) or iodine. Irritants (eg: Olbas oil) or lit cigarettes are to be discouraged since they can cause the ticks to regurgitate and therefore increase the risk of disease. It is best to get a travelling companion to check you for ticks; if you are travelling with small children, remember to check their heads, and particularly behind the ears.

Spreading redness around the bite and/or fever and/or aching joints after a tick bite imply that you have an infection that requires antibiotic treatment, so seek advice.

This means that fruit you have washed and peeled yourself, and hot foods, should be safe, but raw foods, cold cooked foods, salads, fruit salads prepared by others, ice cream and ice are all risky. It is rarer to get sick from drinking contaminated water but it happens, so stick to bottled water. If you suffer a bout of diarrhoea, it is dehydration that makes you feel awful, so drink lots of clear fluids, ideally infused with sachets of oral rehydration salts, but any dilute mixture of sugar and salt in water will do you good, for instance a bottled soda with a pinch of salt added. If the problem persists, seek medical help.

Bilharzia

Also known as schistosomiasis, bilharzia is an unpleasant parasitic disease transmitted by freshwater snails in lakes and rivers. It cannot be caught in hotel swimming pools or the ocean. If you do swim in a lake or river, try to stay away from the reedy banks. You can test for bilharzia at specialist travel clinics, ideally six weeks or longer after exposure, and it is easy to treat at present. Remember you do not have to have symptoms to have the disease.

HIV/AIDS

East Africa has one of the world's highest rates of HIV infection, and other sexually transmitted diseases are rife, so if you do indulge, use condoms or femidoms to reduce the risk of transmission.

Skin infections

Ethiopia has a varied climate, but where it is hot and humid then wounds (even a mosquito bite or small nick) are more likely to become infected and need to be kept clean, dry and covered. Use dry antiseptic sprays such as Savlon Dry rather than creams. **Prickly heat** is a fine pimply rash that can be alleviated by cool showers, dabbing (not rubbing) dry and applying talc, and sleeping naked under a fan or in an air-conditioned room. **Fungal infections** also get a hold easily in hot moist climates so wear 100% cotton socks and underwear and shower frequently.

Wild animals

Don't confuse habituation with domestication. Ethiopia's wildlife is genuinely wild, and certain widespread species such as hippo or hyena might attack a person given the right set of circumstances. Such attacks are rare, however, and they almost always stem from a combination of poor judgement and poorer luck. A few rules of thumb: never approach potentially dangerous wildlife on foot except in the company of a trustworthy guide, never swim in lakes or rivers without first seeking local advice about the presence of crocodiles or hippos, never get between a hippo and water, and never leave food (particularly meat or fruit) in the tent where you'll sleep.

Never swim in croc-infested water! (SS)

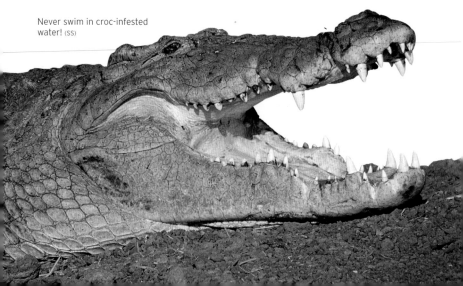

Rabies

All warm blooded mammals potentially carry rabies so any bite, scratch or lick over an open wound, or more rarely saliva into the eyes, mouth or nose can be an exposure. The animal doesn't have to look unwell either. Any skin wound should be scrubbed with soap and running water for at least 15 minutes then apply antiseptic if you have any. Get straight to medical help. If you have not had the pre-exposure vaccine (three doses over a minimum of 21 days) then you will need Rabies Immunoglobulin (RIG – either human or horse) and five doses of vaccine. RIG is hard to come by and expensive and may mean evacuating to another country. If you have had all three pre-exposure doses of vaccine before travel then you no longer need the RIG, just two further doses of vaccine three days apart. It is well worth investing in the pre-exposure course however long you are travelling and always if you are working with animals.

Snake and other bites

Snakes are very secretive and bites are a genuine rarity – only a small fraction of snakebites deliver enough venom to be life-threatening, but it is important to keep the victim calm and inactive, and to seek urgent medical attention. Certain **spiders and scorpions** can also deliver nasty bites. In all cases, the risk is minimised by wearing closed shoes and trousers when walking in the bush, and watching where you put your hands and feet, especially in rocky areas or when gathering firewood.

Banking and foreign exchange

The **Ethiopia birr** (also sometimes referred to as the dux or, a little confusingly, the dollar) is one of the strongest currencies in Africa, with exchange rates in 2012 at roughly US$1 = birr 17, €1 = birr 23 and £1 = birr 28, a pleasant change from the decimal shifts required to calculate prices in many African countries. Notes are printed in denominations of birr 100, 50, 10, 5 and 1, and coins to the value of 50, 25, 10, 5 and 1 cent are minted. If you have cash, the quickest way to exchange money in Addis Ababa is at a **foreign-exchange bureau**, which offer similar rates to banks but are less bogged down in paperwork. You can also exchange money at most branches of the **Commercial Bank of Ethiopia** (CBE) or **Dashen Bank**. Banking hours in Addis Ababa are from 09.00 to 12.00 and 14.00 to 16.00 weekdays, but the CBE branch at Bole Airport is open every day of the week.

Tipping and guide fees

The qualified guides who work in Ethiopia's main historical centres usually charge a fixed rate of around US$10-20 per party per day. Elsewhere, for a knowledgeable professional guide, expect to pay US$2 for up to two hours and US$1 for every hour thereafter. In both cases it is best to agree a price upfront.

Tipping waiters is not the established custom in Ethiopia, but it is acceptable. At upmarket restaurants such as those in government hotels, the 10% tip customary in many Western countries is a fair-to-generous guideline. In local restaurants and bars, a few birr will be greatly appreciated by the recipient. It is also customary to tip drivers and guides at the end of a tour, though the actual amount is totally at your discretion.

If you are drawing money against a **Visa** credit or debit card, the Dashen Bank and CBE have ATM machines dotted throughout Addis Ababa (including two at the airport and several at the Hilton and Sheraton hotels) and in most other large cities. If you only have a **MasterCard**, it is possible to get a cash advance at the bank in the Hilton Hotel, at a fee. Outside of banks and ATMs, credit cards are of limited use except to settle room and restaurant bills at the Addis Ababa Hilton and Sheraton, and a few other top hotels in the capital and around the country. ATMs outside Addis Ababa can also be temperamental, so it pays to do all your foreign exchange dealings in the capital.

Food and drink

Eating out

Contrary to some people's expectations, Ethiopia is liberally endowed with good eateries, though the vast majority of restaurants outside of Addis Ababa adhere strictly to the local cuisine, which is quite unlike that of any other African country. The staple carbohydrate is *injera*, a large, pancake-shaped substance made from *tef*, a nutty-tasting grain that is unique to Ethiopia, and supplies more fibre-rich bran and nutritious germ than any other grain, containing 15% protein, 3% fat and 82% complex carbohydrates. To make *injera*, a *tef* dough is fermented for up to three days before it is cooked, the result of which is a foam-rubber texture and a slightly sour taste reminiscent of sherbet. *Injera* is normally served with a bowl of *wat* stew. The ritual is to take a piece of *injera* in your hand and use it to scoop the accompaniment into your mouth. If you dine with Ethiopians, it is normal for everyone to eat off the same plate.

There are two types of **wat** sauce: *kai wat* is red in colour (*kai* literally means 'red') and flavoured with hot *beriberi* (chilli peppers), onions and garlic; *alicha wat* has a yellowish colour and is generally quite bland. There is a widely held belief among Ethiopians that no *faranji* ('foreigner') can tolerate spicy food, so best to specify which type you want. Or, if you're not overly fond of spicy food, order *wat misto*, which consists of half-portions of *kai* and *alicha wat*, sometimes served in separate bowls and sometimes mixed together.

Most *wat* is made from **meat** (*siga*). The most common meat in the highlands is lamb (*bege*), while in drier areas you will most often be served with goat (*figel*). Beef (*bure*) is also eaten, mostly in large towns. In towns near lakes, **fish** (*asa*) predominates. I have also come across *tripe wat* – which is the same as our tripe but pronounced *trippy*. The official national dish of Ethiopia is **doro wat**, made of chicken, but this is to be avoided if you are hungry, as it is traditional to serve only a lonely drumstick or wing in a bowl of sauce. Normally *kai wat* consists of meat boiled in the *kai* sauce, but you may also come across *tibs kai wat*, which means the meat was fried before the sauce was added. If the meat is minced prior to cooking, then the dish is known as *minje tabish*.

Vegetarian *wats* are served mainly on Wednesday and Friday, the Orthodox fasting days, and can be made from puréed beans (*shiro wat*), halved beans (*kik wat*) and lentils (*misr wat*). *Shiro tegamino* is an especially delicious thick paste, whereas standard *shiro wat* tends to have a liquid consistency. The normal dish on fasting days is *atkilt bayinetu*, which consists of dollops of various vegetarian *wats*, as well as piles of spinach (*gomon*), beetroot (*kai iser*) and vegetable stew (*atkilt alicha*) heaped discretely in a circle on the *injera*.

Fried meat (*siga tibs*) is also very popular in Ethiopia, as is **boiled meat** (*siga kekel*). *Shakila tibs* consists of fried meat

A vegetarian selection served on *injera* is typical fare on fasting days. (SS)

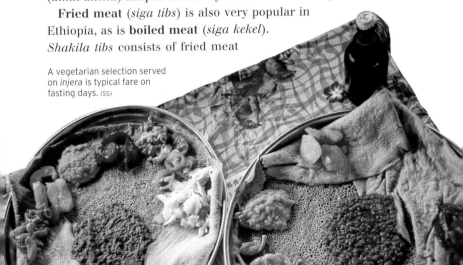

served in a clay pot that contains a charcoal burner. Other dishes, found mainly in large towns, are **crumbed meat or fish cutlet** (*siga* or *asa kutilet*), **roast meat** (*siga arosto*), **steak** (*stek*) and a mildly spicy brown **stew** (*gulash*). Then there is *kitfo*, a very bland form of fried mince, and *kitfo special*, the same dish but uncooked, which should be avoided purely for health reasons as should *kurt* (pronounced court), which is raw sliced beef.

A popular **breakfast** dish, and a useful fallback in the evening if you don't fancy anything else that's on offer, is *inkolala tibs* – literally fried eggs, but more like scrambled eggs, cooked on request with slices of onion (*shinkuts*), green pepper (*karia*) and tomato (*tamatim*). Another common breakfast dish is *yinjera firfir*, which consists of pieces of *injera* soaked in *kai wat* sauce and eaten with – you guessed it – *injera*. Note that *firfir* literally means 'torn-up': *inkolala firfir* is exactly the same as *inkolala tibs*, but hacked at a bit before it is served. Also popular at breakfast is *ful*, a spicy bean dish made with lots of garlic, a refreshing change from eggs when you can find it.

If you feel like a break from *injera* (and you will), many restaurants serve **pasta** (look out for variant spellings such as *spiggttii* or *makarronni*) skimpily topped with a spicy sauce. Even in the smallest villages you can usually find fresh, crusty **bread** (*dabo*) as an alternative accompaniment. Many hotels in Addis, and government hotels throughout the country, serve standard Western food such as roast chicken, fish kebabs, roast meat and steaks.

The variety of food at local restaurants decreases during the fasting weeks of Ethiopian Lent, which generally occupies most of March and April, since Orthodox Christians will only eat vegetarian dishes during this period. Most non-vegetarians travelling in off-the-beaten-track areas get a bit frustrated by this, whereas vegetarians will find it a good

Ordering food

Menus are normally printed in Amharigna script so you will have to ask what's available ('*Magi min ale?*'). As a rule, you won't understand a word of the rushed reply, so you'll probably have to suggest a few possibilities yourself. The way to phrase this is to start with the type of meat or vegetable (prefaced with *ye*), then the type of dish. In other words, fried goat is *yefigel tibs*, fish cutlet is *yasa kutilet*, *kai wat* made with lentils is *yemisr kai wat*, and *alicha wat* made with beef is *yebure alicha wat*. If all else fails, ask for *sekondo misto*, which consists of small portions of everything on the menu.

Pastry shops

An attractive feature of Ethiopia is the numerous pastry shops in Addis Ababa and other medium to large towns. These generally serve a selection of freshly baked iced and plain cakes, wonderful biscuits and good bread, along with coffee, tea and puréed fruit juice. Pastry shops are great for sweet-toothed breakfasts and snacks, and you'll walk away with plenty of change from a dollar.

time to travel. It doesn't affect travellers so much in Muslim areas, nor will it alter the variety of food on offer at tourist-oriented restaurants.

On the **snack** front, look out for *ashet* (roasted maize cobs); the cry of the kids who sell it, which sounds remarkably like 'shit', should attract your attention. *Kolo* is a delicious snack of roasted grains or pulses, sometimes covered in spice, and sold by the handful for a few cents.

Drinks

The Kaffa province of Ethiopia is thought to be where **coffee** originated, and the coffee bean accounts for more than half of Ethiopia's exports. As a consequence, many Ethiopians are coffee-addicts and their espresso-style coffee (*buna*), served with two spoons of sugar, is rich, sweet and thoroughly addictive. Coffee with milk is *buna watat*. In small towns, sweet **tea** (*shai*) is more widely available than coffee. You'll often be invited to join a traditional coffee ceremony, wherein the fresh beans are roasted over charcoal, ground while the water is boiled, then used to make three successive pots of coffee.

Ethiopia's prime soft drink is fresh **fruit juice**, most commonly banana, avocado, papaya, orange and guava, with availability dependent on season and location, and the quality is generally superb. If in doubt, ask for *espris*, which consists of layers of all available juices. The usual brand soft drinks – Coca-Cola, Fanta, etc – are widely available and very cheap. The generic name for soft drinks is *leslasa*. Locally bottled carbonated mineral water is widely available; it is asked for by the brand name, which is *Ambo* in central, south and western Ethiopia, and *Babile* (pronounced 'bubbily' – I'm not sure if this is coincidence) in the east. Still water is also available.

The most popular **local tipple** is *tej*, a mead-like drink made from honey (*mar*) or sugar (*isukalama*). *Mar tej* is a considerable improvement on most African home brews and very alcoholic, but still something of an acquired taste. Locally brewed **beer**, made from millet or maize, is called *tella*. Acceptable bottled lager is sold throughout

Traditional coffee ceremony in Lalibela (SS)

Khat

(AZ)

This mildly stimulating leaf, traditionally popular with Muslims (who are forbidden from drinking alcohol), is eaten throughout Ethiopia. Eating *khat* is generally a social thing. A few people gather in a room, each grab a few branches, pick off the greenest leaves, pop them into their mouths one by one, mush it all up into a cud, chew for a few hours and then, with whatever strength is left in their jaw, spit out the remaining pulp. Ideally, you devote the afternoon to eating *khat*, then go for a few beers to neutralise the sleeplessness that the leaves induce. The leaves taste very bitter so a spoonful of sugar helps it all go down. The centre of *khat* cultivation (and mastication) is Harar, but you can get the stuff at markets all over the country. It's not expensive, but do take along an Ethiopian friend to ensure you locate the best quality stuff.

Sticking with leaves green and mind-altering, it should be clarified (despite Ethiopia's link with Rastafarianism), smoking marijuana is illegal, and generally less socially acceptable than in most Western countries. You should certainly not assume that an Ethiopian male with plaited hair is adorned for anything but religious reasons.

Ethiopia, with popular brands being Castel, Bati, Bedele, St George, Harar and Dashen. **Wine** is brewed locally; the result is indifferent but affordable, especially if bought directly from a shop. Imported **spirits** are served in most bars at very low prices for generous tots.

Shopping

Shops are generally well stocked by African standards, though readers unfamiliar with African conditions should realise that this is a very relative statement. Basic goods are widely available; luxuries are not. Most medium to large towns have stationery shops, good pharmacies, music shops and general stores. Even in small towns you'll find kiosks that sell most things you're likely to want – batteries, pens, paper, soap, washing powder, dry biscuits, boiled sweets, bottled drinks, toilet rolls (which Ethiopians rather endearingly call *softi*), mosquito spray and incense (useful for rooms with drifting toilet smells).

Most towns and villages have **markets**. In larger towns these will be open every day but the main market day throughout the country is Saturday. In some towns, especially small towns that serve large rural areas, there is an additional market day. Market days are usually the best days to visit off-the-beaten-track areas, as there will be far more transport. Buying from markets rather than shops actively puts money into the hands of a local community.

Ethiopia offers some excellent opportunities for **handicraft** shopping, though it is important to distinguish between so-called Airport Art (modern 'ethnic-like' artefacts, often made in the Far East) and authentic items. Tourists can help support local artisans by buying locally made items such as basketwork and *agelgils* (*injera*-holders), traditional silver crosses, textiles, religious paintings and manuscripts, woodwork, gourds, calabashes, stonework and pottery. Local incense, *beriberi* (the spice used in *kai wat* – see page 95), and Ethiopian tea and coffee make good presents too, while music lovers might want to stock up on cassettes and CDs of Ethiopian music, which are very cheap at stalls in the Mercato and elsewhere.

Where handicrafts are concerned, it is always best to buy at source if possible (baskets in Harar, *agelgils* in Bahir Dar, Jimma stools in Jimma, stonework in Axum, Falasha goods outside Gondar, calabashes in the Omo Valley, and so on). That said, there is little that cannot also be found somewhat more expensively in Addis, in particular halfway up Churchill Road, in the streets around Tewodros Square and in the tourist section of the Mercato. Prices are not fixed, except in expensive hotels, but some appropriate haggling between two stores will quickly give you an idea of a target price.

Fresh produce abounds at Jijiga's colourful market (SS)

Buying antiques

Be aware that many of Ethiopia's ancient treasures have been removed from the country in recent years, most infamously the 6kg gold Lalibela Cross stolen from the Church of Medhane Alem in Lalibela in March 1997 and returned two years later. Many smaller items have gone, too, and the Ethiopian authorities are understandably cracking down on what tourists can take out of the country. Indeed, readers are encouraged to think twice before they buy genuine antiquities – aside from depleting the country of its cultural resources, many such items will have been stolen from their real owner for resale to tourists.

Media and communications

Television
Ethiopia's domestic television service isn't much to get excited about. The nightly news service is in Amharigna, though you may catch the odd bit of international news in English. A recent development is the spread of satellite television, especially the South African-based multi-channel service DSTV and the Arabsat service out of Saudi Arabia. This is something of a mixed blessing – it's great when you want some news from home or to watch live sport, but there are times when it seems impossible to find a bar or restaurant where the atmosphere isn't dominated by a television shouting at the clientele.

Telephone
The **international telephone code** is +251. Ethiopia has a decent telephone service when compared with most parts of Africa. There are telecommunications centres in most towns, and even functional phone booths. Playing by the books, it is generally easiest to make international calls from the telecommunications centre on Churchill Avenue in Addis Ababa. Calls are cheap, but expect to wait anything between ten minutes and an hour for your call to be placed. Much less hassle and even cheaper are the officially forbidden VOIP internet kiosks found in Addis Ababa and many larger towns.

Mobile (cell) phone coverage is excellent in terms of geographic range, but the network is often overloaded due to high volume. You should be able to buy an Ethiopian SIM card at a kiosk at the Bole Airport for around US$30. An excellent alternative, especially for short trips, is to rent a phone and/or SIM card from someone in Addis. Several hotels offer this service at a reasonable fee, or you can contact Red Zebra Executive Solutions (ⓜ +251 911 24 05 65 ⓔ info@redzebraes. com ⓦ www.redzebraes.com), which charges around US$10 per week for a SIM card. Airtime is bought through prepaid scratch cards which are available in most towns. Some international mobile phones work in Ethiopia, but at much higher airtime rates.

Internet and email

The only server that currently operates in Ethiopia is the state-run Ethionet, which is effectively a monopoly protected by law, though there is some talk of private servers being permitted and introduced in the near future. This means that all locally hosted Ethiopian email addresses have the same suffix (@ethionet.et).

Reliable **internet cafés** are dotted all around Addis Ababa, and are very inexpensive, but rather slow by international standards. Elsewhere, internet usage and access lags far behind that of many neighbouring countries, though most large towns offer some sort of service, ranging from almost as good as Addis Ababa (Bahir Dar, Hawassa, Harar, Dire Dawa, Jimma, Gondar) to slow and costly (Lalibela, Axum).

Business and time

In Addis Ababa and other large cities, formal business hours are broadly similar to those in Europe or North America, typically running from around 08.30 to 17.30 Monday to Friday with an hour taken at lunch, but this is not rigid and many small businesses keep longer hours. **Museums and other historical sites** generally keep similar hours, but also open on Saturdays and Sundays (perhaps for slightly shortened hours). **National park and other natural sites of interest** are typically open to day visitors from around sunrise to sunset (say 06.00 to 18.00). However, most **churches** of interest to tourists have no fixed opening hours beyond mass times, and may close almost anytime at the whim of the priest.

In villages and small towns, the notion of fixed opening hours is often quite meaningless. Generally your guide will know when best to visit any specific site of interest, though even this is not infallible.

Time

Ethiopia, as with most of its neighbours, operates on East Africa Time, three hours ahead of GMT/UTC and eight hours ahead of US Eastern Standard Time. There is no daylight saving in place, as the country's

If it's 2005, we must be in Ethiopia ...

In September 2007, Ethiopia began a yearlong millennium celebration that probably had the rest of the world scratching its head. According to the Ethiopian calendar, 11 September marked the start of the year 2000. Why such a difference? For the answer you have to go back to 1582, when the rest of the Christian world abandoned the Julian calendar in favour of the revised Gregorian calendar. Ethiopia never has followed suit, so it remains seven years and eight months 'behind' the rest of the Christian world.

The Ethiopian calendar consists of 13 Months (hence the old tourist marketing slogan '13 Months of Sunshine'), of which 12 endure for 30 days each, while the remaining month is only five days (or six in leap years). The first month of the Ethiopian year, Meskerem, coincides with the last 20 days of September and the first ten days of October. The months that follow are Tekemt, Hidar, Tahsas, Tir, Yekatit, Megabit, Miyazya, Genbot, Sene, Hamle, Nahase and the short month of Pagumen. Ethiopian New Year falls on 11 September, which means that Ethiopia is seven or eight years behind Western time, depending on whether the date is before or after 11 September. For instance, the year that we consider to be 2013 will be 2005 in Ethiopia from 1 January to 10 September, and 2006 from 11 September to 31 December. In practice, most institutions used by tourists - banks, airline reservation offices, etc - run on the Western calendar, but you might get caught out from time to time.

equatorial location means that sunrise and sunset fall at a relatively similar time (around 06.30 and 18.30) throughout the year. Note that while most Westernised and tourist-oriented institutions use the familiar 24-hour clock, a regular cause of confusion in Ethiopia is that time is measured in 12-hour cycles starting at 06.00 and 18.00, so that their 07.00 is our 01.00, and vice versa! Most local people use and think in local time, and even fluent English-speakers will sometimes absent-mindedly say '9 o'clock', for instance, when they mean '3 o'clock' – so when in doubt, check.

Cultural etiquette

Ethiopians won't easily take offence at a minor *faux pas* committed by a tourist. That said, like anywhere else, it does have its rules of etiquette, and there is some value in ensuring that allowances are not made too frequently.

Probably the most important single custom that needs to be absorbed by visitors is the importance of **formal greetings**. As in the West, shaking hands is normal upon a first meeting between people of the same gender, but lightly rather than with a tight grip. People also usually greet each other elaborately, and while tourists aren't expected to do the same, it would be very rude to blunder into conversation or interrogative mode without first exchanging greetings – a simple 'How are you?' or '*Salaam!*' delivered with a smile will be adequate. The titles *Ato* and *Woizero* (essentially 'Mr' and 'Madam') are used to address a man and married woman respectively.

The public display of certain emotions is regarded to be in poor taste, most obviously any **informal public show of affection** – such as holding hands, kissing or embracing – between males and females. It is also considered bad form to show anger publicly, and losing your temper will almost certainly be counterproductive when dealing with obtuse officials, dopey waiters and hotel employees, or uncooperative drivers. Male and female **homosexuality** is not only unacceptable to most Ethiopians, but strictly illegal and punishable by up to five years imprisonment.

An important area of etiquette relates to **church visits**. Never just blunder into a church without first taking off your shoes, and checking whether there are different entrances for males and females. During services, try not to be intrusive and avoid taking photographs without the permission of the priest.

There is a **strong Islamic element** in Ethiopia, particularly in the far east, and many Muslim codes of contact also apply to Ethiopian Christians. For instance, most Ethiopians reserve the left hand for ablutions, and may take offence if you use this hand to pass or receive something, or offer it when shaking hands or when eating with your fingers. Even those of us who are naturally right-handed will occasionally need to remind ourselves of this (it may happen, for instance, that you are carrying something in your right hand and so hand money to a shopkeeper with your left), and left-handed travellers will need to make a constant effort.

Dress codes are conservative and most Ethiopians would regard it as offensive for **women** to expose their knees or shoulders (see *Women travellers*, page 82 for more on this), and for **men** to bare their chests publicly. It is also regarded as rather odd for adult men to wear shorts. These customs ought to be taken on board throughout Ethiopia, but particularly in areas where tourists remain a relative novelty, or when dressing to visit a church or mosque.

Ethiopia Highlights

Chapter 5	Addis Ababa and surrounds	107
Chapter 6	Lake Tana Region	131
Chapter 7	Tigrai	155
Chapter 8	Lalibela and the Northeast Highlands	185
Chapter 9	Eastern Ethiopia	215
Chapter 10	Southern Ethiopia	239

Addis Ababa 108

History 109
The city centre 112
The Piazza 115
The Mercato 116
Kiddist Maryam, Kidane Mihret and
  Kiddist Selassie 116
Around Arat Kilo and Siddist Kilo 117
Entoto Maryam 118

Around Addis Ababa: short trips 120

Bishoftu (Debre Zeyit) 120
Mount Zikwala 122
Adama (Nazret) 124
Debre Libanos 124
Melka Kunture prehistoric site 126
Adadi Maryam 126
Tiya stelae field 127
Gefersa Reservoir 128
Ambo and surrounds 128
Menegasha National Forest and Weliso 129

5 Addis Ababa and Surrounds

Situated at the heart of the central highlands, Addis Ababa has been the Ethiopian capital since the late 19th century, and it is also the country's largest city. Almost all tours of Ethiopia start from here, the site of the country's only international airport, and many visitors stop several times at what is the country's most important domestic flight and road hub. Fortunately, Addis Ababa offers plenty of worthwhile sightseeing opportunities, ranging from the excellent National Museum and historic Kiddist Selassie Cathedral to the vibrant Mercato and peri-urban Entoto Hills. For those upon whom a longer stay in Addis Ababa is enforced, it is a good springboard for several day and overnight trips, of which the most compelling are the stelae field at Tiya and nearby rock-hewn church of Adadi Maryam, the wildlife-rich Menegasha National Forest, and the crater lakes at Bishoftu.

Addis Ababa

The world's third-highest capital city, Addis Ababa (which somewhat improbably means 'New Flower', and is often shortened to plain 'Addis') may come as a surprise to anybody harbouring lingering preconceptions about Ethiopia being one large searing desert. Set at an altitude of 2,400m in the central highlands, the city is characterised by a comfortable, temperate all-year climate, and it can be downright soggy between July and August, a three-month period when it typically receives as much rain as London does in a year.

In certain other respects, Addis Ababa and its 3.5 million residents can be somewhat overwhelming to initiates, with beggars, cripples, taxi drivers and hawkers clamouring for your attention, and con artists and pickpockets doing their utmost to divert it (aspects of the city

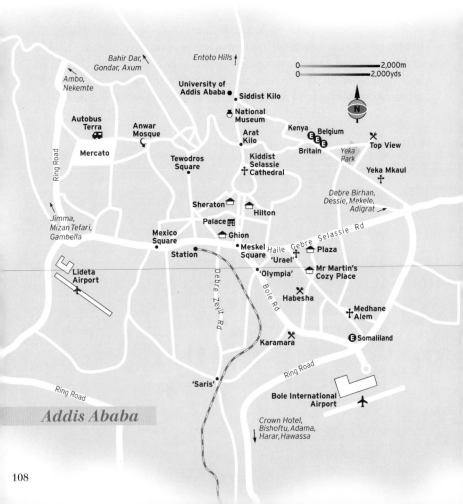

Addis Ababa

Safety in Addis Ababa

Addis Ababa is rife with casual thieves and con artists. The main threat is pickpockets, who tend to haunt the vicinity of the Ghion and Ras hotels, around the railway station, and near the Mercato. Avoid carrying valuables, and be alert to a twin-pronged attack wherein one person distracts you on one side while his pal fishes in a pocket on your opposite side.

Con artists often pose as friendly students, or stop foreigners to ask 'How do you like Ethiopia?', sometimes claiming to be the waiter or gardener at their hotel. A common trick is to ask unsuspecting visitors to a special coffee ceremony or another one-off happening, then to present them with a seriously hefty bill for drinks or food. The bottom line, as in any large city, is to assume that anybody who approaches you in the street has some sort of agenda, and to shake them off quickly, or just ignore them.

from which visitors on organised tours will be reasonably sheltered). Spend a while here, however, and you quickly realise Addis Ababa is all bark and very little bite – petty theft aside, the actual threat to one's personal safety is negligible by comparison to the likes of Nairobi or Johannesburg, or parts of many Western capitals.

Moreover, Addis Ababa is a city with a real urban buzz and a rewarding sense of singularity; a very different prospect to those many African capitals whose governments have attempted – and largely failed – to recreate misplaced pockets of Western urbanity in otherwise under-developed nations. Better still, the city offers more than enough in the way of urban sightseeing and short outings to keep a curious traveller going for days, something you could not say of too many African capitals.

History

Addis Ababa was founded by King Sahle Maryam of Showa – the future Emperor Menelik II – after he abandoned the established Showan capital at Ankober in the mid-1880s, in order to fulfil a prophecy made by his expansionist grandfather Sahle Selassie that one of his successors would establish a great city in the valley below the Entoto Hills. Sahle Maryam initially set up camp high in the hills, but at the end of the cold rainy season of 1886, he relocated to the hot springs known as Filwoha (in the present-day city centre), a site that his wife Taitu found so enchanting that she christened it Addis Ababa – 'New Flower' – and had him build her a house there. Posterity has settled on 1887 as the year in which Addis Ababa became the capital if not of Ethiopia

Practicalities

All **international flights** land at Bole International Airport, which is located at the north end of Bole Road, on the southern periphery of the city, only 5km from the centre. If you haven't arranged a transfer with your tour operator, fret not: fixed-fare taxis can be hired in the airport building, and there are also taxis right outside charging negotiable fares. All **domestic flights** are operated by Ethiopian Airlines and they also leave from and arrive at Bole International Airport. The best **coach** services out of Addis Ababa are the Selam Bus (T 011 554 8800/1 E selam.bus@ethionet.et W www.selambus.com; booking office in front of the central railway station) and Sky Bus (T 011 156 8080/8585; booking office in the Itegue Taitu Hotel).

The Piazza, one of the oldest parts of Addis Ababa, is now a busy shopping area bordering the city centre. (AZ)

Accommodation

Upmarket
Addis Ababa Hilton W www.hilton.com
Addis Ababa Sheraton W www.sheratonaddis.com

Moderate
Addis Regency Hotel W www.addisregencyhotel.com
Ghion Hotel W www.ghionhotel.com.et
Jupiter International Hotel W www.jupiterinternationalhotel.com

Budget
Itegue Taitu Hotel W www.taituhotel.com
Mr Martin's Cozy Place W www.bds-ethiopia.net/cozy-place
Ras Hotel W www.ras-hotels.com

Addis Ababa is a large city, and many roads and landmarks go by two or even three names. The rectangular **city centre** is defined by **Mexico Square** in the southwest, **Meskel Square** in the southeast, the Hilton Hotel in the northeast, and **Tewodros Square** in the northwest. The **main north-south road** is Churchill Avenue, which runs downhill from the City Hall to intersect with Ras Mekonnen Avenue close to the railway station. **Bole Road** runs south from Ras Mekonnen Avenue to terminate at Bole International Airport, 5km out of town. The oldest part of town, known as the **Piazza**, lies immediately north of the city centre. About 1km west of the Piazza, **Addis Ketema** is the site of the vast **Mercato** and **main bus station**.

The easiest way to get around is **private taxis**, which are ubiquitous and cheap: around US$4 from the Piazza to the city centre or Arat/Siddist Kilo, or US$5-10 from the Piazza to the airport.

Addis Ababa is well equipped with **ATMs**; Dashen Bank has the biggest network, followed by the CBE. Reliable ATMs are located in Bole Airport (both in the immigration and public arrivals halls) and there are multiple ATMs at the Hilton and Sheraton hotels. The Dashen Bank at the Sheraton will dispense cash if the ATMs don't work, but at a fee. There are plenty of foreign exchange bureaux dotted around the city: the one at the airport keeps very long hours and the Nib Bank and United Bank in the Hilton are both very efficient.

Eating out

All the hotels listed opposite serve decent food, and there are plenty of stand-alone restaurants to choose from, along with a plethora of bars, cafés and pastry shops. A few established favourites are listed below:

Castelli's ① 011 157 1757/156 3580. Run by the same Italian family for 50 years, this costly stalwart specialises in pasta, grills and seafood.

Cottage Restaurant ① 011 551 6359. Central Swiss restaurant serving excellent continental cuisine.

Habesha Restaurant ① 011 551 8358. This restaurant serves traditional Ethiopian food in a beautiful outdoor area with live music after 20.00.

Karamara Restaurant ① 011 515 8013. Decorated like a traditional *tukul* (a thatched hut), this serves quality Ethiopian food, with traditional music and dancing most evenings.

Top View Restaurant ① 011 651 1573/77. Upmarket restaurant on the footslopes of the Entoto Mountains offering a grandstand view of the city and fine Italian-influenced cuisine.

then of its future emperor, but in reality the shift to Filwoha was more gradual: only in 1889, months before his formal coronation as Emperor of Ethiopia, did Sahle Maryam set about building his own formal palace in the valley.

Menelik's palace in the Entoto Hills was built before Addis was founded. (SS)

Within a few years, concern grew that the New Flower's lack of firewood – which had to be transported 20km from Menegasha – would force it to be abandoned before it reached full bloom. Indeed, by the mid-1890s, Menelik had made tentative plans to relocate his capital west to a site he christened Addis Alem – 'New World' – but these were put on hold when he noticed how quickly a stand of eucalyptus trees planted by a foreign resident had grown. Spurred on by his Swiss adviser Alfred Ilg, Menelik II imported vast quantities of eucalyptus seedlings, and while his subjects were initially unimpressed by the tree's smell, its phenomenal growth rate soon swept such delicacies aside. In 1894, Addis Ababa received piped water, courtesy of Ilg's engineering prowess, and by 1897, its Saturday market – not far from the modern Piazza – attracted up to 50,000 people from the surrounding countryside. Electricity followed in 1905.

By 1913, when Menelik II died, his capital had become, in the words of one contemporary visitor, a 'mushroom city'. Fifteen years later, when Emperor Haile Selassie was enthroned, it was regarded to be the most populous African city between Cairo and Johannesburg. Today, Addis Ababa is also often regarded as the 'capital of Africa', having housed the headquarters of the Organization of African Unity (more recently African Union) since it was founded by Emperor Haile Selassie in 1963. The UN Economic Commission for Africa also has its headquarters in Addis Ababa.

Addis Ababa highlights

The city centre
The modern city centre started to take shape following the arrival of the Djibouti Railway in 1917, and its street plan was finalised during

the Italian occupation. A good place to start a **walking tour** is the junction of Churchill and Ras Mekonnen avenues, site of the rundown neo-colonial **railway station** built by the Parisian architect Paul Barria between 1928 and 1929 and inaugurated by the Empress Zawditu months before her premature death. Following Churchill Avenue northward, the **National Theatre** is of little architectural merit, but it does stage Amharigna plays in the evenings, and lies amid a row of good curio shops and inviting cafés often haunted by pickpockets. The public area to its immediate north is dominated by a geometric statue of the **Lion of Judah**, reputedly erected in 1978 for the men and women who gave their lives in the cross-border war with Somalia. To visit the **Filwoha Hot Springs** that first encouraged Menelik II to move his capital downhill from Entoto, turn right here on to **Atse Yohannes Road** and follow it for about 200m to the Filwoha Spa (which still offers treatments using the natural hot water) and attractively time-warped Finfine Hotel opposite.

The railway station is one of the most striking buildings in central Addis Ababa, but is effectively disused since the closure of the Djibouti Railway. (AZ)

Heading uphill on Churchill Avenue, the **Postal Museum** next to the main post office displays every stamp issued by the Ethiopian postal service since its foundation a century ago. The nearby **National Library** houses 355 ancient church manuscripts, the country's largest collection, the oldest being a 15th-century document retrieved from the monastery of Hayk Istafanos. One of the most interesting buildings in this part of town is the **Mega Theatre**, a rectangular double-storey stone construction that dates to the 1920s and was originally named the Club

The Red Terror Martyr's Museum evokes the horrors perpetrated by the Mengistu regime. (AZ)

de l'Union. A combined cinema, bar, dancing hall and casino, it acquired a rather seedy reputation that earned it the soubriquet of Satan Bet – Devil's House – from suspicious Ethiopians, a name still in casual use today.

Heading eastward from the railway station along Ras Mekonnen Avenue, the **Addis Ababa Stadium**, built in the mid-1960s, has been the site of most home football international matches ever since – including Ethiopia's fondly remembered home victory in the third Africa Nations Cup. A few hundred metres further, **Meskel Square** is an important landmark, notable for being one of the scariest pedestrian road crossings you're ever

likely to navigate. Next to the square, the new **Red Terror Martyrs' Memorial Museum** (Ⓦ www.redterrormartyrs.org ⊘ 08.30–18.30) is dedicated to the victims of President Mengistu's 'red terror' campaign – displays include riveting black-and-white photos dating from the 1975 coup, as well as some chilling relicts of the genocidal era that followed.

Uphill from Meskel Square, the **church of Kidus Istafanos**, built during the Haile Selassie era, stands in an attractive green garden and has a mosaic depicting the martyrdom of its namesake St Stephen above the main entrance. On festival days and Sundays, white-robed worshippers congregate here in a scene characteristic of rural Ethiopia, but transplanted to the big city. The neighbouring **Africa Hall**, also constructed by Haile Selassie, to serve as the headquarters of the Organisation of African Unity, in known for the immense stained-glass mural created by the lauded

local artist Afewerk Tekle. Further uphill, to the left, a pair of steel gates guards the verdant grounds of the **Imperial Palace** built in 1955 to mark the occasion of Haile Selassie's 25-year jubilee, but closed to the public.

The Piazza

Prior to the 1938 Italian construction of the present-day Mercato and simultaneous expansion of the more southerly modern centre, the area widely known as the Piazza (but more correctly as Arada) was the city's economic pulse and site of its most important bank, market, hotel and shops. **Arada Market**, described by one European visitor as 'picturesque chaos', was held around a sprawling sycamore fig on what is today **De Gaulle Square**, peaking in activity on Saturdays, which is also when public executions were held right through until the early years of Haile Selassie's rule. An important landmark in this area, **St George's Cathedral** was founded by Menelik in 1896 to commemorate the victory over Italy in the Battle of Adwa, though the church itself dates from 1905–11.

The Piazza (SS)

The Piazza remains an important upmarket(ish) shopping area, dominated by post-Italian occupation constructions, but with several Armenian-influenced gems of the Menelik era still tucked away. The most accessible of these, the **Itegue Taitu Hotel**, the city's oldest hostelry, is practically unchanged in appearance since it was built for Empress Taitu in 1907, and is well worth a look for the spacious architecture, period furnishings and excellent national restaurant. Other interesting buildings close to the Itegue Taitu include the **bar** next door, which has gone somewhat downhill since it was consecrated as a Greek Orthodox church to accommodate the Greek hotel manager circa 1915, and the stone **Bank of Abyssinia**, which dates to 1905. Around the corner, next to the Omar Khayyam Restaurant, a fabulously sprawling **five-storey house designed by Minas Kherbekian** (the Armenian architect who also designed the Taitu) was the tallest in the city prior to the Italian occupation.

The Mercato
Reputedly the largest market on the African continent, the Mercato sprawls across a vast grid of roads lined with stalls, kiosks and small shops. Here, you can buy just about any product known to mankind: the latest local cassettes or CDs; traditional Ethiopian crosses, clothes and other curios; vegetables, spices and pulses; custom-made silver and gold jewellery; and enough *khat* to keep the entire population of Somaliland masticating for a week. Prices are generally negotiable, but be warned that pickpockets are rife.

Kiddist Maryam, Kidane Mihret and Kiddist Selassie
This trio of **historical churches**, situated to the north of Menelik II Avenue, is most easily reached by following a little road that circles the back of the hill towards Arat Kilo. The oldest of the churches, **Kiddist Maryam**, built by Empress Zawditu in 1911, has four Axumite-style colonnaded arches on each of its exterior walls and carved lions guarding the entrance. To the left of Kiddist Maryam, **Kidane Mihret** is a circular church noted for its interior paintings and nearby sacred springs, which produce holy water used for baptism ceremonies.

Arguably the most interesting of the three churches, with its Arabic façade and interior lavishly decorated by ecclesiastical paintings, is the **Kiddist Selassie** or **Holy Trinity Cathedral** (⊙ 07.00–18.00 Mon–Fri, 09.00–18.00 Sat–Sun), the cornerstone of which was laid by Haile Selassie in 1933. Several members of the Ethiopian aristocracy are buried here, as is the famous suffragette and Ethiopian sympathiser Sylvia Pankhurst. More recently, Kiddist Selassie was chosen as the

Ceiling detail at Holy Trinity Cathedral (SS)

final resting place of Emperor Haile Selassie, who was laid to rest in a granite tomb inside the church on 5 November 2000, 25 years after his brutal death, following a colourful reburial procession attended by a substantial international Rastafarian contingent including Rita Marley.

Around Arat Kilo and Siddist Kilo

The two major traffic roundabouts dubbed Arat Kilo and Siddist Kilo are – as their Amharigna names suggest – respectively situated about 4km and 6km north of the city centre, and are easily reached by minibus from Meskel Square or the Piazza area. The back roads running to their west form one of Addis Ababa's oldest residential quarters, an area strongly associated with the Armenian Orthodox community that took refuge there at the invitation of Menelik II in response to its persecution by Turkish Muslims, and had an important influence on the development of the city's music scene and pre-Italian occupation architecture. A great many characterful **old Armenian buildings** are dotted close to the junction of Tewodros and Welete Yohannes streets, among then the city's oldest extant house, a one-storey thatched residence built by Krikorios Bogossion circa 1886 and still in the same family – interested visitors may be invited to take a look around the period-furnished interior.

About halfway between the two, the superb **National Museum of Ethiopia** (⊘ 08.30–17.00 daily) houses some excellent modern displays on human evolution, including a replica of the 3.5-million-year-old skull of Lucy (or Dinquinesh – 'thou art wonderful' – to Ethiopians), an *Australopithecus afarensis* women whose fossilised remains were discovered in eastern Ethiopia in 1974. Also worth the nominal admission price are several pre-Judaic and pre-Axumite artefacts dating back to the 1st millennium BC, among them a stone statue of a seated female, and a 2m-high throne adorned with engravings of ibex.

Siddist Kilo itself is dominated by the **Yekatit 12 Monument**, a towering column topped by a statue of a lion and dedicated to the Ethiopians who died in a punitive massacre that followed the attempted assassination of the Italian Viceroy Graziani on 19 February 1937. Also situated at Siddist Kilo is the **Lion Zoo,** the one place in Ethiopia where you can be certain of seeing a (caged) Abyssinian lion – descendants of the pride that accompanied Haile Selassie.

Continuing straight uphill from Siddist Kilo, the University of Addis Ababa is the site of the excellent **Museum and Library of the Institute of Ethiopian Studies** (⊘ 08.00–12.00 & 13.00–17.00 Tue to Fri, 10.00–17.00 Sat–Sun, whose exemplary ethnographic displays and collections of musical instruments – relating not only to the monotheistic highlanders, but also to the fascinating animist cultural groups of South Omo, and the Afar of the eastern deserts – are housed on the upper floors of a former palace of Haile Selassie. The first floor of the building is dedicated to a varied array of artefacts and household objects.

Entoto Maryam

Prior to the foundation of Addis Ababa, the Entoto Hills to the north of the present-day city centre were the short-lived site of Menelik's capital. The only obvious relic of this era, however, is the **Entoto Maryam Church**, where Menelik was crowned in 1882. It is an octagonal building with a traditionally painted interior that can only be viewed during and immediately after church services, which are held daily, ending at around 09.00. In the church compound, the **Entoto Saint Mary, Emperor Menelik and Empress Taitu Memorial Museum** (⊘ 08.30–17.00 Tue–Sun), which opened in 1987, houses an interesting collection of religious items and ceremonial clothing dating from Menelik's time.

Prayer time at Entoto Maryam (TK/S)

Around Addis Ababa: short trips

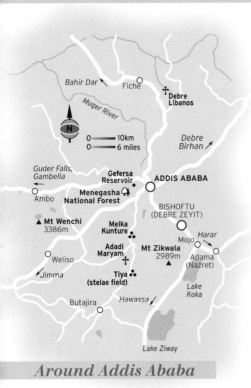

Around Addis Ababa

Addis Ababa lies at the centre of an area rich in historical, scenic and natural interest, and many worthwhile sites are dotted within a 100km radius of the city. In many cases, these sites to some extent replicate superior and better-known attractions further afield. For instance, the combination of the Tiya stelae field and the rock-hewn church of Adadi Maryam – possibly visited in conjunction with the Melka Kunture prehistoric site – would be especially rewarding to anybody unable to visit the likes of Lalibela and Axum in the north, while birdwatchers who don't make it to Bale National Park are pointed to the combination of the Gefersa Reservoir and Menegasha National Forest. Other excellent sites are Bishoftu with its plentiful crater lakes and the ancient monastery of Debre Libanos, the latter the most reliable site for spotting the unique gelada monkeys outside the Simien Mountain National Park.

Around Addis Adaba highlights

Bishoftu (Debre Zeyit)

Less than one hour's drive southeast of the capital, Bishoftu is Ethiopia's ninth-largest town, and the site of its main airforce base and training centre, as well as the veterinary facilities of Addis Ababa University. It is often referred to as Debre Zeyit ('Mount of Olives'), the official 'Christian' name imposed on the town by Haile Selassie in 1955, but it reverted to the original Oromo name of Bishoftu in the late 1990s. It also lies at the epicentre of one of Africa's most accessible field of **crater lakes**, two of which practically lie within the town centre, making it an excellent goal for a day trip out of the capital, or first stop before heading further east or south.

The **most central lake**, also called **Bishoftu**, is set at the base of a 90m-deep crater only 100m south of the main road from Addis Ababa, but invisible from it. The prettiest lake is probably the 1km² **Lake Hora**,

Practicalities

Any tour operator can arrange **day or overnight trips** to the sites described below, either as a stand-alone trip out of Addis Ababa, or as a prelude to explorations further afield. If you are looking to **visit multiple sites**, Tiya, Adadi Maryam and Melka Kunture could all be fitted into a long day trip out of Addis Ababa, one particularly rewarding to those who aren't visiting the northern historical circuit. For **nature and wildlife enthusiasts**, a loop through Ambo, Mount Wenchi and Menegasha Forest is recommended.

Bishoftu and Adama are **well-equipped towns** with numerous banks, ATMs, internet cafés, restaurants and snack bars, as to a lesser extent is Ambo, but the other sites listed below are all quite remote with limited facilities.

Accommodation

Upmarket
Dire International Hotel Adama Ⓦ www.direinthotel.com
Dreamland Hotel and Resort Bishoftu Ⓣ 011 437 1520-2
Kuriftu Resort and Spa Bishoftu Ⓦ www.kurifturesortspa.com
Negash Lodge Weliso Ⓦ www.negashlodge.com

Moderate
Abebech Matafaria Hotel Ambo Ⓣ 011 236 2365/6
Ambo Ethiopia Hotel Ambo Ⓔ ttadesse_2008@yahoo.com
Bekele Molla Hotel Adama Ⓦ www.bekelemollahotels.com
Salayish Lodge and Park Bishoftu Ⓦ www.salayishlodge.com
Wabe Shebelle Spa Sodore Ⓦ www.wabeshebellehotels.com.et

Budget
Bishoftu Afaf Hotel Bishoftu Ⓣ 011 433 8299
Ethio-German Park Hotel Debre Libanos Ⓣ 011 156 3213
Forestry Headquarters Cottages Menegasha Forest Ⓣ 011 515 4975

View of Lake Bishoftu Guda (HS)

which is set in a thickly wooded crater, teeming with birds, some 2km north of the town centre. A footpath leads from the rim to the lakeshore, where a recreation resort sells drinks and basic meals, and has a few boats for rental.

A short distance further north, **Lake Kiriftu** is the site of the premier spa resort in the Addis Ababa area, while **Bishoftu Guda** is a large and very attractive lake with lushly vegetated shores. Also worth a mention, though it is doesn't lie within a crater, is **Lake Chelekleka**, a shallow seasonal floodplain pan whose open waters often support a profusion of waterfowl.

Mount Zikwala

Of recent geological origin, Zikwala – a **dormant volcano** marked as 'Xiquala' on Fra Mauro's world map of 1459 – rises to an altitude of 2,989m some 30km southwest of Bishoftu, dominating the skyline for miles around. The **juniper forest** on the crater rim supports **colobus monkeys** and several **bird species** endemic to Ethiopia, but the main attraction is the beautiful sacred lake set in the middle of the 2km-wide crater, which reputedly glows at night, and the associated **monastic church of Zikwala Maryam**. Points of interest here include a crack between two rocks through which, according to the monks, only the pure of conscience can squeeze, and a sacred stone said to mark the grave of Gebre Manfus Kidus, one of the Egyptian monks who founded the monastery in the 4th century. Zikwala is especially worth visiting

The Donkey Sanctuary
Hilary Bradt

Visitors are often dismayed at the state of the working donkeys in Ethiopia (which has the second-largest number of donkeys in the world, after China). A Devon charity, The Donkey Sanctuary, has a highly effective project in Ethiopia, working with the owners to improve their understanding of donkey care, such as how to prevent harness sores by using the locally made padded pack-saddles, and reduce the currently high incidence of traffic accidents involving donkeys.

I talked to Asmamaw Kassaye, the head vet at the Donkey Sanctuary in Ethiopia. He told me its headquarters are in Debre Zeit but with mobile units in five different locations. With so much poverty around you would expect donkey welfare to be pretty low down in priorities, but of course to a rural person a donkey is the equivalent of a car; without one he loses his ability to earn money. Asmamaw showed me a photo of a donkey brought in strapped to a flat-bed cart, pulled by another donkey. The vets successfully cured it of its colic.

To learn more about their work while in Ethiopia or to make a donation during your visit, phone the headquarters in Addis Ababa (℡ 011 618 5708, ℡ 91 333 3591 or ℡ 91 160 3911). Once home, donations can be made through the sanctuary website Ⓦ www.thedonkeysanctuary.org.uk.

(TDS)

on 5 Tekemt and 5 Megabit (normally 15 October and 14 March), when it forms the scene of an impressive religious festival dedicated to Gebre Manfus Kidus.

Adama (Nazret)

The third-largest town in Ethiopia and capital of its largest federal region Oromia, Adama – officially known as Nazret, a corruption of Nazareth, from the last years of the imperial era until the late 1990s – is perched at an altitude of 1,600m on the fertile plateau that divides the narrowest stretch of the Ethiopian Rift Valley from the central highlands. It is an unusually vibrant and modern town by comparison to anywhere else in Ethiopia other than Addis Ababa, boasting an excellent range of restaurants, hotels and internet cafés, though facilities are aimed more at weekenders from Addis Ababa than at international visitors. The main focal point for tourism here is the **hot springs resort of Sodore**, situated 25km south of Adama on a stretch of the Awash River whose forested banks host vervet monkeys and a varied birdlife, while crocodiles and hippos also make an occasional appearance. The riverine forest also offers excellent birding.

Debre Libanos

The renowned **medieval monastery** of Debre Libanos is set in the spectacular 700m-deep Wusha Gadel ('Dog Valley'), 100km north of Addis Ababa, off the surfaced road towards Bahir Dar. It was founded in 1284 by Abuna Tekle Haymanot, the priest who was not only instrumental to the spread of Christianity in this part of Ethiopia and the reinstatement of the so-called Solomonic dynasty after centuries of Zagwe rule, but who also subsisted on one seed annually for a full seven years all the while standing on one leg and praying. Debre Libanos usurped Hayk Istafanos as the political centre of the Ethiopian Church in the mid-15th century – it was here that Emperor Lebna Dengal formally received the first Portuguese mission to Ethiopia in 1520 – and it retained its political significance until the Italian occupation, when – as a perceived hotbed of patriotic anti-Italian sentiment – the monastery was razed and its inhabitants massacred by the fascist troops at the bidding of Viceroy Graziani. It remains an important pilgrimage site, and while the modern church – built by Haile Selassie in the 1950s – is of limited architectural merit, the surrounding countryside is truly spectacular and it is the most reliable site close to Addis Ababa for sightings of the endemic **gelada monkey** and iconic **lammergeyer**.

Also of interest on the main road close to Debre Libanos, is a lichen- and moss-stained **stone bridge**, built at the cusp of the 19th and 20th centuries by Ras Darge, a relation of Menelik II, that spans the Gur River before it plunges for several hundred metres over a cliff edge to eventually flow into the Jemma, a tributary of the Nile.

The stone bridge spanning the River Gur was built in the late 19th or early 20th century. (AZ)

Melka Kunture prehistoric site

Situated on the south face of a gorge along the Awash River, some 50km south of Addis Ababa by road, Melka Kunture is one of the most important Stone Age sites in Ethiopia. Numerous stone cleavers and hand-axes and other tools have been unearthed along the river, and it has also yielded fossils of several extinct mammal species, including forms of hippo, giraffe, gelada and wildebeest. *Homo erectus* fossils dating back from between 1.5 and 1.7 million years have also been found at the site, along with what are possibly the oldest-known cranial fragments of *Homo sapiens*, estimated to be more than 500,000 years old. An informative site **museum** spread across four *tukuls* displays a collection of prehistoric skull replicas modelled after findings throughout Africa, and an **open-air excavation site** and a **prehistoric animal butchering site** lie a short walk away. Everything is well described on wall panels, and the curator is usually delighted to welcome a few visitors to his lonely patch.

Adadi Maryam (AZ)

Adadi Maryam

A particularly worthwhile goal for visitors who won't make it to Lalibela or Tigrai, Adadi Maryam, the southernmost extant **rock-hewn church** in Ethiopia, is reached via a 13km-long turn-off signposted to the right about 5km past Melka Kunture. The church's original name has evidently been forgotten – 'Adadi' is the Oromo name for a type of bush that grows in the vicinity – but a persistent local tradition associates its excavation with King Lalibela's visit to nearby Mount Zikwala in AD1106. This assertion is supported by its architecture: a subterranean semi-monolith encircled by a wide tunnel containing a few disused monastic cells, Adadi Maryam is smaller and more roughly hewn than its counterparts at Lalibela, but it resembles them far more closely than it does any rock-hewn church in Tigrai. Adadi Maryam was attacked by Ahmed Gragn in the early 16th century, causing severe damage to the large cross above the entrance, and it subsequently fell into disuse. After being rediscovered by local hunters during the reign of Menelik II, the church was rehabilitated, and it has been in active use ever since. More extensive restoration work took place over 1996–98, funded by the Swiss Embassy.

Tiya stelae field

Inscribed as a UNESCO World Heritage Site in 1980, this mysterious and haunting spot, only 30km south of Adadi Mayram, marks the northern limit of a belt of at least **160 stelae (obelisk) fields** stretching through southern Ethiopia from Dilla to Negele Borena. Remarkably little is known about the origin of these stelae or of the meaning of the symbols carved upon them, but recent excavations have revealed that they mark the 700-year-old mass graves of males and females who were laid to rest in a foetal position having died aged between the ages of 18 and 30. The stelae field at Tiya comprises more than 40 stones, some standing 2m tall, though several had

Mystery still surrounds the engravings on the stones at the Tiya stelae field. (SS)

collapsed prior to being re-erected in their original position by French archaeologists. Nearly all the stones are engraved with what appear to be stylised swords (suggesting perhaps that the deceased were soldiers), plain circles (which seem to denote that a female is buried underneath that stele), and what looks like a pair of podgy leaves rising on a stem from a rectangular base (quite possibly symbolising the enset or false banana, a plantain still widely grown in southern Ethiopia). On some stones is carved what looks like a Greek 'E', a symbol for which no plausible interpretation has been put forward.

Gefersa Reservoir

Set at an altitude of 2,600m in the Akaki catchment area, 18km west of Addis Ababa along the Ambo road, this large reservoir was created in 1938 to provide drinking water for the expanding capital. The lack of fringing vegetation makes the reservoir rather bland visually, but it is popular with **birdwatchers** as a good place

Rouget's rail (IY/FLPA)

to look for a few endemic species not easily seen at the main stops along the northern historical circuit. These include the ubiquitous **wattled ibis** and more localised **blue-winged goose**, as well as **Abyssinian longclaw**, **Rouget's rail** and **black-headed siskin**.

Ambo and surrounds

Situated on the Huluka River 125km west of Addis Ababa, the small town of Ambo – home to Ethiopia's most popular brand of mineral water – was temporarily renamed Hagare Hiwot ('Healthy Country') under Haile Selassie, who was partial to bathing in the therapeutic hot springs that lie in the town centre. Still the centrepiece of a low-key resort and accompanying swimming pool, these springs ensure that Ambo remains a popular weekend break from the capital, but in truth it is of limited interest to tourists except as a base to explore a few local sites. One of the most accessible of these is the **Guder Falls**, on the Nekemte road about 15km past Ambo, which carries an impressive volume of water in the rainy season, and lies in a forest patch rattling with monkeys and birds. It's supposed to be best on Sundays, when the sluice gates are opened for Ethiopian weekenders.

The most popular attraction in the Ambo area is **Mount Wenchi**, a dormant volcano that rises to an elevation of 3,386m alongside the dirt road that connects Ambo to Weliso. Wenchi's picturesque caldera, settled and quite densely cultivated, encloses a 4km² crater lake dotted with small islands, one of which hosts the **monastery of Wenchi Chirkos** whose foundation is variously attributed by some to the 15th-century Emperor Zara Yaqob and the 13th-century saint Tekle Haymanot. An extensive plateau covered in Afro-alpine heather and moorland surrounds the crater, and a few relic patches of natural forest remain in the area.

Menegasha National Forest and Weliso

The largest remaining tract of **indigenous forest** in the Addis Ababa region, the magnificent Menegasha National Forest incorporates some 2,500ha of closed canopy juniper, hagenia and Podocarpus forest at altitudes of 2,300–3,000m on the southern and western slopes of Mount Wechecha. This forest has been preserved by imperial decree since the mid-15th century, when Emperor Zara Yaqob, concerned at the high level of deforestation, arranged for a large tract of junipers to be replanted with seedlings from the Ankober area, and it was set aside as a state forest by Menelik II in the late 1890s. Today, five colour-coded **walking trails**, ranging in length from 0.3km to 9km, run out of the park headquarters, variously taking in a lovely waterfall as well as the 3,385m peak of Mount Wechecha. It is also a great place for **wildlife enthusiasts**: large **mammals** include the colobus monkey, the endemic Menelik's bushbuck, as well as the more elusive leopard, and a long list of **forest birds** includes the endemic yellow-fronted parrot, black-winged lovebird, banded barbet, Abyssinian woodpecker, Ethiopian oriole and Abyssinian catbird. The forest is reached via the small town of Weliso, which straddles the Jimma road 100km southwest of Addis Ababa.

Bahir Dar and surrounds 132

History 133
Around town 136
Lake Tana monasteries 138
Blue Nile Falls 142
Gish Abay 143

Gondar and the Simiens 144

History 145
Royal Enclosure 147
Simien Mountains National Park 150
Gorgora 152

6 Lake Tana Region

Ethiopia's largest lake, extending over 3,673km^2, Tana lies at an altitude of 1,830m in a shallow basin formed 20 million years ago by a lava extrusion. The primary source of the Blue Nile, the lake was known to the ancient Egyptians as 'Coloe', and to the ancient Greeks as 'Pseboe', the 'copper-tinted lake ... that is the jewel of Ethiopia'. The main regional gateway, Bahir Dar, lies on the southern lakeshore close to the spectacular Blue Nile Falls, and several historic island monasteries. Another popular attraction, a short distance north of the lake, is the city of Gondar, which served as the imperial capital from the early 17th until the late 19th century. For wildlife lovers, Tana is renowned for its varied birdlife and plentiful hippos, while Gondar forms the springboard for hikes into Simien Mountain National Park, a scenic stronghold for the handsome gelada monkey and endangered Walia ibex.

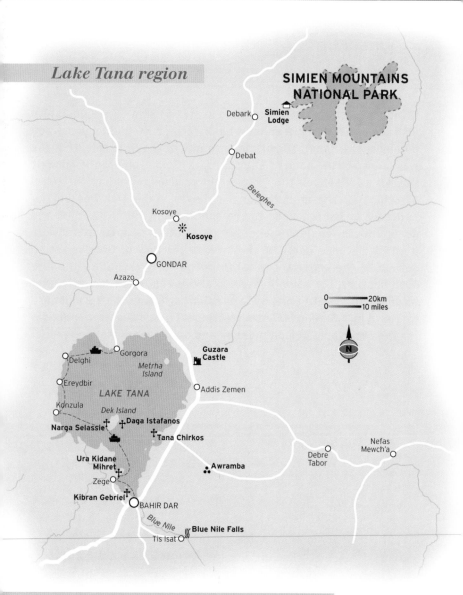

Lake Tana region

SIMIEN MOUNTAINS
NATIONAL PARK

Debark
Simien
Lodge

Debat

Beleghes

Kosoye
☀
Kosoye

GONDAR

Azazo

0 ———— 20km
0 ———— 10 miles

N

Delghi
Gorgora
*Metrha
Island*

Ereydbir
**Guzara
Castle**

LAKE TANA

Addis Zemen

Konzula
Dek Island

Narga Selassie
Daga Istafanos

Tana Chirkos

Ura Kidane
Mihret

Awramba

Debre
Tabor

Nefas
Mewch'a

Zege

Kibran Gebriel

BAHIR DAR

Blue Nile
Blue Nile Falls

Tis Isat

Bahir Dar and surrounds

With its palm-lined avenues and pretty lakeside vistas, this large and
neatly laid-out city on the southern shore of Lake Tana possesses
a tropical ambience unusual for northern Ethiopia. As with so many
large Ethiopian towns, Bahir Dar offers an intriguing juxtaposition
of urban modernity and rustic traditionalism, the latter epitomised
by the bustling daily central market. It is a popular first stop on the

northern historical circuit, both in itself and as a base for exploring the renowned Blue Nile Falls and remote island monasteries of Lake Tana. Other less popular attractions include the most remote source of the Nile at Giash Abay, and the idiosyncratic atheistic community at Awra Amba in the highlands east of Lake Tana.

Market, Bahir Dar (AZ)

History

Links between Lake Tana and the classical world are reflected in the design of its papyrus *tankwa* boats (which bear a striking resemblance to boats used in ancient Egypt) and the presence of pre-Christian Jewish sacrificial pillars on the island of Tana Chirkos. The southern shore was the focal point of Ethiopian politics between the late 13th-century collapse of the Zagwe Dynasty and the foundation of Gondar almost 400 years later. A succession of temporary capitals were established in the region back then, and it was here that several battles took place between the Christian empire and the Islamic army of Ahmed Gragn in the early 16th century.

Fishermen on Lake Tana still use traditional *tankwa* boats (AC)

Practicalities

Most visitors with time limitations **fly** to Bahir Dar from Addis Ababa, or to/ from elsewhere on the northern historical circuit. At least one flight daily operated by Ethiopian Airlines connects Bahir Dar to Addis Ababa, Gondar, Axum and Lalibela, and each of these legs takes around one hour. The airport lies about 3km west of the town centre, and unless you are booked into a hotel with a shuttle service or are being met by a tour operator, you'll have to get a taxi into town, which shouldn't cost more than US$5 per group.

Bahir Dar lies 560km from Addis Ababa on a recently improved and fully surfaced **road**, which can now be covered in one day, whether in a private vehicle, or using the Sky or Selam **coaches**. Tourists can also now make use of the weekly *MV Tananich* **ferry** between Bahir Dar and Gorgora, an expensive and enjoyable trip, with an overnight stop at Konzula in either direction, but prone to delays. Once in Bahir Dar, **getting around town** is easy enough by **minibus** or **taxi**. There are also many operators offering **boat trips** to the Lake Tana monasteries, or bus trips to the Blue Nile Falls.

Foreign-exchange facilities are available at the Dashen Bank or Commercial Bank of Ethiopia. **Internet cafés** are now dotted all around town; the two on

Accommodation

Upmarket
Kuriftu Lake Tana ⓦ www.kurifturesortspa.com
Tana Hotel ⓦ www.ghionhotel.com.et

Moderate
Papyrus Hotel ⓦ www.papyrushotel.net.et
Summerland Hotel ⓔ gogobahirdar@yahoo.com

Budget
Ghion Hotel ⓔ ghionbd@ethionet.et
Tana Pension ⓣ 058 220 1302

As recently as the early 1950s, Bahir Dar was little more than a sleepy lakeshore village, overshadowed politically and economically by Gondar to the north and Debre Markos to the south. The initial stimulus for its modern growth was the decision to build a hydroelectric plant at the nearby Blue Nile Falls, and it has since emerged as an important

Bahir Dar street scene (AC)

the main waterfront road next to Ethiopian Airlines are recommended, as is the one in the Ghion Hotel.

Eating out

The out-of-town **Tana Hotel** and relatively inexpensive **Ghion Hotel** serve decent food but stand out mainly for their unbeatable lakeshore settings. For Ethiopian food, reliable bets include the stalwart **Blue Jayz Restaurant**, **Tana Restaurant** (part of the Tana Pension), **Amanuel Restaurant** or pricier but very reliable **Enkutatash Hotel #2. Cloud Nine Pastry** stands out for its tasty confectionaries and juices, and **Tana Pastry**, **Mugera Pastry** and **Central Pastry** are also recommended.

The **Balageru Cultural Club** next to Amanuel Restaurant offers lively traditional music and dancing from all over Ethiopia, starting at 20.00 and lasting for three hours or so.

centre of industry and tourism, with a population that recently passed the 200,000 mark. The city's importance was further boosted when it was chosen ahead of Gondar, Dessie and Debre Markos – formerly the respective capitals of the defunct provinces of Gondar, Wolo and Gojjam – as the capital of the Amhara region in the redrawn federal map of 1995.

Bahir Dar

LAKE TANA

Tana

Football stadium

Blue Nile Springs Hotel, Source of the Nile, Debre Margam Monastery, Bezawit Mill & palace, Gondar

Kiriftu Lake Tana hotel, Zege, airport (3km)

Ferry jetty
(For Zege, Dek & Gorgora)

Enkutatash Hotel #2

Ghion

Lake Tana Transport Authority

Football field

Minibus to Zege

Dar Gioyorgis Church

Polytechnic

Commercial Bank of Ethiopia

Amhara Development Association

Regional Admin

Telecom

Dashen

Ethiopian Airlines

Dashen

Tourist office

Summerland

Textile factory

Mullu Alem Cultural Centre

Blue Jayz Bar & Restaurant

Amanuel

City Council

Mosque

Cloud Nine Pastry

Tana Pension & Pastry

Balageru Cultural Club

Bank of Abyssinia

Central Pastry

Commercial Bank of Ethiopia

Bus station

N

0   200m
0   200 yards

Football field & park

MARKET

Addis Ababa (560km)

Minibus park

Police

Water Ministry

Commercial Bank of Ethiopia

Blue Nile Falls

University

Bahir Dar and surrounds highlights

Around town

Bahir Dar is essentially a modern town, but it boasts one significant antiquity in **Dar Giyorgis**, a waterfront church near the main traffic roundabout. Founded at least 400 years ago, the original church building was knocked down to make way for a larger and more modern edifice in the Haile Selassie era, but the compound also houses a disused two-storey stone tower, architecturally reminiscent of the Gondarine palaces, whose construction is attributed to the Jesuit priest Pedro Páez during the reign of Susneyos.

Bahir Dar is famous for its goatskin *injera*-holders. (AZ)

Close by, the scenic **Ghion Hotel** has lovely grounds, with the lake lapping its lawns, pelicans huddling on the waterfront, and the likes of white-cheeked turaco, paradise flycatcher and spotted eagle owl resident in the giant *ficus* trees. Also worthwhile, the **central market** is one of the largest in Ethiopia, and well stocked with traditional handicrafts. The local speciality is a goatskin *injera*-holder called an *agelgil*, traditionally used by herdsmen as a 'picnic basket', but the locally produced white *shama* cloth is also popular with souvenir hunters.

The out-of-town **Tana Hotel** is set in large, thickly wooded lakeshore grounds that host a rich variety of birds, ranging from kingfishers and herons to colourful woodland dwellers such as double-toothed barbet, banded barbet, Bruce's green pigeon and white-cheeked turaco. Continue past the hotel for another 1km or so to reach the **bridge** that spans the Nile as it exits Lake Tana, often a good vantage point for spotting **hippos** and **crocodiles**. From here, it's a ten-minute walk to a stretch of lakeshore where traditional papyrus *tankwa* boats cross the water to the 14th-century **Debre Maryam Monastery**, which lacks the impact of the larger island monasteries on Lake Tana, but is friendly and more accessible.

A popular onward option from the Nile outlet involves taking the first right turn after the bridge and following it for about 2.5km to the

Papyrus boats

While visiting the island monasteries of Lake Tana you will likely cross paths with some of the papyrus boats that ferry goods across this enormous lake. Ask your guide to steer alongside and watch the oarsmen power their crafts that are made from bundles of tightly bound papyrus reeds. You'll get some great

photographs of an ancient way of life. Back on shore, take a short excursion to visit one of the local villages where the boats are made.

top of **Bezawit Hill**, site of an ostentatious split-level **palace** built for Haile Selassie in 1967 and used by him on only two occasions during the remaining seven years of his rule. Entrance to the disused palace is forbidden, as is photography of the exterior, but the hill provides an excellent vantage point over the town and Lake Tana, especially at dusk, and there's a chance of seeing hippos in the river below.

Lake Tana monasteries

Practically unknown to outsiders prior to the 1930s, some two dozen monastic churches are scattered across the islands and peninsulas of Lake Tana, most dating to the 14th-century rule of Amda Tsion, though some are older, and others from the more recent Gondarine period. Architecturally, none stands comparison to the rock-hewn churches of Lalibela or Tigrai, but several are beautifully decorated, in particular Narga Selassie and Ura Kidane Mihret, whose **painted walls** serve as a visual encyclopaedia of Ethiopian ecclesiastical concerns. Many of the churches also have incredible **treasuries**, with contents that range from medieval books, crosses and crowns to the mummified remains of former Ethiopian emperors. The conservationist ethic of Orthodox Ethiopian Christianity has ensured that these monasteries support tracts of **natural forest** inhabited by monkeys and plentiful birds.

Motorboat charters to the monasteries can be arranged through any hotel on Bahir Dar, though do be warned that it is difficult to fit more than three into a day trip, and that marine safety guidelines are not up to Western standards. Ura Kidane Mihret, and several other lesser churches on the Zege Peninsula, are accessible by a daily **ferry**, and can also be reached by minibus. All monasteries charge **entrance fees** and most are **closed to women**, the main exceptions being Narga Selassie and Ura Kidane Mihret.

There are more than 20 island monasteries in total, and it would require several days on the lake to see them all. The following are among the most worthwhile, with Kibran Gebriel and Ura Kidane Mihret being a particularly popular combination due to their relative accessibility, while the other three can be visited together on a long day trip out of Bahir Dar.

The Lake Tana monasteries are filled with treasures including medieval books. (AZ)

In conversation with ...
BJ Tours & Trekking

BJ TOURS & TREKKING

What is your favourite itinerary?

The northern historical circuit: Axum, Lalibela, Gondar and the Simien Mountains.

What makes your trips to Ethiopia special?

I have been sharing my home country, Ethiopia, with tourists for many years, both as a guide and as a tour operator, and customer satisfaction has always been my aim. Although I take visitors to all parts of Ethiopia, my local area of Gondar and the Simien Mountains is my favourite. I am the most experienced guide available for trekking and mountain climbing, having made many ascents of the highest mountain in Ethiopia, Ras Dashen (4,620m).

Are your tours good for spotting wildlife?

Ethiopia has some very special animals which are not found elsewhere in Africa. In the Simiens visitors may see the endangered Walia ibex and the gelada monkeys (baboons) which are accustomed to people so you can approach very close. In the Bale Mountains you may also see the Simien wolf.

Does trekking in the Simien Mountains mean that you have to camp?

No, there is a comfortable lodge within the park so it is possible to see the beautiful mountain scenery and wildlife while on a day trip. But to get the most out of the national park it is best to trek for several days. One of my specialities is organising unusual trekking/camping itineraries.

BJ Tours is run by Bedassa Jote, who has been at the centre of Ethiopian tourism for 16 years. He offers a wide variety of tours appealing to all interests. We spoke to Bedassa.

① 058 111 5073 Ⓜ 911 831 629 Ⓔ bjtours@ethionet.et
Ⓦ www.bjtoursandtrekking.com

Kibran Gebriel
The closest monastery to Bahir Dar lies on a tiny, forested crescent – presumably part of the rim of an extinct volcano – and houses the region's largest library of ancient books, including a beautifully illustrated 15th-century *Life of Christ*. Men only.

Ura Kidane Mihret
The forested Zege Peninsula, accessible from Bahir Dar by a daily ferry or more regular minibus service, is studded with medieval churches, of which Ura Kidane Mihret ranks among the most beautiful in the Tana region. Founded in the 14th century, it is covered in a stunning confusion of 100- to 250-year-old paintings that are positively Chaucerian in their physicality, ribaldry and gore.

Tana Chirkos
This small island monastery, separated from the eastern shore of Tana by a narrow marshy corridor, has acquired something approaching cult status since Graham Hancock's book *The Sign and the Seal* publicised the ancient legend that the Ark of the Covenant was stowed there for 800 years prior to being transferred to Axum in the 4th century AD. The monastery itself was founded on the site of an older temple during the 6th-century reign of Gebre Meskel, relics of which include a trio of hollowed-out sacrificial pillars that testify to the island's importance as a Judaic religious shrine in pre-Christian times. Men only.

Daga Istafanos
The largest monastery on the lake, supporting 200 monks, Daga Istafanos lies on a small wedge-shaped island immediately east of the much larger Dek Island. A reliable (and for once apparently uncontested) tradition states that the monastery was founded in the late 13th century by Hiruta Amlak. The church on the island's conical peak, though relatively uninteresting to look at, and not especially old, is reputedly where the Ark of the Covenant was hidden during Ahmed Gragn's 16th-century occupation of Axum. An eerie mausoleum contains the mummified remains of at least five Ethiopian emperors: Yakuno Amlak (1268–93), Dawit I (1428–30), Zara Yaqob (1434–68), Susneyos (1607–32) and Fasilidas (1632–76) – with the latter's facial features still discernible. Men only.

Narga Selassie
Situated on the western shore of Dek, the largest island on Lake Tana, this ornately decorated monastery was built in the 18th century for Princess

The stunning paintings at Ura Kidane Mihret are between 100 and 250 years old. (AZ)

Mentewab. The stone walls surrounding the compound are typically Gondarine, and a riotous and absorbing collection of ecclesiastic art is supplemented by an incongruous etching of the explorer James Bruce, a close associate of Mentewab, puffing away on his pipe.

Blue Nile Falls

Only 30km after it exits Lake Tana, the Blue Nile plunges over a 45m-high rock face into a steep narrow gorge to form one of Africa's most spectacular waterfalls, known locally as Tis Abay ('Smoke of the Nile') or Tis Isat ('Smoking Water'). The 18th-century Scottish traveller James Bruce, often but incorrectly credited as the first European to see the waterfall (it was described two centuries earlier in the memoirs of the Portuguese priest João Bermudes), eulogised it as:

> A magnificent sight, that ages, added to the greatest length of human life, would not efface or eradicate from my memory; it struck me with a kind of stupor, and a total oblivion of where I was, and of every other sublunary concern.

Unfortunately, the waterfall has been a somewhat capricious sight since 2003, with up to 95% of the Nile's water being diverted to power a hydroelectric plant, and it is often difficult to determine when it is flowing normally. It's a 30-minute walk from Tis Abay village to the

Blue Nile Falls are a popular day excursion from Bahir Dar. (AZ)

Awra Amba

(PT)

The community of Awra Amba (Ⓦ www.awraamba.com) was founded in 1972 to demonstrate that the best escape route from poverty and hunger is not religion or prayer but education and hard work. The community believes in one creator who made all people equal, and it accords pride of place not to a mosque or a church, but to a well-stocked school library. Its 400 members follow egalitarian non-sexist and non-racist policies, welcoming people of all religions and ethnic backgrounds. Its main source of funding is a weaving co-operative that produces hand-spun cotton and wool shamas, scarves, shirts and blankets, which cost significantly less than in most other parts of the country. Awra Amba lies about 60km from Bahir Dar along the Woldia road.

main viewpoint, crossing the river below the falls on a large stone bridge called Agam Dildi, built in the 1620s for Emperor Susneyos, and passing through dense riverine woodland alive with birds.

Gish Abay

Protected within the grounds of **Gish Mikael Monastery**, this spring is the starting point of the Gilgil Abay (Calf Nile), the most voluminous river to flow into Lake Tana, and ultimate source of the Blue Nile. The **sacred spring**, which reputedly has healing powers, was visited by the Spanish priest Pedro Páez in 1613, by the Portuguese missionary Jerónimo Lobo in 1629, and by James Bruce in 1770. Close by, a **trio of holy springs** known locally as the Father, Son and Holy Spirit emerges from a hole above a cave into a warm natural pool where it is possible to swim. The closest town, Sekala, lies 35km along a side road running northeast from Tilili (near Kosober, on the main road between Debre Markos and Bahir Dar). It is forbidden for anybody who has already eaten anything that day to see the holy water, and travellers who arrive in the afternoon risk being turned away on that suspicion.

143

Gondar and the Simiens

The largest and most immediately impressive of Ethiopia's three major ex-capitals, Gondar is perhaps less enduringly memorable than its more ancient counterparts Axum and Lalibela. It is a very pleasant city, with a laidback and rather countrified mood by comparison to, say, Addis Ababa or Bahir Dar. Its focal point is the **Royal Compound**, or Fasil Ghebbi, which is named after the city's founder Emperor Fasilidas (also known as Fasil) and was inscribed as a UNESCO World Heritage Site in 1979. The half-dozen **stone castles** protected within the tall compound walls, built over the course of the 17th and 18th centuries, have led to Gondar being dubbed the Camelot of Africa.

Also of interest are **Fasilidas's Bathing Pool**, the beautiful **church of Debre Birhan Selassie**, and **out-of-town palaces** built by Fasilidas's predecessor Emperor Susneyos and by the Empress Mentewab, an

Practicalities

Ethiopian Airlines **flies** daily between Gondar and Addis Ababa, Bahir Dar, Axum and Lalibela. The airport is about 20km out of town, just off the main Bahir Dar road, but taxis meet all flights. There are also daily Sky and Selam **buses** to Gondar from Addis Ababa, a 12-hour journey, and regular road transport runs there from Bahir Dar and Gorgora. Within Gondar, **taxis** are widely available in the city centre, and cheap **minibuses** run out to the suburbs.

Accommodation

Upmarket
Goha Hotel ⓦ www.ghionhotel.com.et
Landmark International Hotel ⓦ www.gonderlandmark.com
Simien Lodge (Simien Mountain National Park) ⓦ www.simiens.com. See advert, page 153.

Moderate
Atse Bekaffa Hotel Ⓔ atsebekafahotel@yahoo.com
Capra Walia Inn Ⓔ caprainn@yahoo.com
Gorgora Port Hotel (Gorgora) Ⓣ 058 164 7003
Hotel Imet Gogo (Debark) ⓦ www.hotelimetgogo.com.et
Quara Hotel ⓦ www.quarahotelgonder.com

associate of the explorer James Bruce. Juxtaposed against the distinctive early Gondarine architecture, much of the modern town centre dates from the Italian occupation of 1936–41, and hints of Art Deco and other pre-war European styles can be detected in many of the rundown buildings that line the central Piazza. Gondar is also the obvious base from which to stage day trips or longer treks into the scenic Simien Mountains National Park, Ethiopia's most popular hiking destination.

History

Gondar was founded in the wake of a tumultuous century during which the Christian Empire of the Ethiopian Highlands fought, and almost lost, a crippling war with its Islamic neighbours, and then suffered a period of intense internal religious conflict sparked by Emperor Susneyos's declaration of Catholicism as the state religion. In 1632, Susneyos abdicated in favour of his son Fasilidas, who reinstated the Orthodox

Most operators in Gondar can organise day or longer trips to the Simien Mountains. It is also possible to make all your **hiking arrangements** in Debark, the town closest to the entrance gate for Simien Mountains National Park.

Both branches of the Commercial Bank of Ethiopia offer a **foreign-exchange** service, as does the generally more efficient Dashen Bank. Gondar seems to suffer from a paucity of **internet cafés** by comparison with nearby Bahir Dar, with Golden Internet (next to Sofa Juice) and Galaxy Internet (next to the Circle Hotel) being the best bets.

Budget
Belegez Pension ⓣ 058 111 4356
Simien Park Hotel (Debark) Ⓦ www.simienparkhotel.com

Eating out

Try the **Tuscany Restaurant** for pizzas and Italian fare, the **Golden Gate Restaurant** for Chinese food, or the **Fogera** and **Quara hotels** for Ethiopian fare. Of the smaller eateries, the **Ras Bar and Restaurant** is known locally for its excellent *injera*.

Traditional music and dancing can be enjoyed most nights at the **Balageru Bar** and the **Minas Bar & Nightclub**.

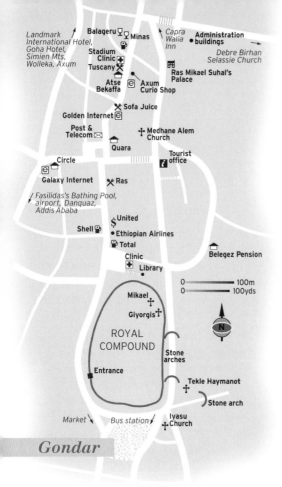

Gondar

Church, expelled all Portuguese settlers from his empire, and decided that replacing his father's temporary capital at Danquaz with a permanent capital would help restore stability to his empire.

In 1635, Emperor Fasilidas chose as his capital the small village of Gondar, with its strategic hilltop location at an altitude of 2,120m in the southern foothills of the Simien Mountains, fulfilling an ancient tradition that the next capital would have an initial 'G'. By the time of Fasilidas's death in 1667, Gondar had become the largest and most important city in the empire, with a population in excess of 60,000. It retained its position as the capital of Ethiopia for 250 years, though this status was increasingly nominal from the late 18th century onwards as the central monarchy gradually lost importance to powerful regional rulers. In 1855, Gondar was formally supplanted as capital when Emperor Tewodros II moved the imperial capital to Magadala.

Gondar declined further in significance as a result of two Mahdist attacks – in June 1887 and January 1888 – with most of its historic churches being burnt to the ground on the latter occasion. The city enjoyed something of a revival during the Italian Occupation, when the Royal Compound was used as the Fascist's military headquarters, and it remained in Italian hands until November 1941, six months after Addis Ababa was captured by the Allied Forces. From then until 1994, it was capital of the Begemder, a province subsequently absorbed into the Federal Region of Amhara. It remains the fourth-largest city in Ethiopia, with a population approaching the 250,000 mark.

Gondar and the Simien Mountains highlights

Royal Enclosure

Also known as the **Fasil Ghebbi**, this walled 70,000m^2 compound of 17th-century castles and buildings lies at the heart of the city centre and gives it much of its character. The most impressive building within the compound is the **restored three-storey castle** built by Fasilidas circa 1640, a stone building that displays a unique blend of Portuguese, Axumite and Indian influences, and whose roof offers views all the way south to Lake Tana. The other major relic of the Fasilidas era is the **Royal Archives**, which served as the Italian headquarters during World War II, and was partially destroyed by British bombs as a result. The castle built by Emperor Iyasu (1682–1706) is one of the largest in the compound, and the most ornately constructed, but it was partially damaged by an earthquake in 1704, and the ground-floor ceiling collapsed under the British bombardment. Emperor Bakafa (1721–30) also left his mark on the Royal Compound by building a castle, some stables and an immense banquet hall. Queen Mentewab, the regent for Bakafa's son, Iyasu II (1730–55), was the last of Gondar's castle builders, having constructed the fine building now used as a gift shop. Of the **three churches** set within separate compounds within the main walls of the Royal Compound, the oldest is **Gemjabet Maryam**, built by Fasilidas.

Fasilidas's Castle is the most impressive of the buildings within the Royal Enclosure. (SS)

Historic sites in and around Gondar

The central royal compound is undoubtedly Gondar's prime historical attraction, but the city's suburbs and surrounding hills host a wealth of other sites dating from the time when this area was the focal point of Ethiopian politics.

Fasilidas's Pool

Enclosed by a turreted stone wall and overlooked by a two-storey building, this 2,800m² sunken **bathing pool**, 2km from the town centre, may be the earliest of Emperor Fasilidas's constructions, pre-dating his famous castle. Though sometimes referred to as a swimming pool, it has probably always been used ceremonially rather than for royal leisure pursuits. The pool plays a central part in the **Timkat Festival**, with thousands of white-robed worshippers converging on its edge – a sight not to be missed, should you be around Gondar at the time.

Kuskuam

Set 5km out of town on the slopes of Debre Tsehai, this partially ruined **palatial complex** was constructed as the residence of the fondly remembered Empress Mentewab after the death of her husband Emperor Bakafa in 1730. The best preserved building is the **banquet hall**, whose engraved outer walls must be

The Kuskuam complex (KFK)

at least 10m high, while the **church of Kuskuam Maryam**, rebuilt during the Italian occupation, is also elaborately decorated, though none of the paintings pre-date 1970.

Debre Birhan Selassie

The only **17th-century Gondarine church** to survive the 1888 Mahdist attack on the city completely unscathed – legend has it, thanks to the intervention of a swarm of bees – lies about 1km out of town along the road to Debark. It was built to the same directions as Solomon's Temple in Jerusalem as an intended resting place for the Ark of the Covenant. The superb artwork inside, attributed to the 17th-century artist Haile Meskel, includes the much-photographed ceiling with its 80 cherubic faces, and some rousing Biblical scenes.

Danquaz

Situated 20km south of modern Gondar, Danquaz was the last of several semi-permanent capitals established by Emperor Susneyos in the early 17th century, and it was also used by Emperor Fasilidas for the first three years of his reign. Historically important as it may be, there isn't much left to capture the imagination of the casual visitor, though its proximity to the airport makes for an easy diversion on the way in or out of town.

Wolleka

This **village** 5km from Gondar along the Axum road was vacated by its original Falasha occupants between 1985 and 1992, when most of Ethiopia's 'Black Jews' were airlifted to Jerusalem to liberate them from the repressive Mengistu regime. All that remains today is the old synagogue, which mimics a typical circular Ethiopian church, but with a Star of David on its roof.

The old synagogue, Wolleka (MV)

Tana highlights

RAINBOW
TOURS

We recommend two nights in Bahir Dar staying at either Abbay Minch - situated in a former coffee plantation so fantastic for birders - or the more upmarket Kuriftu Resort & Spa. Take a drive along the shores of Lake Tana to Gondar and experience the Simien Mountains on a three-day to two-week mule-trekking trip. Look out for the Walia ibex at Chennek, and geladas around Sankaber. Sankaber is also home to Africa's only rose, the rose of Abyssinia.

Simien Mountains National Park

Established in 1969 and made a UNESCO World Heritage Site nine years later, the 220km² Simien Mountains National Park protects the western part of the eponymous mountain range, a series of incised plateaux characterised by sheer 1,000m-high cliffs and rugged pinnacles and buttresses. The range includes at least a dozen peaks that top the 4,000m mark, among them the 4,620m Ras Dashen, which is the fifth-highest mountain in Africa (and lies just outside the park boundaries). Situated about 100km north of Gondar and best accessed from the small town of Debark, the park is best known for the stupendous scenery lauded by Rosita Forbes as 'the most marvellous of all Abyssinian landscapes', but it is also the most important stronghold for the endemic **gelada monkey**, **Walia ibex** and northern race of **Ethiopian wolf**, as well as hosting one the world's densest populations of the spectacular bearded vulture (w**ammergeyer**), which is frequently seen at close range at the campsites.

The park can be explored by **4x4**, along the single dirt road that branches eastward from Debark, and passes through Sankaber and Chennek campsites *en route* to the Bwahit Pass (but note that a new road is planned, running from Sawre to Janamora, to bypass the main escarpment). With an early start, it is possible to cover this road as a **day trip** out of Gondar, though this is a less satisfactory approach than an **overnight trip** based at Simien Lodge (the only accommodation within the park) or nearby Debark, and the rushed timeframe might arguably encourage the driver to speed in what is a fragile environment. Even as a day trip from Gondar, sightings of the charismatic gelada and handsome lammergeyer are a near certainty, but you need to spend longer to stand a fair chance of sighting Walia ibex or Ethiopian wolf.

The Simiens are the most important stronghold of the Gelada monkey. (YDB)

A less efficient but far more satisfactory way to explore the Simiens is **on foot or by mule**, following an extensive network of tracks used by local people to travel between the villages on the lower slopes or to reach the high pastures for grazing animals. Trekking routes vary from a couple of days to two weeks in duration, taking you through small villages and terraced fields in the lower valleys, before reaching a series of dramatic cliffs and escarpments. Beyond the escarpments you reach the beautiful alpine meadows and the rugged wilderness of the high peak areas. A popular route is the **five-day** (four-night) **trek** sleeping at Sankaber, Chennek (for two nights, going to the summit of Bwahit or the viewpoint on the way to Ras Dashen on the day in-between), then at Sankaber again on the way back to Debark.

Aside from the upmarket **Simien Lodge, accommodation** within the park comprises an inexpensive dormitory at **Sankaber Camp**, and the **Ethio-Austria Community Hostel** located just past Simien Lodge. Elsewhere there are several **campsites** for self-sufficient travellers, the

(PR)

Kosoye viewpoint

Local legend states that when Queen Elizabeth II of England was driven between Gondar and Axum in 1965, this viewpoint 32km from Gondar appealed to her so much that she instructed her driver to stop there for tea. True or not, this is a genuinely lovely spot, and a recommended half-day excursion out of Gondar for those who don't have time to get to the Simiens proper. From the road, there are sweeping views across the lowlands to the Simien Mountains, while a one-hour walk along the cliffs offers a good chance of seeing gelada and guereza monkeys, as well as birds of prey such as lammergeyer.

most important being Gich and Chennek, or you can stay in **village huts**. Simien hikes remain very affordable compared to other major mountains in East Africa and can be arranged through any operator or directly with the park headquarters at Debark.

Gorgora

This little-visited port town on the Lake Tana shore 60km south of Gondar is the northern terminus of the lake ferry from Bahir Dar, and a highly **rewarding spot for birdwatchers**. Founded in medieval times, Gorgora also boasts several buildings of historic interest. These include the **Monastery of Debre Sina Maryam**, which lies five minutes' walk from the town centre, and permits women visitors. Founded circa 1334, it is of interest for its carved Axumite windows and frames, and some of the oldest, most complex and vivid murals to be seen anywhere in the Tana region. The church's greatest treasure is a glass-covered portrait of the 'Egyptian Saint Mary': an utterly implausible legend has it that this painting was made when Mary was exiled to Egypt, and the local priests claim that it lights up spontaneously from time to time, and has the capacity to revive dead children.

Debre Sina Maryam (DC)

On a peninsula roughly 10km west of Gorgora stands **'Old Gorgora'** and the **ruined palace**, constructed by Emperor Susneyos between 1625 and 1630 with Portuguese assistance. The building isn't in the greatest shape, but it is of some interest architecturally as an immediate precursor to the more renowned palaces of Gondar, and it can be visited by boat. Also worth seeing is the abandoned **Gorgora Cathedral**, built several kilometres out of town by the Jesuit priest Pedro Páez after he was granted land there by his friend Emperor Susneyos.

Axum and surrounds   **156**

History   156
Axum Museum   160
The main stelae field   161
Maryam Tsion Church   162
Mai Shum   162
King Ezana's Park and King Basen's Tomb   163
Adwa and Abba Garima Monastery   166
Yeha   166

Eastern Tigrai   **169**

History   170
Adigrat   173
Debre Damo Monastery   173
Wukro   174
Abreha we Atsbeha rock-hewn church   175
Hawzien and Gheralta   178
Mekele   178
Eyesus Hintsa Church   183

7 Tigrai

The most northerly of Ethiopia's federal regions, Tigrai (also spelt Tigray) has a distinctly different character to the rest of the country. Historically and culturally, it has strong links with neighbouring Eritrea, stretching from the days of the Axumite Empire to the liberation war that toppled Mengistu in 1991. The region is named after the Tigraian people, descendants of the Axumites who still dress mostly in traditional style, and whose lifestyle harks back to Biblical times. Scenically, its mountainous sandstone rockscapes and terraced slopes possess a stark angularity distinct from the more curvaceous green hills elsewhere in the Ethiopian Highlands, while its trademark stone houses lend the towns and villages an orderly permanence rare in Africa. For tourists, the most important site is Axum, a pivotal fixture on the northern historical circuit. The region also boasts some of the country's finest ancient churches, ranging from Debre Damo Monastery to the dozens of rock-hewn sanctuaries carved into the cliffs around Wukro and Mekele.

Axum and surrounds

The oldest town in Ethiopia, holiest city of the Ethiopian Orthodox Church, and former capital of one of the world's greatest empires,

Tigrai

Axum – also spelt Aksum – today is smaller than you might expect, and rather inauspicious on first contact. But while it might lack the immediate impact of Lalibela or Gondar, the city is scattered with startling antiquities, most notably the ancient **Church of Maryam Tsion** and nearby stelae field, but also a selection of mysterious **catacombs**, ruined **palaces**, **multi-lingual tablets** dating from the time of Christ, and much more besides. Axum is also a useful base for exploring several other more remote sites of historic interest, ranging from the towering pre-Christian temple at Yeha to the small town of Adwa, where Emperor Menelik famously repelled the Italian invasion in 1896.

History

The early history of Axum is integral to that of Ethiopia itself. Nevertheless, only a tiny fraction of known archaeological sites around the city have been excavated, and new sites are discovered at a faster pace than the established ones are investigated, so that almost anything written about the city is based on sketchy foundations. As the prominent archaeologist Stuart Munro-Hay wrote in 1991:

> Of all the important ancient civilisations of the past ... Aksum still remains perhaps the least known ... Its history and civilisation has been largely ignored, or at most accorded only brief mention, in the majority of recent books purporting to deal at large with ancient African civilisations, or with the world of late antiquity.

Tradition asserts that the town was established by King Aksumai, a great-great-grandson of Noah, and that it was later the birthplace of the Queen of Sheba, whose eldest son, fathered by King Solomon, became King Menelik I, the founder of the so-called Solomonic Dynasty. No physical evidence exists to confirm this rather tenuous story, but it does seen reasonably certain that Axum existed in its current location by around 500BC, and the *Periplus of the Erythraean Sea*, a Greek document written in the 1st century AD, confirms it was by then the centre of an important global trade empire, ruled by a King called Zoscales (who was 'miserly in his ways and always striving for more, but otherwise upright, and acquainted with Greek literature') and served by the port of Adulis in present-day Eritrea.

A key event in the history not only of Axum but of Ethiopia itself was the conversion of the twin kings Ezana and Saizana to Christianity, whereupon they made it the state religion, took the throne names Abreha and Atsbeha, and founded the church of Maryam Tsion in Axum (as well, legend has it, as several of the rock-hewn churches in eastern Tigrai). The Axumite empire was then at its peak, stretching west from its capital as far as the Sudanese Nile, and east across the Red Sea to Yemen.

Axum's political significance declined during the 7th century, when the wave of Arabic expansionism associated with the emergence and rise of Islam resulted in the loss of its Red Sea trade routes. Indeed, by the 9th century, it seems that Axum, though still the spiritual home of Ethiopian Christianity, had been usurped as capital by the yet-to-be-located city of Kubar. It was at around this time that the city was attacked by Queen Yodit, who reputedly razed the original church of

The Axum area is rich in unexplored archaeological sires and fresh excavations take place regularly. (GS/C)

Practicalities

At least one Ethiopian Airlines **flight** daily connects Axum to Gondar, Bahir Dar, Lalibela and Addis Ababa. There are also flights between Axum and Mekele on most days. The modern new airport lies 5km out of town along the Adwa road, and **taxis** are available to take you to the city centre. **Buses** or **minibuses** connect Axum to Gondar (switching at Shire-Inda Selassie) in the west, as well as to Adwa, Adigrat and Mekele in the east. Organised tours will include all excursions.

Internet facilities exist at the main tourist hotels, and several independent internet cafés have opened lately. The main road through Axum is liberally endowed with shops selling Ethiopian **handicrafts**, ranging from religious icons and other old artefacts to modern carvings and cotton shama cloth. The **tourist**

Street scene, Axum (TC/A)

Accommodation

Upmarket
Remhai Hotel ⓦ www.remhai-hotel.com
Yeha Hotel ⓦ www.ghionhotel.com.et

Maryam Tsion. Even more destructive was an attack led by Ahmed Gragn in the 16th century. The Portuguese priest Francisco Alvarez, who visited Axum a decade before Gragn's arrival, described it as, 'a large town of very good houses, such that there are none like them in the whole of Ethiopia, and very good wells of water, and worked

Ethiopian handicrafts on sale, Axum (RP)

office (① 034 775 3924), located along the road towards the stelae field, just east of the main roundabout, is a good source of local information and is also where you pay the entrance fee that covers the various secular historical sites dotted around town. An excellent companion for anybody with a serious interest in Axum's archaeological sites is Gian Paulo Chiari's *Guide to Aksum and Yeha*, published in 2009 by Arada Books.

Moderate
Exodus Hotel ⓦ www.exodushotel.com

Budget
Africa Hotel ⓔ africaho@ethionet.com
Kaleb Hotel ⓦ www.kalebhotel.com

Eating out

The **Remhai Hotel** is the pick for international food, but the **Yeha Hotel** gets the nudge for the superb view from the patio. The restaurant at the **Africa Hotel** is pretty good, too, while the **Café Abyssinia** has good Ethiopian dishes. For pastries and coffee, try **Habesha Coffee and Juice** and **Tela Café**.

masonry, and also in most of the houses ancient figures of lions, dogs and birds, all well made in stone'. Yet a century later, according to Manuel de Almeida, Axum had been reduced to nothing 'a place of about a hundred inhabitants [where] everywhere there are ruins to be seen'.

Axum

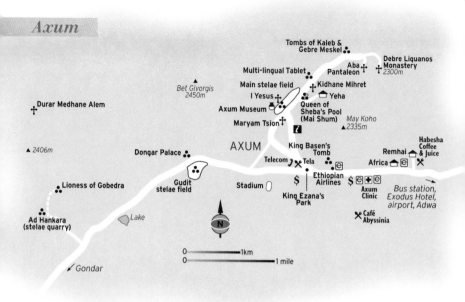

The earliest excavations at Axum were conducted during the first three months of 1906 by the Deutsche-Aksum Expedition (DAE). Panoramic photographs taken at the time suggest that the town then supported a population of a few thousand, with settlement concentrated to the northwest of Maryam Tsion, while the present-day city centre comprised uninhabited plains. This eastward expansion has continued in recent years, with most of the development east of the Axum Touring Hotel dating to the post-Derg era. The modern town of 50,000 inhabitants has also gained some presence in recent years as a result of a newly surfaced main road bisected by a neat row of young palms.

Axum and surrounds highlights

Axum Museum

The best place to start a tour of Axum, the site museum, situated behind the main stelae field, houses a selection of displays that collectively illustrate just how cosmopolitan and technologically advanced the ancient city was. A collection of ancient rock tablets is inscribed in a variety of languages that includes the early consonant-based form of Sabaean from which derived the Ge'ez of Christian Axum, as well as modern Amharigna script. Also present is an array of Axumite household artefacts, ranging from a water filter to drinking glasses imported from Egypt, a collection of ancient Axumite coins (the most recent minted in the 6th century AD), and a 700-year-old leather Ge'ez Bible, decorated with illuminations. In addition, a series of explanatory posters, funded by an American–Italian archaeological research project, provides an overview of Axum's history, the major archaeological sites and the various artefacts found at them.

The main stelae field

Axum's most striking archaeological site is the main stelae field, which lies next to the museum opposite the church of Maryam Tsion. Here, around 75 stelae of various shapes and sizes are concentrated within an area of less than 1,000m². These include the largest such monolith ever erected: a collapsed stele, traditionally attributed to the 3rd-century King Remhai, decorated with a door and 12 windows, that weighs 500 tons and would tower 33m above the ground were it standing. The collapse of this stele is linked by tradition to Queen Yodit, who destroyed many of Axum's finest buildings, but scholarly opinion is that it probably toppled soon after being erected, or even during the process of erection, due to the small area of the base.

The **second-largest Axumite stele**, which stands 26m high, was relocated to Rome during the Italian occupation, after being carved into three blocks for ease of transportation. Several years of negotiation between the Ethiopian and Italian governments culminated with its return to its rightful home in 2005, and it is currently stabilised by an elaborate jungle of scaffolding. The largest fully intact stele (and **third-largest** ever erected at Axum) is a slightly tilted 23m-high monolith whose carved door and nine windows are thought to symbolise the door and nine chambers of the tomb of its creator King Ezana.

Catacombs beneath the main stelae field (AP/C)

Below the stelae lie various partially excavated **catacombs**, of which Remhai's tomb, which comprises 12 underground vaults made with large granite blocks held together by metal pins, is open to the public. Another nearby excavation is the **Tomb of the Mausoleum**, which opened for the 2007 millennium celebration.

Paintings in the Church of Maryam Tsion (SS)

Maryam Tsion Church

Opposite the stelae field, the compound of Maryam Tsion ('St Mary of Zion') has housed a church of that name since King Ezana built one over an old pagan shrine in the 4th century. The **original Maryam Tsion Church** was Ethiopia's first and comprised 12 temples, but it was later destroyed by Ahmed Gragn or Queen Yodit, depending on which tradition you choose to believe, but parts of the foundations are still in place. Its handsome stone replacement is widely attributed to King Fasilidas, and it strongly resembled the 17th-century castles built by the same king at Gondar. There are some good paintings and musical instruments inside the church, but entrance is forbidden to women.

Also in the compound, its ugly **spire** competing with the ancient stelae for horizon space, is a typically overblown cathedral, built under Haile Selassie in the 1960s. Other sites of interest are the so-called **Throne of David**, where the Axumite emperors were once crowned, and the **sanctified outbuilding** where Axum's most famous religious artefact, the supposed Ark of the Covenant, is kept under lock and key.

Mai Shum

Often referred to as the **Queen of Sheba's swimming pool**, Mai Shum is a small **reservoir** situated at the northern end of the stelae field, where the tracks to the Yeha Hotel and the Tomb of Kaleb converge. Traditions regarding the excavation of the pool are widely divergent. Some say that Mai Shum was created some 3,000 years ago as a bathing place for the Queen of Sheba, others that it was dug by Bishop Abuna

Queen of Sheba's swimming pool (AC)

Samuel during the early 15th century. While the notion that the Queen of Sheba ever unrobed to dip in Mai Shum seems a touch fanciful, there is reason to think that the pool, and the stone steps leading down to it, were excavated in Axumite times. Indeed, the phrases *Mai Shum* and *Ak Shum* (from which Axum derives) both translate as 'Water of the Chief' in different local dialects, implying that the town is named after the pool alongside which it was founded.

King Ezana's Park and King Basen's Tomb

Two major historical sites lie within the modern town centre. The first is **King Ezana's Park**, where a 4th-century tablet inscribed in Sabaean, Ge'ez and Greek stands in its original location, alongside pillars from what was presumably Ezana's palace, a stele, a tomb and an innocuous-looking stone slab that might easily be mistaken for a park bench but was in fact used for cleaning corpses. Not far from the park, marked by the customary stele, is a **subterranean tomb associated with King Basen**, whose rule may have coincided with the birth of Christ. Entered via a man-high tunnel, this tomb differs from those in the main stelae field in that it isn't built from stone blocks but chiselled into the rock – making it reminiscent of the more recent graves carved into the walls surrounding the churches at Lalibela.

King Ezana's stone (AC)

Five excursions close to Axum

Several important sites lie within a 5km radius of the city centre; most can be visited on foot if you so choose, though most tours will include any such excursions.

The tombs of Kaleb and Gebre Meskel

On a hilltop 2km north of the town centre stand the 'two houses under the ground, into which men do not enter without a lamp', mentioned by the Portuguese priest Francisco Alvarez. A credible local tradition maintains that these tombs, which are adorned with stone crosses rather than stelae, were excavated below the palaces of the powerful 6th-century Emperor Kaleb and his successor Gebre Meskel. About halfway up the hill, a trilingual tablet inscribed under King Ezana was uncovered accidentally by a farmer in the 1980s – leaving one to wonder what else might still lie undiscovered beneath the soil around Axum.

Underground tombs of Kaleb and Gebre Meskel (CB/H/C)

Debre Liqanos Monastery

From Kaleb's Palace, a clear path to the right leads after 20–30 minutes' walk to a 6th-century hilltop monastery founded by Abba Liqanos, one of the 'Nine Saints'. The original Axumite church, thought to have been converted from an older non-Christian temple, was replaced several centuries ago, but fragments such as the pillar next to the baptismal font can still be seen.

Panteleon Monastery

This attractive 6th-century monastery, situated 5km out of town on a euphorbia-clad pinnacle known as Debre Katin, hosts one of the oldest churches in the country, founded by its namesake, another member of the 'Nine Saints'. It is said that Panteleon spent the last 45 years of his life praying and healing the sick from the confines of a narrow monastic cell where he would spend his entire day in a standing position. Abba Yared, the contemporary of Gebre Meskel who invented the notation of Ethiopian ecclesiastical music and compiled the Mazgaba Degwa ('Treasury of Hymns'), reputedly spent much of his life here.

Dongar and the Gudit stelae field

Popularly associated with the Queen of Sheba, **Dongar Palace** more likely dates to the 7th century AD. All that is left is the floor plan and entrance stairs, sufficient to confirm it was probably the most impressive palace ever built around Axum, comprising at least 50 rooms and boasting an elaborate drainage system. It is also where many of the more unusual relics now housed in Axum's museum were found. On the opposite side of the road, a field of unadorned stelae includes a 22.5m-high monolith that reputedly marks the grave of the Queen of Sheba. For reasons that are unclear, locals refer to the site as the **Gudit stelae field** (Gudit being an alternative rendition of Yodit, the 9th-century Falasha queen who razed much of ancient Axum). Both sites lie about 30 minutes' walk from town along the Gondar road.

Ad Hankara and the Gobedra Lioness

Alongside the Gondar road, perhaps 3km past Dongar, **Ad Hankara** is the hillside quarry where all the stelae that stand outside Axum were quarried.

One partially carved stele lies *in situ*, and it is a total mystery how the others were transported to their present site. A short walk uphill leads to the **Gobedra Lioness**, a 3.27m-long outline figure of a crouching lion etched into a flat rock face. Tradition asserts that the Archangel Mikael was attacked by a lion here, and repelled it with such force that it left an outline in the rock. The cross carved alongside it is probably a more recent addition.

The Gobedra Lioness is one of the most mysterious and underated historical sites around Axum. (TK/S)

Adwa and Abba Garima Monastery

Slightly larger than Axum, and a more important centre of industrial and population growth, the neat little town of **Adwa** has an attractive setting amid the stark granite hills so typical of Tigrai. Of greater interest than the town itself, and only 10km away by road, **Abba Garima** is another monastery associated with an eponymous member of the 6th-century 'Nine Saints'. It was from Abba Garima that Menelik II observed the Italian troops as they approached Adwa prior to Ethiopia's decisive victory over the aspirant colonists in 1896. A year later, Ras Alula, the accomplished military tactician who famously defeated a contingent of 500 Italian troops at Dogali in January 1887, died at Abba Garima of wounds sustained at the Battle of Adwa; his modest tomb stands outside the rear entrance of the church, and several of his possessions are held in the treasury.

The church at Abba Garima is said to be 1,500 years old. It looks far newer than that, but the twin stelae and bowl-like rocks that stand in front of its main door might well date to Axumite times. The **treasury** contains a fantastic collection of ancient crowns, crosses and other artefacts donated by various emperors and nobles over the centuries, including a silver cross with gold inlays that once belonged to Gebre Meskel, and the crown of Zara Yaqob. The extensive **library** includes an illuminated Gospel supposedly written and illustrated in one day by Abba Garima himself. It's probably not *quite* that ancient, but some experts reckon it dates to the 8th century, which would make it the oldest-known manuscript in Ethiopia.

Ibex engravings at Yeha (AC)

Yeha

Situated 50km northeast of Axum, Yeha today is not so much a village as a cluster of rustic stone houses, but it was once the region's most important city, founded at least 2,800 years ago, and capital of a pre-Axumite empire called Damot for centuries prior to being usurped by Axum. Yeha's most remarkable antiquity is a well-preserved 2,500-year-old stone **temple** that stands 12m high and comprises up to 52 layers of masonry. Little is known about the religion practised here, but

What is your favourite part of the country?

It depends on the time of year, and my mood. The stark beauty of the Gheralta Mountains in Tigray; the people, forests and mountains of West Omo; the smell from the earth after rains in the Afar region; Lake Tana in the early morning – these images flash through my mind and I want to hit the road.

What makes your trips to Ethiopia special?

The fact that they are not my trips, but are usually itineraries that have evolved from discussions with our clients. Many people have done the research and know exactly what they want to do and how long it will take. But people are different, with their own specific interests and requirements, and it is these differences we like to explore. We discuss all the options – places to see, where to stay, how to get there – and come up with the trip that the client wants.

Which tour would you recommend for a first time visitor to Ethiopia?

More than 60% of visitors to Ethiopia come for the Historic Route, and I advise people to try not to miss Lalibela, but one person's Lalibela is another person's Prince Ruspoli's turaco. Wish lists and 'must sees' vary from visitor to visitor.

What kind of involvement do your tours have with local communities?

Our company is always seeking ways to maximise benefits to host communities, and we have, for example, facilitated training programmes for hoteliers and guides in Lalibela, bringing in top tourism professionals from Ireland. It's an ongoing programme we want to replicate elsewhere.

Tony Hickey, the owner and founder of Ethiopian Quadrants Plc, has been involved in Ethiopia for nearly 40 years. A tourism and development activist, he is currently serving his third term as an elected board member of the Ethiopian Tour Operators Association (ETOA), of which he was a founding member.

Ⓣ + 251 (0) 11 515 7990 Ⓔ ethiopianquadrants@ethionet.et
Ⓔ ethiopianquadrants@gmail.com Ⓦ www.ethiopianquadrants.com

Religious services

For a journey back in time, observe a religious service at one of the churches that dot the highlands. Christianity arrived here in the 4th century, and the theology and traditions of the Ethiopian Orthodox Church developed without Western influence. Most of the hymns were written in the 6th century and attending a service can be a memorable and mesmerising experience. Ask your guide first, but try visiting early in the morning or even in the middle of the night.

appearances link it with the pagan faith of the Sabaean civilisation of present-day Yemen. Inscriptions refer to a deity called Ilmukah, abundant engravings of ibex indicate that this animal was of some religious significance, and a few statues of dreadlocked women found nearby (and now housed in the National Museum in Addis Ababa) suggest a fertility cult of sorts.

One of the reasons why the temple at Yeha is in such good condition is that it became the centre of a monastic Christian community in the early 6th century. This church was founded by Abba Afse, yet another one of the 'Nine Saints', who was guided there by an angel after having spent 12 years at Abba Garima. It seems credible that the high stone monastery surrounding the ancient temple dates from this era, and the remarkable treasure house contains many ancient illuminated manuscripts and crowns.

Illuminated manuscript, Axum (AP/C)

Eastern Tigrai

Less developed for tourism than Axum, eastern Tigrai has a rather remote and stoic character, partly a function of its relatively stark landscapes, and partly because of the hardship it suffered under the Mengistu regime and during the border war with Eritrea. It is the site of the likeable Tigraian capital Mekele and the smaller but equally congenial town of Adigrat, but its main attraction is a cluster of around **100 rock-hewn churches** described by the British academic Ivy Pearce as 'the greatest of the historical-cultural heritages of the Ethiopian people'. These churches are mostly still in active use, and several are decorated with venerable paintings and house sacred medieval artefacts.

Sensitivity towards an older way of life is a prerequisite for exploring the Tigraian churches. So, too, is patience and humour. If you possess

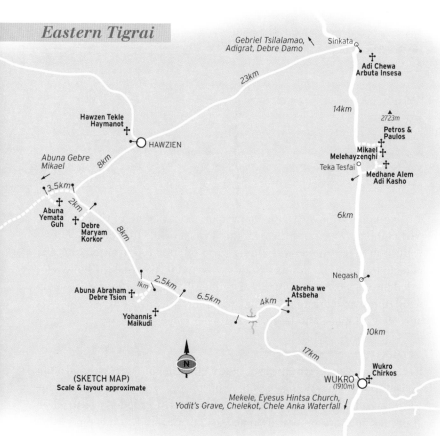

Eastern Tigrai

Gebriel Tsilalamao, Adigrat, Debre Damo

Sinkata

Adi Chewa Arbuta Insesa

23km

14km

2723m

Hawzen Tekle Haymanot

Petros & Paulos

HAWZIEN

Mikael Melehayzenghi

Abuna Gebre Mikael

8km

Teka Tesfai

Medhane Alem Adi Kasho

3.5km

Abuna Yemata Guh

2km

Debre Maryam Korkor

8km

6km

1km

2.5km

Negash

Abuna Abraham Debre Tsion

6.5km

4km

Abreha we Atsbeha

Yohannis Maikudi

10km

N

17km

Wukro Chirkos

(SKETCH MAP)
Scale & layout approximate

WUKRO
(1910m)

Mekele, Eyesus Hintsa Church,
Yodit's Grave, Chelekot, Chele Anka Waterfall

Practicalities

By air, the gateway to the region is Mekele, whose airport, about 5km from the city centre, is serviced by daily Ethiopian Airlines flights to/from Addis Ababa, and most days there are also flights to/from Axum, Bahir Dar, Gondar and Lalibela. **Taxis** to the airport are available from the city centre.

By road, allow half a day to drive from Axum to Adigrat along a variable surface, and two hours from Adigrat to Mekele. Coming from the south, Mekele lies 780km from Addis Ababa along a mostly asphalt road that you could cover in one long day with a very early start, although you might be best advised to allow two days which is more realistic.

Several road routes exist between Mekele and Lalibela: the most direct

Accommodation

Upmarket
Gheralta Lodge (near Hawzien) ⓦ www.gheraltalodgetigrai.com

Moderate
Abreha Castle Hotel (Mekele) ⓔ castle@ethionet.et
Axum Hotel (Mekele) ⓦ www.axumhotels.com

Budget
Atse Yohannis Hotel (Mekele) ⓣ 034 440 6760-22
Geza Gerelase Hotel (Adigrat) ⓣ 034 445 2500

those qualities, however, this is in many respects the most rewarding part of the northern historical circuit, exposing one to Biblical scenes – white-robed worshippers chanting and swaying in prayer, or standing outside the church sharing rough *injera* and beakers of alcoholic *tella* – that provide an almost surreal reminder that the religion we associate with American televangelism and quaint European country churches is at root every bit as Middle Eastern as Islam or Judaism.

History
It is anybody's guess why the rock-hewn churches of Tigrai were so often carved into relatively inaccessible cliff-faces – was it for security, for spiritual isolation or simply because cliff-faces are good places to carve churches, and are inherently inaccessible? Certainly, if keeping away

option, via Abi Aday and Sekota, could be covered in a day at a push, but most tourist vehicles prefer the longer but smoother route via Woldia.

Visiting the rock-hewn churches listed in this section can be frustrating without an experienced Tigrigna-speaking guide and common obstacles faced include the key being unavailable, timing clashes (many priests will not allow tourists into their church during special masses, for instance) and unnecessary requests for permits. A good guide will do his best to smooth the way, but do make allowances for the fact that the churches are not primarily tourist attractions but active shrines

There are several **banks** with ATMs and foreign-exchange facilities in Mekele and to a lesser extent Adigrat, and both towns have a few **internet cafés**. Other towns in the region have limited facilities.

Top View Guesthouse (Wukro) ℮ topview_gh@peoplepc.com
Weldu Sebagadis Modern Hotel (Adigrat) ℮ helenzz2002@yahoo.com

Eating out

There is no shortage of good eateries in **Mekele.** Try the top-notch **Axum Hotel** or **Abreha Castle Hotel**, the latter with pleasant outdoor seating, for good Western food, or the more homely **Yordanos Restaurant** or **Habesha Village Restaurant** for local food. The pick of the restaurants in **Adigrat** are the two hotels listed above or the stand-alone **Sami Restaurant**. There are plenty of basic local eateries in **Wukro** and **Hawzien**, but none that stand out.

outsiders *was* the objective, then the excavators did an admirable job judging by the obscurity in which many of these churches languished throughout the first century of regular European presence in the area. Indeed, when the first exhaustive list of Ethiopian rock-hewn churches was published, as recently as 1963, fewer than ten such edifices were listed for Tigrai.

Only three years later, at the 1966 Conference of Ethiopian Studies, Dr Abba Tewelde Medhin Josief, a Catholic priest from Adigrat, caused a veritable buzz when he announced the existence of 123 rock-hewn churches in Tigrai. Over the next three years, the British academics David Buxton, Ivy Pearce and Ruth Plant collectively visited 75 of these churches and published several papers based on their formative research. By 1973, the full list of confirmed rock-hewn churches in

Many Tigraian churches are carved into what were existing caves or crevices in impregnable-looking cliff faces. (AZ)

Tigrai had been extended to 153, of which all but 26 were still in active use. However, the 1974 revolution put paid to any further research in the region, and nothing of consequence has been published about the Tigraian churches since that time.

The antiquity of the Tigraian rock-hewn churches is a matter of conjecture. Every church has at least one oral tradition regarding its excavation – and some have several somewhat contradictory ones – often dating it back to the 4th-century reign of the twin emperors Abreha and Atsbeha. By contrast, David Buxton, an authority on Axumite architecture, believed the Tigraian churches were from the 10th century or later, and in a 1971 publication he divided them into five broad chronological styles. The oldest church, according to Buxton, is Adi Kasho Medhane Alem, which he regarded as a relatively crude attempt to reproduce the classic built-up Axumite style in rock. The likes of Wukro Chirkos and Abreha we Atsbeha, with their cruciform plans, are dated to the 11th and 12th centuries, while the cliff churches of the Gheralta, excavated in the 13th and 14th centuries, post-date their counterparts at Lalibela.

Ironically, Buxton's suggested dates of excavation, like those ascribed to the churches by oral tradition, are often quoted as immutable fact. It should be noted, therefore, that Buxton himself not only took great pains to emphasise that his chronological scheme was no better than provisional, but that he also routinely phrased his opinions in the guise of educated guesses. Indeed, it is perfectly possible that many churches have been excavated in stages, and that some have been expanded from pre-Christian rock-hewn temples dating back to the first half of the 1st millennium BC. Whatever the truth of the matter, these extraordinary shrines have mostly been in active use for at least 700 years, possibly a lot longer, and they retain an aura of spirituality that seems to have seeped into the very rock into which they are carved.

Eastern Tigrai highlights

Adigrat

The second-largest town in Tigrai, with an estimated population of 70,000, Adigrat is located at the pivot of the roads to Axum, Mekele and neighbouring Eritrea. It's a bustling, friendly, rather cosmopolitan town, with strong historical and cultural links to Eritrea, but its economy has suffered from the loss of international trade since the border closed in the late 1990s. It has a busy market where Tigraian coffeepots and cloths are sold alongside the nationally renowned honey that comes from nearby Alitena. Just behind the market, the **church of Adigrat Chirkos** is covered in fine 19th-century paintings, and its balcony offers a great view over the town. Otherwise, it is of interest mainly as the closest town to the **Debre Damo Monastery** and as a potential base for exploring the rock-hewn churches along the road to Wukro.

Debre Damo Monastery

An oft-neglected highlight of northern Ethiopia is the monastery of Debre Damo, which stands on a 3,000m-high *amba* (flat-topped hill) north of the Adigrat road. It is something of a mystery how the monastery's founder Abba Aregawi reached the site – one tradition has it that a flying serpent whisked him to the top – and the only way to get there today is by ascending a 15m-high cliff with the aid of a leather rope. The original 6th-century stone church, built up with layers of thick wood and whitewashed stone, is perhaps the finest extant example of ecclesiastic Axumite architecture, and may well be the oldest non-rock-hewn church in Ethiopia. A secondary church stands on the spot where Abuna Aregawi reputedly vanished into thin air at the end of his mortal existence. On the main

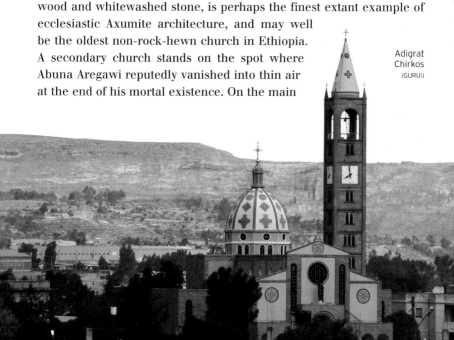

Adigrat
Chirkos
(GURUi)

Visiting Debre Damo is only for those with a head for heights. (PR/S/C)

cliff, there are several cramped hermit caves whose inhabitants subsist on bread and water lowered from the monastery by rope. Women are not allowed to visit the monastery, and the ascent is recommended only to those with a head for heights.

Wukro

The largest town between Adigrat and Mekele, Wukro supports a permanent population of around 22,000, as well as a more transient military quota associated with its strategic importance in the wake of the Eritrean border war. It forms a useful base for visiting a number of rock-hewn churches (including **Wukro Chirkos**, on the outskirts of town, see page 177), though sadly facilities aren't nearly as good as in Mekele or Adigrat. In addition to the rock-hewn churches, the site known as **Yodit's Grave**, a plain stone cairn 3km south of Wukro, is reputedly where the destructive Queen Yodit was swept into the afterlife by a killer whirlwind after her raid on the nearby church of Abreha we Atsbeha.

Visiting Tigrai

Ethiopian Quadrants PLC
To the four corners of the country

If you have the time, Tigray is best savoured by road. Whether you come up from Gondar or from Lalibela, you are assured of fantastic scenery. It's rich in history, with new discoveries all the time, the latest being the mines of Queen Sheba in the Gheralta area. Tigray bore the brunt of the struggle against

the military regime, but has recovered and is fast developing. Mekele by night is worth exploring - even Axum by night has a lot of surprises!

Abreha we Atsbeha rock-hewn church

Regarded by many experts to be the finest rock-hewn church in Tigrai, Abreha we Atsbeha lies 17km from Wukro along the good but mountainous dirt road that continues for another 14km to Dugem at the base of the Gheralta Escarpment. The church's imposing façade, reached via a flight of stone stairs, is partially cut free from the cliff and was reputedly added after Queen Yodit burnt the original exterior. The cruciform interior is very large – 16m wide, 13m deep and 6m high – and has a beautifully carved roof supported by 13 large pillars and several decorated arches. The well-preserved and beautifully executed murals are relatively recent, many dating from the reign of Yohannis IV, and depict a complete history of the Ethiopian Church. Local tradition states that the church was excavated in AD335–40 by the twin kings for whom it is named, and whose mummified bodies are preserved in a box stored in the holy of holies. Another tradition relates that Queen Yodit attacked Abreha we Atsbeha and ran off with some sacred rocks that gave off a supernatural light, and which were responsible for her being blown to death a few hours later outside Wukro. It is the target of a major pilgrimage on 4 Tekemt (normally 14 October).

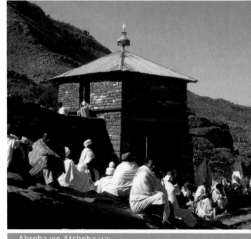

Abreha we Atsbeha (AZ)

The Adigrat–Mekele Road: four church sites and a mosque

For those with time restrictions, at least seven rock-hewn churches lie within walking distance of the main road between Adigrat and Mekele. Running from north to south, these are:

Gebriel Tsilalmao

This large church of unknown antiquity, 3km north of the village of Mai Megelta, is supported by unusually thick cruciform columns decorated with some quite recent-looking paintings. Notable features include the neatly cut arches, the engraved roofs of the six bays, two windows cut in Axumite style, an entrance with a built-up porch, and a large room in the back bisected by a column. A pair of evidently disused hermit cells is carved into the outer wall. The riparian woodland around the church and permanent marsh patch on the opposite side of the gorge support grivet monkeys and endemic birds such as white-cheeked turaco and Rouget's rail.

Adi Chewa Arbuta Insesa

This church is situated immediately east of Sinkata, a quietly attractive village of stone houses that straddles the Mekele road 35km south of Adigrat at the junction of a side road to Hawzien. It's a large church with several unusual features, including a domed ceiling almost 5m in height (the deepest of its kind in any Tigraian church) and strange red-and-yellow stencil-like figures on the thick columns.

Teka Tesfai

The most accessible cluster of Tigraian churches lies 2km east of the main Adigrat–Mekele road, some 10km south of Sinkata. It consists of three old churches and one new one within 2km of each other. Its showpiece is Medhane Alem Adi Kasho, a very old church described by Ruth Plant as 'one of the truly great churches of the Tigrai'. It has an imposing exterior cut free from the rock behind, and a cathedral-like interior whose roof is dense with patterned etchings. Very different in style, the recently disused Petros and Paulos Melehayzenghi is a ledge church notable for its primitive but fascinating paintings of angels and saints. Its tabot is now housed in the new Church of Petros and Paulos, carved below it between 1982 and 1996. Finally, Mikael Melehayzenghi, carved into a domed rock outcrop, is notable for a vivid painting that depicts Christ saving Adam and Eve from (or possibly abandoning them to) a pair of ferocious dragon-like creatures at the Last Judgement.

Medhane Alem Adi Kasho has been described as 'one of the truly great churches of the Tigrai'. (AZ)

Negash

Something of an anomaly in the heart of rock-hewn church territory, this small hilltop village 20km south of Sinkata is Ethiopia's oldest Islamic settlement, founded by refugees (including Muhammad's daughter and two of his future wives) at the dispensation of Emperor Asihima in AD615. Some Ethiopians rank it the most holy Islamic town after Mecca, and its large modern mosque was reputedly built on the site of the 7th-century original. An Islamic cemetery of similar pedigree was recently discovered here too.

Wukro Chirkos

The single most accessible rock-hewn church in Tigrai, situated only 500m from the town of Wukro, Wukro Chirkos juts prominently from a low cliff. Claimed locally to date from the 4th-century rule of Abreha and Atsbeha, its interior consists of a large domed reception area and three rooms, and there are some notable ceiling frescoes that must date to the 16th century or earlier, since they were partially destroyed when the church was burnt by Ahmed Gragn. Because the church is attached to a town, it is nearly always open, and visitors will be made welcome even during services.

Hawzien and Gheralta

Situated about 20km west of the main Adigrat–Mekele road, in a fantastic spaghetti-western landscape of flat dry plains and towering rock outcrops, Hawzien is the closest town of substance to the Gheralta Escarpment, a tall sandstone spine whose upper reaches are studded with several dozen rock-hewn churches. Not necessarily the oldest such edifices in Tigrai, nor even the most architecturally impressive, the **Gheralta churches** are probably the most captivating to the casual visitor, thanks to their magnificent setting, atmospheric interiors and wealth of old paintings and treasures (see box, page 180, *Five fine Gheralta churches*). Comparatively disappointing, but lying only five minutes' walk from town, **Hawzien Tekle Haymanot** is a modern built-up church whose rock-hewn sanctuary reputedly started life as a pre-Christian temple and is now off-limits to lay visitors.

Hawzien is of some inherent historical interest, appearing as it does on the oldest-known maps of Tigrai, and being the site of **four stelae** of similar vintage to the so-called Gudit stelae outside Axum. The town was reputedly founded by the Sadqan – 'the Righteous Ones' – a group of zealous Christian exiles said to have been as numerous 'as the army of a king' and to have subsisted only on grass. The Sadqan fled the worldly Roman Church in the late 5th century to preach their ascetic 'heresies' to Ethiopians. They were accorded the official protection of King Kaleb of Axum, but legend holds that this didn't greatly impress the local animist tribes, who eventually massacred the intruders. Heaps of bones believed to date from this genocide are preserved at several sites associated with the Sadqan. More recently, Hawzien was the target of one of the most vicious public excesses of the Mengistu regime, when its marketplace was bombed from the air in 1988, an unprovoked civilian massacre in which an estimated 2,500 people died.

Mekele

Sprawling across a hill-ringed basin at an altitude of 2,100m, the Tigraian capital is a modern city that was little more than a village when Emperor Yohannis IV relocated there in 1881, and built the palace that served as the main imperial residence during the latter part of his reign. It is now the sixth-largest city in Ethiopia, with a fast-growing population estimated at 200,000, and its contradictions – modern high-rises towering above rows of rustic stone homesteads, besuited mobile-phone-clasping businessmen hurrying past rural Tigraians ambling towards the market in their traditional attire – seem to encapsulate those of 21st-century Ethiopia. It is also one of the most pleasant cities in the country – clean, vibrant, overwhelmingly Tigraian, largely unaffected

Tigraian women in traditional robes on a dirt road at the base of the Gheralta Escarpment. (CB/H/C)

Five fine Gheralta churches

The churches are accessible from a 70km road loop connecting Sinkata and Wukro on the main Adigrat–Mekele road via Hawzien and Abreha we Atsbeha. The main cluster lies to the southwest of a roughly 10km stretch of road connecting the villages of Megab (8km southwest of Hawzien) to Dugem (14km west of Abreha we Atsbeha). Reaching any individual church generally involves a steep return hike of at least two hours, which means that only the fittest of travellers could consider visiting more than two in the course of one day. The following churches are the most worthwhile for those with time restraints:

15th-century murals in Abuna Yemata Guh (GS/C)

Abuna Yemata Guh

The most spectacularly sited rock-hewn edifice in Ethiopia, this small but very beautiful church is carved into the top of tall perpendicular rock pillars on the southwest horizon of Megab. The interior is decorated with well-preserved 15th-century murals, regarded to be 'the most sophisticated in Tigrai' by Ruth Plant. There are stunning views from the narrow ledge that leads to the church, looking over a sheer drop of roughly 200m. The one-hour hike there involves clambering up a sheer cliff face using handgrips and footholds, and cannot be recommended for unfit travellers, or anybody with a tendency to vertigo.

Abuna Gebre Mikael

Situated on the Koraro Escarpment about 15km southwest of Guh, this little-visited church, reputedly carved by its 4th-century namesake, is set in the base of a 20m-high cliff. It has an ornate carved exterior whose brightly coloured paintings are lit by four windows and an imposing wooden doorway. The steep 45-minute walk involves some clambering and jumping between rocks, but nothing as risky as the ascent of Abuna Yemata Guh.

Debre Maryam Korkor

This monastic church is set on a small plateau atop a sheer-sided 2,480m-high mountain a short distance southeast of Guh. The built-up façade is rather off-putting, but the cavernous interior, supported by 12 cruciform pillars and seven arches, is very atmospheric. The fine artwork on the walls and columns is said to date from the 13th century. The hike there takes the best part of an hour, with the option of using the shorter 'men's route' (scrambling up footholds and handgrips on a 60° rock face), or the less vertiginous 'women's route'. *En route*, the footpath passes a partially collapsed rock-hewn church that once served as a **nunnery**, as well as the disused **church of Abba Daniel Korkor**, set above a sheer precipice with stunning views over the surrounding plains.

Abuna Abraham Debre Tsion

It is difficult to argue with Ruth Plant's estimation that this is 'one of the great churches of the Tigrai, both from the architectural and devotional aspect'. A monastic cliff church carved into a rusty sandstone face high above the village of Dugem, it has an impressive and ornate exterior, while the interior boasts the largest ground plan of any rock-hewn church in the region. Arcing behind the main church, a rock-hewn passage leads to a **decorated cell** that was once the personal prayer room of Abuna Abraham. Amongst the church's treasures is a beautiful 15th-century ceremonial fan, 1m in diameter, and comprising 34 individual panels, each painted with a figure of a saint. The track to Debre Tsion starts 3.5km southeast of Dugem, and involves a steep but otherwise easy 30- to 40-minute hike to the summit and the church.

Yohannis Maikudi

Lying 2km southeast of Debre Tsion as the crow flies, this atmospheric 130m² rectangular church is notable for its Axumite doors, one reserved for male worshippers, the other for females. The walls and roof are dense with well-preserved and evocative 300-year-old paintings of Old and New Testament scenes, very different in style from other church paintings in Gheralta. Yohannis Maikudi can be visited on its own or in conjunction with nearby Debre Tsion. The walk, whether from Debre Tsion or from the end of the motorable track used to reach Debre Tsion, takes about one hour.

Ceremonial fan at Abuna Abraham Debre Tsion (DCr)

by tourism and refreshingly free of chanting children and self-appointed guides – with a good selection of affordable accommodation, decent restaurants and tempting pastry shops.

The town's premier tourist attraction, the **Yohannis IV Museum** (☉ 08.30–12.30 & 13.30–17.30 Tue–Thu & Sat–Sun), sited in the palace built for the eponymous emperor in the early 1880s, hosts some rather esoteric displays of royal paraphernalia and offers a great rooftop view over town. Other relics of Mekele's time as imperial capital are the **churches of Tekle Haymanot, Medhane Alem** and **Kidane Mihret**, all built in the 1870s. Also well worth a visit, the legendary **market** situated a couple of blocks west of the city centre is the urban terminus of the camel caravans that carry blocks of salt mined in the Danakil to Tigrai. The main market day is Monday, but the salt caravans often arrive on other days.

Further afield, the small village of **Chelekot**, set on a green hill 17km south of Mekele, was a far more important settlement than Mekele in the early 19th century, when it housed the court of the Ras Wolde Selassie, probably the most powerful regional ruler in Ethiopia at the time. The main point of interest today is **Chelekot Selassie**, an impressive example of the circular *tukul*-style church covered in beautiful 19th-century paintings. Another interesting outing is the 60m-high **Chele Anka Waterfall**, which tumbles into a gorge at Debir 8km southwest of Mekele, and is particularly dramatic during the rainy season. A steep footpath leads from the lip of the gorge to the base of the waterfall, where locals say the pool is safe for swimming.

The salt caravan *en route* to Mekele from Danakil (AZ)

Chele Anka Waterfall (AZ)

Eyesus Hintsa Church

Located 60km south of Mekele, this recently rediscovered rock-hewn church, devoted to Jesus, has been refurbished with the assistance of the UK-based Eyesus Hintsa Trust. Carved out of sandstone, most likely during the 14th century, it is impressive both for its size and unique design features. The façade features five large round windows reminiscent of portholes, while the interior is elaborately carved in the Axumite style, with six massive stone pillars topped by arches and a large domed ceiling. A nearby museum houses church antiquities, and a second rock-hewn church, the **Church of St Michael**, is built into a limestone cave a short distance away. The entire site is situated in a scenic river valley that is teeming with birds and wildlife. Your best chance of finding the priest and gaining entrance is right after the morning service, usually 06.00–08.00, or the after the evening service at 17.00.

Lalibela and surrounds   187

History   187
Around town   189
Bilbilla   196
Nakuta La'ab Monastery   200
Asheton Maryam Monastery and
   Mount Abuna Yosef   201

Northeast Highlands   202

Dessie and Hayk   203
Gishen Debre Kerbe Monastery   205
Makdala Hill   205
Bati   208
Menz and the Guassa Plateau   208
Debre Birhan and Ankober   210

8 Lalibela and the Northeast Highlands

The main tourist focus in this part of Ethiopia, indeed in the whole country, is the strange isolated town of Lalibela, set high in the remote mountains of Lasta. It is here that the Ethiopian rock-carving architectural tradition reaches its undisputed apex in the form of the dozen or so rock-hewn churches whose excavation is popularly associated with the medieval king for which the town is named. Often visited as a stand-alone fly-in destination, Lalibela is actually one of many worthwhile sites in the highlands northeast of Addis Ababa. Other less-celebrated highlights include dozens of churches as venerable as their counterparts at Lalibela, but generally more remote and isolated, so more of an adventure to visit. Elsewhere, the extensive Afro-alpine moorland of the Guassa Plateau provides an important refuge for numerous endemic bird and mammal species, including Ethiopian wolf and gelada monkey, while hikes operated by TESFA offer an opportunity to experience rural Ethiopia in the raw.

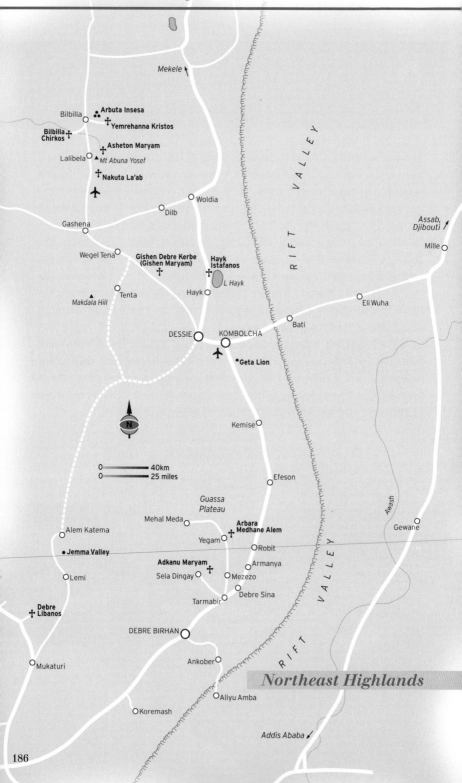

Mekele

Bilbilla
Arbuta Insesa
† **Yemrehanna Kristos**

Bilbilla
Chirkos †
† **Asheton Maryam**
Lalibela ▲ Mt Abuna Yosef
† **Nakuta La'ab**
✈

Woldia
Dilb
Gashena

RIFT VALLEY

Assab,
Djibouti

Wegel Tena
Gishen Debre Kerbe
(Gishen Maryam)
†
Hayk
Istafanos
†
L Hayk

Mille

▲ Makdala Hill
Tenta
Hayk

Eli Wuha

DESSIE
KOMBOLCHA
Bati
✈
• Geta Lion

N

0 ——— 40km
0 ——— 25 miles

Kemise

Efeson

Guassa
Plateau

Mehal Meda
Arbara
Medhane Alem
†
Yegam
Robit

Awash

Gewane

Alem Katema

• **Jemma Valley**

Adkanu Maryam
Sela Dingay
†
Armanya
Mezezo

Lemi

Debre Sina

Tarmabir
Debre
† **Libanos**

DEBRE BIRHAN

RIFT VALLEY

Mukaturi
Ankober

Northeast Highlands

Koremash
Aliyu Amba

Addis Ababa

Lalibela and surrounds

No matter how many rock-hewn churches you visit elsewhere in Ethiopia, Lalibela exists on an altogether different architectural and spiritual plane. Often listed as the unofficial eighth wonder of the ancient world, the church complex here is all the more impressive because, as opposed to being a sterile archaeological site, it is an active Christian shrine that's formed the spiritual focal point of the devout highland town for at least seven centuries. The churches in town warrant a stay of at least two nights, and are best explored over two separate sessions to avoid fatigue, but Lalibela can also be used as a base to explore the truly majestic highland countryside of **Lasta**, whether on an organised TESFA hike or *en route* to any of several stand-alone churches and monasteries dotted around the surrounding mountains, a list that includes the remarkable built-up Axumite **Church of Yemrehanna Kristos** near Bilbilla.

History

The excavation of Lalibela's rock-hewn churches is shrouded in legend. Formerly known as Roha, the town was the capital of the Zagwe Dynasty, which ruled over Ethiopia from the 10th century until the mid-13th century. The most famous of the Zagwe kings was Gebre Meskel Lalibela, who reigned circa 1180–1220, and was later made a saint by the Ethiopian Orthodox Church for his widely accepted role as the mastermind behind the rock-hewn churches in the town that now bears his name. The story goes that Lalibela was covered by a swarm of bees as a child, which his mother took as a sign that he would one day become the king himself. (One reported translation of Lalibela is 'the bees recognise his sovereignty', which isn't bad for four syllables; another more mundane and succinct translation is 'miracle'.) This prophecy displeased the incumbent king, his elder brother Kedus Harbe, who poisoned the teenage Lalibela to prevent the prophecy from coming true. Instead of killing Lalibela, however, the poison cast him into a deep sleep that endured for three days.

King Lalibela (WC)

Whilst sleeping, Lalibela was transported to heaven by an angel and shown the city of Jerusalem, which he was ordered to replicate in a rock-hewn form. Rather neatly Kedus

The Church of Bet Gebriel-Rafael is thought to date back to the 1st millennium. (AZ)

Harbe had a simultaneous vision in which Christ instructed him to abdicate in favour of his younger brother. As soon as he was crowned, Lalibela set about gathering the world's greatest craftsmen and artisans in order to carve the churches, at least one of which was excavated overnight with the assistance of angels! In practice, assuming the excavation of churches was initiated by Lalibela, it is unlikely the work could have been completed in his lifetime, and it may well have extended into the early 15th century. However, one school of thought has it that several of the churches at Lalibela – including Bet Mercurios, Bet Gebriel-Rafael and Danaghel – date back to the 1st millennium and were probably originally constructed for secular purposes and restyled as churches in the Lalibela era.

The various churches of Lalibela were excavated using one of two different methods. Bet Giyorgis and the churches in the northwest cluster are mostly excavated from below the ground, and are surrounded by courtyards and trenches, so that they mimic normal buildings. Several of these churches are monoliths or three-quarter monoliths – free from the surrounding rock on three or four sides – a style of excavation that is unique to Ethiopia. The churches of the southeast cluster are similar to many churches in Tigrai, in that most of them were excavated from a vertical rock face by exploiting existing caves or cracks in the rock.

The churches had certainly been around for a while when the Portuguese explorer Pêro da Covilhão, who travelled overland to Ethiopia from Seville, became the first European to see them circa 1500. The priest Francisco Alvarez was taken to see Lalibela in 1521, and later wrote: 'It wearied me to write more of these works, because

Ethiopia's art

Ethiopia has a vibrant and growing community of internationally respected artists. In Addis Ababa, ask your guide about current shows at art galleries or on display at some of the finer restaurants. There is also plenty of art to appreciate outside the capital, especially the distinctive icons and murals on display at any of the churches. Those at Gondar's Debre Birhan Selassie are the most famous but there many less well-known art treasures in places like Lalibela.

it seemed to me that they would accuse me of untruth ... there is much more than I have already written, and I have left it that they may not tax me with it being falsehood.' The next reported European visitor to Lalibela was Miguel de Castanhoso, probably in the early 1540s. Not long after this, Lalibela was reputedly the victim of a fierce mid 16th-century attack by Ahmed Gragn, but there is no sign of fire or other damage in the churches today, and the description of Lalibela in the only surviving written account of the event suggests that locals might have duped the jihadists into attacking the nearby church of Ganata Maryam instead.

Oddly, three centuries would then pass before another European visited Lalibela in the form of the German explorer Friedrich Gerhard Rohlfs, who arrived some time in the late 1860s. Lalibela was still legendarily inaccessible as recently as the 1950s, when no road there existed, and the likes of Thomas Pakenham took four days to reach it on mule-back from Dessie. Until 1997, it remained largely cut off during the rainy season, when no flights could land and the road there was frequently impassable. All that has changed, however, with post-millennial Lalibela now being serviced by a surfaced airstrip and two all-weather gravel roads, one running south to Gashena and the other north to Sekota.

Lalibela and surrounds highlights

Around town

Lalibela is a strikingly singular town. The setting alone is glorious, perched as it is at an altitude of 2,630m, among wild craggy mountains and vast rocky escarpments whose stark grandeur recalls the

Practicalities

Daily **flights** connect Lalibela to Addis Ababa, Gondar, Bahir Dar and Axum, landing at the new airport 25km from the town centre along a surfaced road passing Nakuta La'ab Monastery. All flights are met by private operators offering a one-way transfer to town. There is no surfaced road to Lalibela but there is the choice of three routes: from Bahir Dar or Gondar via Werota and Debre Tabor (allow around eight hours in a private 4x4), from Dessie or Mekele via Woldia (allow four hours from Woldia), and from Axum via Adwa and Sekota (allow a full day with a very early start). At the time of writing, there is still no direct all-weather road to Lalibela from Addis Ababa.

Once in **Lalibela**, all the churches in town can be explored **on foot** from any hotel. However, a **4x4** or **mule** is required to visit most of the churches out of town, the one exception being Nakuta La'ab, which lies within easy walking distance.

The recent opening of a branch of the **Commercial Bank of Ethiopia**, on the main square next to the Ethiopian Airlines office means that Lalibela finally has a reliable facility for foreign exchange. Email and **internet services** are now widely available, but speed and availability are unreliable and prices are quite high. For **curio hunters**, the main clusters of craft stalls are on the

Accommodation

Upmarket
Jerusalem Hotel ⓦ www.lalibelajerusalemhotel.com. See advert, page 211.
Lal Hotel ⓦ www.lalhoteltour.com. See advert, page 212.
Mountain View Hotel ⓦ www.mountainsviewhotel.com
Roha Hotel ⓦ www.ghionhotel.com.et
Tukul Village Hotel ⓦ www.tukulvillage.com

Moderate
Alef Paradise Hotel ⓔ alparahotel@yahoo.com
Lalibela Hudad Ecolodge ⓦ www.lalibelahudad.com. See advert, page 213.
Seven Olives Hotel ⓦ www.sevenoliveshotel.com

Budget
Asheton Hotel ⓔ asheten_hotel@yahoo.com
Lalibela Hotel ⓔ lalibelahotels@gmail.com
Private Roha Hotel ⓣ 033 336 0094

central square and along the road between the Lal and Roha hotels. Also close to the Roha Hotel is a fine art shop run by a self-taught local artist. Next to the tourist office, the House of the Lalibela Artisans sells locally made cloth, pottery and baskets, with proceeds benefiting the community.

The scenery around Lalibela is truly spectacular. (JH/C)

Eating out

Most tourist-oriented hotels serve a good mix of Ethiopian and Western dishes, with the **Lal Hotel** offering perhaps the best food, and the **Seven Olives Hotel** scoring top marks for alfresco ambience. Also recommended are the restaurant at the **Blue Lal Hotel**, the **Blue Nile Restaurant** and the **Serkies Restaurant**. The **Old Abyssinia Coffee House** is an excellent new bar housed in an authentic mud-wall *tukul*, tastefully decorated with locally made furniture and wall-hangings; if you call ahead, traditional dancing can be arranged. To stock up on dried food before trekking to one of the monasteries, **My Supermarket** opposite the Blue Nile Restaurant has a fair range of imported goods.

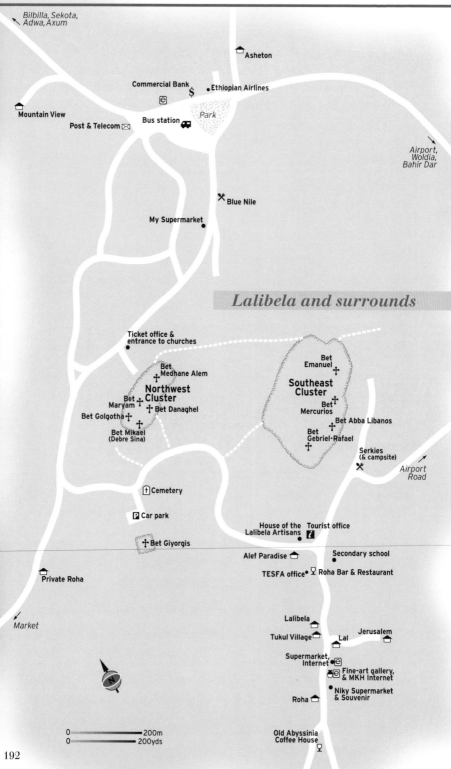

Bilbilla, Sekota,
Adwa, Axum

Asheton

Commercial Bank
Ethiopian Airlines

Mountain View

Park

Post & Telecom
Bus station

Airport,
Woldia,
Bahir Dar

Blue Nile

My Supermarket

Lalibela and surrounds

Ticket office &
entrance to churches

Bet
Emanuel

Bet
Medhane Alem

**Northwest
Cluster**

**Southeast
Cluster**

Bet
Maryam

Bet Danaghel

Bet
Mercurios

Bet Golgotha

Bet Abba Libanos

Bet Mikael
(Debre Sina)

Bet
Gebriel-Rafael

Serkies
(& campsite)

*Airport
Road*

Cemetery

Car park

Bet Giyorgis

House of the
Lalibela Artisans

Tourist office

Alef Paradise

Secondary school

TESFA office

Roha Bar & Restaurant

Private Roha

Market

Lalibela

Tukul Village

Lal

Jerusalem

Supermarket,
Internet

Fine-art gallery,
& MKH Internet

Niky Supermarket
& Souvenir

Roha

Old Abyssinia
Coffee House

0   200m
0   200yds

N

White-robed figures at Fasika (Easter) celebrations, Lalibela (DC)

uKhahlamba-Drakensberg of South Africa and Lesotho. The town's **traditional houses**, now only seen away from the main road, are circular two-storey stone constructs unlike those built anywhere else in Ethiopia. The main attraction, however, is undoubtedly its **rock-hewn churches**, which are generally divided into two clusters, each of which feels a bit like a subterranean village and requires around three hours to visit.

The two clusters of churches are separated by the Jordan River – so named by King Lalibela after he returned from Jerusalem – of which the northwest cluster comprises seven churches, and the southeast five, with a 13th church, Bet Giyorgis, standing discrete from both (see the box texts, page 196 and 198).

While it might be naïve, even a touch patronising, to talk in terms of unchanging cultures in the 21st century, wandering between the churches in the thin light of morning – white-robed hermits emerging from their cells Bible-in-hand to bask on the rocks, the chill highland air warmed by Eucharistic drumbeats and swaying chants – you can't help but feel that you're witnessing a scene that has been enacted here every morning for centuries. It is not just the rock-hewn churches that

In conversation with...

Why should travellers consider visiting Ethiopia over another African country?

There are many great destinations in Africa, but Ethiopia is truly unique. First, the sheer diversity of scenery, highlights and experiences that Ethiopia offers is very hard to beat. There is a fantastic book of Ethiopian photographs by Carol Beckwith and

Angela Fisher entitled *Ethiopian Ark* – this sums up perfectly Ethiopia's appeal. It has elements of all that visitors hope to find in Africa: interesting cultures, history, beautiful scenery, and wildlife. Secondly, it has undoubtedly one of the most hospitable cultures in the world and is quite safe. Just like any country, there are areas that you should avoid, but these are mostly in remote regions where the average traveller is not going to venture.

Which of your tours would you recommend to a first time visitor to Ethiopia?

Ethiopia has a wide variety of destinations, but the scenic northern circuit, which is a tour through the historically important towns of Bahir Dar, Gondar, Axum and Lalibela should be on every visitor's priority list. The main sites are easily accessible yet there are opportunities to spot wildlife, especially in the Lake Tana region. Each of these towns has a modern airport so it's an ideal itinerary for those with a limited amount of time.

What are some of the highlights of an Ethiopian tour?

The churches of Lalibela are spectacular and it's remarkable that so relatively few people in the world have ever heard of them. Also, meeting some of the tribes in the South Omo Valley is just as unforgettable but for entirely different reasons. At one end of the spectrum there is this culture with roots that go back thousands of years to a sophisticated and powerful empire, and at the other end, there are these isolated tribes living a very traditional lifestyle. The contrast is amazing. If you enjoy trekking, both the Simien and Bale mountains

Awaze Tours

are ideal. Yet, really, what most visitors take away from their tour is the entire 'Ethiopian Experience'. A lot of the time it's the seemingly small, day-to-day encounters with Ethiopians that will never be forgotten. At Awaze Tours we don't want our clients to travel in a 'bubble' – we want them to experience firsthand the wonderful hospitality and humour of the Ethiopian people.

Are there any travellers you advise not to take this trip?

We're often asked if single women can travel safely. This anxiety probably arises because of difficulties experienced in other countries in this part of the world, but the vast majority of Ethiopians really do feel responsible for their 'guests', and women are especially well respected. Ethiopian culture also holds senior citizens in high regard and older travellers will certainly feel welcome. However, medical facilities are limited, especially outside the capital, so seniors, like all travellers should consult with their physician when planning their trip. Unfortunately, wheelchair ramps, hotel rooms with adaptations for disabled, etc are very rare. Hopefully this will begin to change for both our guests and for Ethiopia's disabled community.

What are the amenities like? What about the food?

Until recently, the only Western-style, modern hotels in the country were located in Addis Ababa, but very comfortable hotels and lodges are being established throughout the country that still maintain a very Ethiopian flavour. Meal selections are limited outside the capital but you can always find simple, Western meals along the main tourist routes. When possible, we give our guests the option to eat the local cuisine. Ethiopian food can be quite delicious and is an easily acquired taste.

Awaze Tours operates exclusively in Ethiopia and offers both custom and scheduled tours. Whether its historical trips to the north; guided treks in the national parks; or adventures to the remote tribal areas of the south, you're assured a lasting memory of this fascinating and hospitable country.

ⓣ 011 663 4439 ⓔ info@awazetours.com
Ⓦ www.awazetours.com

Lalibela's northwest cluster

Bet Medhane Alem
At the east of the complex, the world's largest monolithic rock-hewn church, measuring 11.5m in height and covering almost 800m², is dedicated to the Saviour of the World. Supported by 36 external and 36 internal pillars, it possesses a classical nobility reminiscent of an ancient Greek temple, leading some experts to think it was modelled on the original 4th-century church of Maryam Tsion at Axum.

Note the Star of David detail, Bet Maryam (AC)

Bet Maryam
Set in a courtyard with two other churches, this 13m-high monolith is thought to have been the earliest church excavated at Lalibela, and its dedication to the Virgin Mary has made it the favourite of most Ethiopians. Carvings of the original Lalibela Cross and the Star of David adorn the ceiling, while a relief of two riders fighting a dragon stands above the entrance. Within the church, a veiled pillar is reputedly inscribed

have survived into the modern era, but also something more organic. More prosaically, however, it is worth noting that many of the churches have been damaged by seepage and are now protected by two large translucent shelters covering each of the main clusters.

Bilbilla
A varied circuit of four churches is focused on the village of Bilbilla, which lies 30km from Lalibela off the road north to Sekota and Adwa. To explore all four churches along this circuit by vehicle takes about eight hours, including walking times of five to 20 minutes each way to the various sites. Three of the churches are rock-hewn, the most worthwhile being the pink-tinged semi-monolith **Bilbilla Chirkos**. Architecturally reminiscent of Bet Gebriel-Rafael with its intricately

with the Ten Commandments in Greek and Ge'ez, as well as the story of how the churches of Lalibela were excavated, and the story of the beginning and end of the world. The local priests say it would be too dangerous to lift the veil to show it to researchers.

Bet Meskel and Danaghel

Carved into the northern wall of Bet Maryam's courtyard, the tiny chapel of **Bet Meskel** ('House of the True Cross') is only 40m² in area, while the atmospheric chapel of **Bet Danaghel** ('House of the Virgin Martyrs') is even smaller. The latter was constructed in remembrance of 50 maiden nuns murdered by the 4th-century Roman ruler Julian the Apostate, as recorded in the *Ethiopian Book of Martyrs*. Also in the courtyard is a pool believed to cure any infertile woman who is dipped into it three times on Ethiopian Christmas – the water is certainly green and slimy enough to suggest a favourable effect on procreativity.

Bet Debre Sina, Golgotha and Selassie

These churches – arguably the most evocative in Lalibela, with a pervasive aura of sanctity – lie in the same courtyard, where they share an entrance and collectively form a semi-monolith. **Bet Golgotha**, the one Lalibela church closed to women, has seven life-size reliefs of saints carved into its walls, while King Lalibela is reputedly buried beneath the floor, giving the surrounding soil healing powers. The **Selassie Chapel**, set within Bet Golgotha, is the holiest place in Lalibela and few visitors have ever been permitted to enter it. The western exit from the courtyard lies at the base of the **Tomb of Adam**, a cruciform hermit's cell decorated with mutilated paintings of the kings of Lalibela.

worked façade, it houses some very old paintings of Maryam, Giyorgis and various other saints, an illustrated 800-year-old Ge'ez history of Kidus Chirkos. One tradition holds that it is the oldest rock-hewn church in Lasta, excavated during the 6th-century

Reputedly 800 years old, this manuscript stored at Bilbilla Chirkos, is among the most ancient in Ethiopia. (AZ)

rule of Emperor Kaleb. Also worth a look are **Bilbilla Giyorgis**, with an imposing façade decorated with a frieze representing the 12 vaults of heaven, and the small sunken semi-monolith **Arbuta Insesa**.

Lalibela's southeast churches

Bet Gebriel-Rafael

This unusual but impressive church is surrounded by a deep rock trench (rather like a dry moat) crossed on a rickety wooden walkway. Recent archaeological studies suggest that both it and nearby Bet Mercurios were excavated as the core of a fortified palatial complex during the 7th and 8th centuries, when the Axumite Empire was disintegrating. The northern façade, its height greatly exaggerated by the trench below, is distinguished by arched niches, showing clear Axumite influences. The interior is surprisingly small and plain, decorated only by three carved Latin crosses.

Bet Abba Libanos

According to legend, this cave church was built overnight by Lalibela's wife and a group of angels. The roof is still connected to the original rock, but the sides and back are separated from the rock by narrow tunnels. The pink-tinged façade, reminiscent of some churches in Tigrai, shows strong Axumite influences in its arched and cruciform windows. A tunnel leads to the Chapel of Bet Lehem, a small and simple shrine that may once have been the private monastic cell of King Lalibela.

Bet Emanuel

The only monolith in the southeast cluster stands 12m high, and art historians consider it to be the finest and most precisely worked church in Lalibela, possibly because it was the private church of the royal family. The exterior of the church imitates the classical Axumite wood-and-stone built-up church typified by Yemrehanna Kristos outside Lalibela. An ornamental frieze of blind windows dominates the church's interior.

Bet Mercurios

Another cave church, this was originally used for secular purposes, possibly as a jail or courtroom, and its interior is partially collapsed. It contains a beautiful if rather faded 15th-century wall frieze of the three wise men, and a recently restored painting of the beatific St Mercurios amid a group of dog-headed men, his sword trailing through the guts of the evil King Oleonus.

Bet Giyorgis

This isolated monolith, a symmetrical cruciform tower, is the most majestic of all Lalibela's churches, and the only one that isn't covered by a modern shelter. About 15m in height, it is excavated below ground level in a sunken courtyard

A passage leading to the cave church at Bet Abba Libanos. (CB/H/C)

enclosed by precipitous walls. The story behind its excavation is that Giyorgis – St George – was so deeply offended that none of Lalibela's churches was dedicated to him that he personally visited the king to set things straight. Lalibela responded by promising he would build the finest of all his churches for Giyorgis. So enthusiastic was the saint to see the result of Lalibela's promise that he rode his horse right over the wall into the entrance tunnel. The holes in the stone tunnel walls are the hoof prints of St George's horse – or so they tell you in Lalibela.

The indisputable gem among the churches around Bilbilla, however, is the **Monastery of Yemrehanna Kristos**, whose built-up church, set within a large cavern, is a particularly fine example of late-Axumite architecture, built with alternating layers of wood and granite faced with white gypsum that give it the appearance of a gigantic layered chocolate cream cake. A reliable tradition maintains that this church was built by its namesake, Yemrehanna Kristos (the third Zagwe ruler and a predecessor of King Lalibela), recorded as ascending to the throne in AD1087 and ruling for about 40 years. Behind the main building, adding an eerie quality to the already dingy cavern, lie the bones of some of the 10,740 Christian pilgrims who, it is claimed, travelled from as far afield as Egypt, Syria and Jerusalem to die at this monastery.

Monastery of Yemrehanna Kristos (PS/A)

Nakuta La'ab Monastery

The most accessible of the outlying churches, the Monastery of Nakuta La'ab is named after its constructor, a nephew of King Lalibela. Along with Lalibela, Nakuta La'ab is the only Zagwe ruler to be included under a recognisable name in all the available lists of Ethiopian kings. One tradition has it that he ruled from this church, which he called Qoqhena, during an 18-month break in Lalibela's monarchy; another is that he succeeded Lalibela but was deposed soon after and took refuge here. The monastery consists of a relatively simple church built around a shallow cave in which several holy pools are fed by natural springs. It has many treasures, including paintings, crosses and an illuminated leather Bible, some of which may have belonged to Nakuta La'ab himself. The monastery can be reached by following the surfaced airport road out of Lalibela, a straightforward walk there takes up to 90 minutes. About halfway out, there is a small gorge where the endemic white-winged and Rüppell's black chat appear to be resident.

Rüppell's black chat (NB/FLPA)

Asheton Maryam Monastery and Mount Abuna Yosef

The monastery of Asheton Maryam, set at an altitude of almost 4,000m on Mount Abuna Yosef, is also associated with Nakuta La'ab, who most probably founded it, and may be buried in the chapel. The cliff church is rougher in execution than other churches in and around Lalibela, but it houses some interesting crosses and other church treasures. Most people go up by mule, but it's only two hours' walk from Lalibela, albeit along a rather steep path strewn with loose stones. The peak of Abuna Yosef makes for a fun yet challenging overnight excursion (see box, *Trekking around Lalibela*, below).

Trekking around Lalibela

Working with local communities in the Lalibela area, TESFA (⑩ www.community-tourism-ethiopia.com) has developed a popular trekking programme aimed at tourists who wish to explore the region's breathtaking scenery and see the local cultures on foot. Most treks begin or end at the town of Filakit, and they follow the escarpment edges of the Meket Plateau, a remote highland area set on a lava bed associated with the formation of the Rift Valley. Treks between the various overnight camps generally take about six hours, and give participants a chance to see local farming techniques and wildlife such as gelada money, rock hyrax and klipspringer. The programme also runs treks to the top of the 4,300m Abuna Mount Abuna Yosef, the closest Afro-alpine moorland to Lalibela, and home to large troops of gelada baboon and a relict population of Ethiopian wolf.

Northeast Highlands

Probably the least visited of the regions covered in this guide, the cool scenic highlands running northeast from Addis Ababa towards the Tigraian border are traversed by the most direct road route between the capital and Lalibela, and are therefore often included in road tours. The region has few established tourist attractions, but it offers some highly rewarding opportunities to explore several little-known but worthwhile sites. Natural attractions include bird-rich **Lake Hayk**, the spectacular escarpment around **Ankober**, and the surprising **Guassa Plateau** – the latter being the most reliable place to see the Ethiopian wolf north of Addis. There are also several **important churches**, among them Hayk Istafanos, Gishen Debre Kerbe and Arbara Medhane Alem. Another popular excursion is to the small town of **Bati**, a cultural melting pot whose Monday livestock market is the largest in Ethiopia.

Practicalities

Flights between Addis Ababa and Dessie (or more accurately the smaller town of Kombolcha 25km to its east) were suspended a few years back. This means that the entire area covered in this section is accessible **by road** only. It is thus most likely to be explored by travellers who are covering the entire northern historical circuit as a road loop out of Addis Ababa, or travelling overland to Lalibela. The more southerly destinations, in particular Debre Birhan, are also frequently visited as a stand-alone road trip out of Addis Ababa, particularly by birdwatchers and other natural history enthusiasts.

Accommodation

Upmarket
Ankober Palace Lodge (Ankober) ⓦ www.ankoberlodge.com.et. See page 129.

Moderate
Eva Hotel (Debre Birhan) ① 011 681 3607
Qualiber Hotel (Dessie) ① 033 111 1548
Tossa Hotel (Dessie) ① 033 111 9225

Budget
Fasika Hotel (Dessie) ① 033 111 2930

Northeast Highlands highlights

Dessie and Hayk

A modern town and notably deficient in character, **Dessie**, former capital of the defunct Wolo region, lies some 400km north of Addis Ababa along the main road to Woldia (the junction town for Lalibela) and Mekele. Set at a breezy altitude of 2,600m below Mount Tossa, it is the fifth-largest town in Ethiopia, supporting a population of 185,000. It was founded in 1882 by Emperor Yohannis IV, who saw a comet while encamped nearby, and immediately set about building a church at the site which he named Dessie – literally 'My Joy' – instigating a skyward arch in the eyebrows of more than one subsequent visitor. In 1888, Dessie became the capital of Ras Mikael Ali, an influential regional leader who became the stepson of Emperor Menelik II in 1893, and went on to father the ill-fated Emperor Iyasu. The only tourist attraction

Dessie lies 400km from Addis Ababa along a well-maintained surfaced road that normally takes five or six hours to cover in a private vehicle. It is 120km south of Woldia along a slightly inferior road that takes around two hours. Other driving times are around 90 minutes from Addis Ababa to Debre Birhan and another 30 minutes to Ankober. Realistically, you need to hire a private 4x4 to visit sites off the main road, such as Makdala Hill, Gishen Debre Kirbe and the Guassa Plateau.

Dessie and to a lesser extent Debre Birhan are well endowed when it comes to **banks** and **internet facilities**, but not so other smaller towns in the region.

Fasika Hotel (Hayk) ① 033 222 0390
Vasco Tourist Hotel (Bati) ① 033 533 0548
Akalu Hotel (Debre Birhan) ① 011 681 1115

Eating out

Dessie has plenty of decent eateries, none better than the popular **Kalkidan Restaurant** (① 033 111 8834), which is famous for its roast lamb. A dozen pastry shops line the main road through Dessie, the pick being the **Palace Café**. **Hayk** is a great place to eat inexpensive fish cutlets at any of half-a-dozen local eateries. Elsewhere, the usual local dishes are available at several restaurants.

in town is the **regional museum** (⊘ 08.30–12.30 & 14.00–17.00 Mon–Fri, 08.30–12.30 Sat–Sun).

Far more attractive than Dessie itself is **Hayk**, which overlooks the beautiful 23km² lake that is also, and somewhat redundantly, known as Lake Hayk (the Amharigna word for 'lake') or Lake Lago. It is a lovely spot: the deep turquoise water, ringed by verdant hills, is still plied by traditional fishermen on papyrus *tankwas*, and the birdlife is superb. Set on a thickly wooded peninsula within easy walking distance of town, the **church of Hayk Istafanos** was reputedly founded in AD862 by a monk from Jerusalem called Kala'e Selama, on a site that formerly supported a cult of pagan snake worshippers. It became a monastery in the mid-13th century under Abba Iyasu Moa, a former apprentice at Debre Damo who died aged 89 in 1293 and is buried within the church. It was the most powerful monastery in Ethiopia from the late 13th to the 15th century, thanks to its role in the restoration of the Solomonic line under Emperor Yakuno Amlak, who had trained for several years under Iyasu Moa. The church **museum** houses several unusual artefacts, including a heavy stone cross that belonged to Iyasu Moa, an illustrated biography of Iyasu Moa written during his lifetime (one of the oldest books in Ethiopia) and hollowed-out sacrificial stones used by the pagans he converted. Women are not permitted to enter the grounds, but they can visit the adjacent **nunnery of Margebeta Giyorgis**, reputedly about 800 years old.

View over Dessie (SS)

Gishen Debre Kerbe Monastery

Often called Gishen Maryam after the oldest of its four churches, this is one of the most revered monasteries in Ethiopia, situated about 90km northwest of Dessie on a massive cross-shaped rock *amba* (flat-topped mountain) off the road to Wegel Tena. Reputedly founded by King Kaleb in the 5th century, the monastery is best known as the home of the piece of the True Cross (on which Jesus was crucified) brought to Ethiopia during the 14th-century reign of Emperor Dawit, and it routinely attracts many thousands of pilgrims over Meskel. This holiest of relics is reputedly stashed Russian doll-style within four boxes (respectively made of iron, bronze, silver and gold) suspended by chains within a closed subterranean chamber at the end of a tunnel 20m below the ground. Gishen Amba has a second, more verifiable claim to fame, as the source of Dr Johnson's morality tale of Rasselas, the prince who was imprisoned in a valley encircled by mountains by the King of Abyssinia. According to Thomas Pakenham, it first served as a royal prison in 1295, when Emperor Yakuno Amlak sent his five sons there, and it held a solid stream of similar captives until it was virtually razed by Ahmed Gragn in the 16th century.

Makdala Hill

It was to Makdala Hill, 100km northwest of Dessie as the crow flies, that an embattled and embittered Emperor Tewodros retreated in 1867, as his dream of a unified Ethiopia crumbled under the strain of internal and external pressures. His once all-conquering army reduced through desertion and rebellion to a tenth of its former size, and his pleas for British alliance unanswered, the emperor abandoned his capital at Debre Tabor and barricaded himself in the hilltop castle at Makdala

In conversation with...

Do you have a favourite destination?

Though we organise trips throughout the country, the cultural sites in northern Ethiopia, particularly the marvellous 13th-century rock-hewn churches of Lalibela (often regarded as the eighth wonder of the world), rank as the best destination. As nature lovers, the rugged Simien Mountains and the Rift Valley region are also rank high.

What is your favourite itinerary?

We run over 200 itineraries, but our favourite is probably the classical route (Lake Tana, Gondar, Axum, the Tigray churches, and Lalibela) combined with the Simien Mountains. This trip gives visitors the chance to enjoy the landscapes, wildlife and one of the highest altitudes in Africa as well as the more cultural aspects of Ethiopia. You can witness ancient civilisations and

meet the locals. Depending on when you visit, you can also experience colourful religious festivals, which comes highly recommended. Because of the diversity this trip offers, we consider it the best option for first-time visitors to Ethiopia. We can also be flexible, allowing for more or less action/adventure/comfort depending on the client's interests and abilities.

What makes your trips to Ethiopia special?

As the first professional tour operator in Ethiopia with over 15 years in the business, we know the country better than anyone else, and we are able to design unique itineraries often to more obscure locations. We are staffed with young, multi-lingual professionals committed to the satisfaction of customers and the development of the tourism industry in the country. Our excellent relationship with various organisations such as federal and regional government offices, the Ethiopian Orthodox Church, and local communities makes for a smooth travel experience every time. Take, for example, the Meskel festival, Timkat, or any other festival in Addis Ababa – we can provide

Paradise Ethiopia

PARADISE ETHIOPIA TRAVEL

VIP badges so that visitors can attend the ceremonies up close. We allow for greater social and cultural interaction by arranging traditional dinner parties and folklore dances as well as Ethiopian coffee ceremonies.

What kind of involvement do your tours have with local Ethiopian communities?

We believe that growth and earning revenue must be reached in an ethical and responsible way. That is why Paradise Ethiopia Travel focuses on setting standards of responsible tourism with the community in which it operates. We participate in development projects and encourage and organise for our customers to do the same; be it building schools and clinics, supporting orphans and widows, or planting trees. We incorporate such projects into our tours so that our customers will have the chance to contribute to the swift economic transformation of the society.

How do you ensure the quality of your tours?

Each trip is careful planned, from advance bookings to assigning the right staff to ensure that the service our customers receive is professional and responsible. During the trip, we stay in touch with guides and drivers to make sure everything is going to plan. We are fully committed to offering superior quality.

We also follow up with the customer after the trip - feedback is invaluable.

Our primary objective is that our customers return home with only happy memories; we want them to feel part of the big Paradise Ethiopia Travel family and our lifetime partner in promoting Ethiopia and our services.

Established in 1997, Paradise Ethiopia Travel operates high-quality customised tours to Ethiopia with profound knowledge and experience, mostly off the beaten track. With a head office in Addis and 11 branches throughout the country, it is the most organised tour operator in Ethiopia. We interviewed Fitsum Gezahegne Lakew, from the company.

Ⓣ 011 662 6623 or 011 551 3494
Ⓔ pet@ethionet. et or fitsum@paradiseethiopia. com
Ⓦ www. paradiseethiopia. com

along with a group of European prisoners to try to lever Britain into giving him military support. This plan backfired, however, when 32,000 British troops were sent to Makdala under the command of Lord Napier with the support of the future Emperor Yohannis IV, leading Tewodros to take his own life. Visiting Makdala requires a bit of perseverance: you first need to obtain a letter of permission from the tourist office in Dessie, then drive the five to six hours to Tenta, stopping at Ajbar to pick up an all-but-obligatory police escort, then undertake an 18km cross-country from Tenta. The scenery *en route* is wonderful, however, and the fortifications erected by Tewodros are still in place, as is Sebastopol, Tewodros's pet name for the unmarked (and unfireable) bronze cannon built for him by the missionaries he took hostage at Gafat.

Bati

Situated 65km east of Dessie (via Kombolcha) at an altitude intermediate to the central highlands and the low-lying Rift Valley, Bati is an important cultural crossroads for the Amhara, Oromo and semi-nomadic desert-dwelling Afar people. For more than two centuries, it has hosted Ethiopia's **largest cattle and camel market**, which attracts up to 20,000 people every Monday, and is well worth the minor diversion should you pass through at the right time. The sheer scale of the phenomenon is impressive, and it also provides a glimpse of a cultural facet of Ethiopia very different from anything in the highlands. Indeed, the Afar – bare-breasted women with wild plaited hairstyles and ornate jewellery, men strutting around with Kalashnikovs slung over their shoulders and traditional daggers tucked away in prominent hide sheaths – seem to belong to another Africa altogether.

En route to the market in Bati (EL)

Menz and the Guassa Plateau

The chilly and fantastically remote highland region known as **Menz** lies to the northwest of the main road between Addis Ababa and Dessie, and is reached by a 100km road that terminates at the small town of Mehal Meda. The area boasts two little-visited but significant attractions, the spooky monastery of Arbara Medhane Alem and the wildlife-rich Guassa Plateau, both readily accessible from the road to Mehal Meda. **Arbara Medhane Alem** is a small cave church and monastery set in a magnificent cliff at the village of Yegam. It is best known for its ancient mausoleum, which is piled high with mummified corpses, some of whose limbs stick out of the wrapping in macabre contortions. A bizarre local tradition suggests that the deceased were angel-like beings who descended from the sky at least 100 years ago.

Set at a mean altitude of 3,200m, the 110km² **Guassa Plateau** is one of the largest Afro-alpine ecosystems in Africa, feeding some 26 streams that eventually flow into the Blue Nile, and it has been managed sustainably by the local community for at least 400 years. Seven endemic mammals are resident, including one of the largest surviving

populations of Ethiopian wolf and several troops of the gelada monkey, both regularly seen from the main road. A checklist of 111 bird species includes 14 endemics, among them the globally threatened Ankober serin, and spot-breasted plover, Rouget's rail, Rüppell's black chat and Abyssinian longclaw. A good place to look for endemic birds (and the Ethiopian wolf) is the marshy area alongside the road about 15km south of Mehal Meda road.

The Guassa Plateau supports Afro-alpine vegetation and wildlife similar to the Bale Mountains. (JK)

Debre Birhan and Ankober

A friendly highland town of 70,000 souls, **Debre Birhan** – 'Mountain of Light' – was founded by Emperor Zara Yaqob after he witnessed a miraculous nocturnal light there (probably Halley's Comet) in 1456. Fifty years later, it was captured by Ahmed Gragn and abandoned to the Oromo, only to be reclaimed by the Showan monarchy in the early 18th century, and served as a secondary capital to four successive Showan emperors in the 19th century. Little indication of Debre Birhan's former importance survives today. Nevertheless, the **church** built by Emperor Menelik II in 1906, on the site first selected by Zara Yaqob, is one of the country's most beautiful and spiritually affecting modern churches, and the interior is decorated with some marvellous paintings – including one of Zara Yaqob looking at a celestial body, modelled on Halley's Comet when it passed over at the beginning of the 20th century. The **woollen carpets and blankets** for which Debre Birhan is famous can be bought directly from the co-operative that manufactures them at a shop near the Telecommunications building.

The remote small town of **Ankober**, one of the coldest in Ethiopia, is set at 3,000m on the eastern edge of the Rift Valley escarpment about

40km east of Debre Birhan. The town's name literally translates as the 'Anko's Gate' (Anko probably being a person's name), a reference to its medieval role as a tollgate along the trade route between the highlands and the Afar Depression. From the early 18th century until 1878 (when Emperor Menelik II relocated his capital to the Entoto Hills) it was the capital or joint capital of Showa, and it is studded with ruined palaces as well as the extant churches dating to the early 19th century. Ankober is popular with **ornithological tours** as the best place to see the Ankober serin (a rather nondescript seedeater first described in 1979), which is often seen on an escarpment alongside the scenic road from Debre Birhan, along with troops of gelada monkey and other localised bird species including lammergeyer, moorland and Erckell's francolin, blue rock thrush, Somali starling and the endemic blue-winged goose and Abyssinian longclaw. The **spectacular road** that descends around 1,500m over 15km between Ankober and the small town of Aliyu Amba is worthwhile not only for the scenery, but also for offering access to the **Melka Jebdu River** (3km out of Aliyu Amba) one of only two reliable sites for the distinctively marked yellow-throated serin, among the most localised of Ethiopia's endemic birds.

LALIBELA HUDAD
ላሊበላ ሁዳድ

Perched on a "desert island" plateau overlooking the town of Lalibela is a community run ecolodge that offers an invigorating mix of relaxation and adventure. Spectacular views, abundant wildlife and people steeped in tradition will leave you with memories to last a lifetime.

Ours is an authentically ecological retreat, completely off grid, sharing our profits with the local community and working to protect endangered habitats. We serve only wholesome locally sourced organic dishes, provide evening campfire entertainment and enjoy a star-studded sky like no other. Stay in one of our tukul suites and sample our rustic and homely highland hospitality.
Visiting us will make your stay in Ethiopia complete.

We also offer:
- Wildlife watching (including a resident troupe of baboons)
- Trekking and hiking
- Village visits and community workshops
- Yoga retreats
- Visits to nearby churches such as Asheton Maryam and Yemerhane Kirstos

Harar and the far east   216

History   217
Historic Harar   221
Dire Dawa   225
Babile and surrounds   225
Mount Kundudo   226
Kulubi   227

The northern Rift Valley   228

Awash National Park   228
Yangudi Rassa National Park   231
Assaita and surrounds   231
Danakil Depression   235

9 Eastern Ethiopia

By contrast to the central highlands, the far east of Ethiopia is predominantly Islamic, with strong historic links to the ancient Somali ports of Zeila and Berbera. Its most popular tourist focus, often visited as a fly-on appendage to a tour of the northern historical circuit, is the characterful and agriculturally bountiful highland citadel of Harar, which ranks as the fourth-holiest city in the Islamic world after Mecca, Medina and Jerusalem. Much of the rest of eastern Ethiopia lies within an arid, low-lying and very thinly populated part of the Rift Valley, whose southern reaches are alleviated by the perennially muddy waters of the Awash River (part of which is protected in the attractive Awash National Park). Further north, this gives way to the compellingly forlorn and desolate Danakil Depression, a searing sub-sea level landscape pockmarked with multi-hued mineral deposits, vast salt pans and belching volcanoes.

Eastern Ethiopia

Danakil Depression

Mile

ASSAITA

DJIBOUTI

Dikhil

KOMBOLCHA

Gewane
Wildlife
Reserve

E T H I O P I A

N

0 ———— 40km
0 ———— 25 miles

Ahmar Mountains

DIRE DAWA

Kulubi

Kombolcha

Jijig

**Alleghedi
Wildlife Sanctuary**

Mieso

Gara Muleta
▲3405m

HARAR

Hirna

Fedis

Babile

● **Valley of Marvels**

**Awash
National Park**

Metahara

Abse Teferi

Kuni

Arbereketi

Arba Gugu Mountains

**AWASH
SABA**

**Kuni Muktar
Mountain
Nyala Sanctuary**

**Babile
Elephant
Sanctuary**

Awash

Harar and the far east

The regional transport focus is **Dire Dawa**, the second-largest city in
Ethiopia, with a population estimated at 600,000. Of greater interest
to visitors, however, is **Harar**, the walled hilltop citadel which easily
ranks as one of the most pleasant cities in Ethiopia. Lively, friendly and
stimulating, Harar – with its 90-odd mosques – boasts an aura of lived-
in antiquity and a strong sense of cultural integrity, while its fertile

surrounds are notable for their mild highland climate and as a producer of high-quality coffee and *khat*. Further afield, the **Babile area** is noted for the scenic **Valley of Marvels**, which forms part of the vast **Babile Elephant sanctuary**, home to the last pachydermal population in the Horn of Africa.

History

One of the oldest cities in Ethiopia, Harar is mentioned in an early 14th-century Arabic manuscript, and its oldest mosque was founded in the 12th century. One tradition suggests it was a Christian city that went by a different name until the arrival of its Arabian patron saint, Sheikh Abadir Gey, in the 10th century. According to this tradition, it is Sheik Abadir who renamed the city Harar, and organised its first Islamic administrative system. More contentiously, another tradition claims

Traditional Harar houses

About 100 traditional Harar houses survive more or less intact, the oldest reputedly built in the 18th century for Emir Yusuf. As viewed from the outside, these houses are unremarkable rectangular blocks occasionally enlivened by an old carved door. But the design of the interiors is totally unique to the town. The ground floor is open plan, and is dominated by a carpet-draped raised area where all social activity takes place. The walls are decorated with small niches and dangling items of crockery, including the famed Harar baskets, some of which are hundreds of years old. Above the main door are grilles

from where carpets are hung to indicate there is a daughter of marriageable age in the family. When the carpets come down, newlyweds in Harar take residence in a tiny corner cell, where they spend their first week of wedlock in cramped, isolated revelry, all they might need being passed to them by relatives through a small service window.

(AZ)

that it was founded in the 7th century by a contemporary follower of the prophet Muhammad, who saw the hill on which the city stands as a shining light during his ascent to heaven, and was told by an angel that it was the Mountain of Saints.

Practicalities

Harar may be the premier tourist attraction in the far east, but Dire Dawa serves as the main regional gateway, with Ethiopian Airlines running at least two **flights** daily to the modern airport, which lies about 5km from the centre. All flights to Dire Dawa are met by charter and shared **taxis**, and regular **minibuses** run along the surfaced road from there to Harar, taking about one hour. The Sky and Selam **Bus** both run direct daily services from Addis Ababa to Harar and Dire Dawa, a tolerably comfortable nine-hour trip in either instance.

Accommodation

Upmarket
Selam Hotel Dire Dawa ① 025 113 0219/20

Moderate
Belayneh Hotel Harar ① 025 666 2030
Heritage Plaza Hotel Harar ⑭ www.plazahotelharar.com. See advert page 237.
Peacock Hotel Dire Dawa ① 025 111 3968/130 0168
Ras Hotel Dire Dawa ① 025 111 3255

Budget
Tewodros Hotel Harar ① 025 666 0217
Tsehay Hotel Dire Dawa ① 025 111 1023

Eating out

In Dire Dawa, the pick is the **Paradiso Restaurant**, set in an atmospheric old house along the Harar road, and offering a varied selection of Italian and Ethiopian dishes, including excellent lasagne and various roast meats. **In Harar**, the **Heritage Plaza** and **Belayneh** hotels both have decent restaurants, while **Fresh Touch Restaurant** along the main road features pizzas and stir-fries. Harar is well endowed with bars, of which the **Bar Cottage**, with its organic banana-leaf walls, is almost as cosy as the name suggests.

Medieval market in Harar (AC)

Harar's rise to modern prominence dates to 1520, when Sultan Abu Bekr Mohammed of the Walashma Dynasty relocated there from the Somali port of Zeila. Five years later, the militant Somali-born leader Ahmed Gragn killed the Sultan of Harar, and used the city as the base from which to launch a succession of bloody and destructive raids on the Christian empire of the Ethiopian Highlands. Gragn died in battle in 1543, but the *jihad* continued, culminating in a 1559 retaliatory attack on Harar led by the Ethiopian emperor Galawdewos, who was killed and had his head paraded around town on a stake. The tall protective walls that enclose Harar were built in the 1560s to repel attacks from the pagan Oromo, who had taken advantage of the devastating Muslim–Christian conflict to occupy much of southern Ethiopia.

In 1647, Emir Ali Ibn Daud founded a ruling dynasty under which Harar became the most populous and important trade centre in the

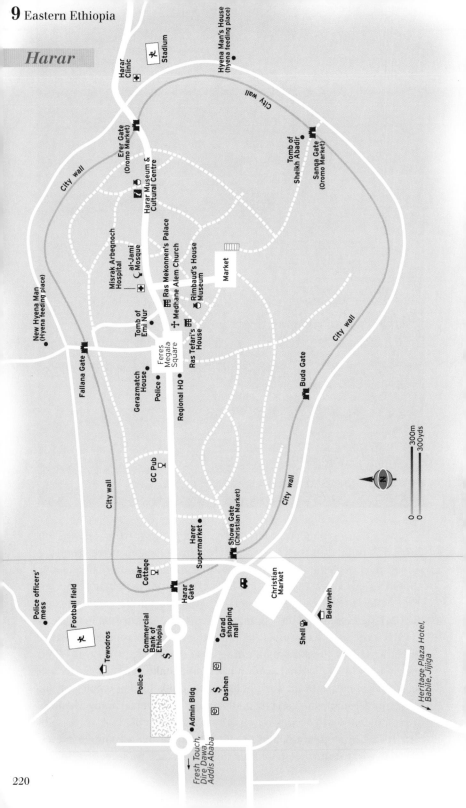

Harar

Stadium

Harar Clinic

Hyena Man's House (hyena feeding place)

City wall

Erer Gate (Oromo Market)

Tomb of Sheikh Abadir

Sanqa Gate (Oromo Market)

Harar Museum & Cultural Centre

Misrak Arbegnoch Hospital

al-Jami Mosque

Ras Mekonnen's Palace

Medhane Alem Church

Rimbaud's House Museum

Market

New Hyena Man (Hyena feeding place)

Tomb of Emi Nur

Feres Megala Square

Ras Tefari's House

Fallana Gate

Gerazmatch House

Police

Regional HQ

Buda Gate

City wall

300m
300yds

N

City wall

GC Pub

0
0

City wall

Harer Supermarket

Showa Gate (Christian Market)

Police officers' mess

Bar Cottage

Football field

Harar Gate

Christian Market

Belayneh

Tewodros

Commercial Bank of Ethiopia

Garad shopping mall

Shell

Heritage Plaza Hotel, Babile, Jijiga

Police

Admin Bldg

Dashen

Fresh Touch, Dire Dawa, Addis Ababa

region. At this time, only Muslims were allowed to enter the walls of the city, which was the source of more rumour than substance in the Christian world until the arrival of the British explorer Richard Burton, who spent ten anxious days in what he referred to as 'the forbidden city' in 1855. Another famous 19th-century visitor was the French poet Arthur Rimbaud, who moved to Harar in 1880, set himself up as a trader and was based there until his death in 1891.

Harar's autonomy ended in 1887, when it was captured by the future Emperor Menelik II of Ethiopia. Menelik warded off religious sectarianism by including several members of the old Emir's family in his new administration, which he headed with a Christian governor, Ras Mekonnen (the father of the future Emperor Haile Selassie). Then the most important trading centre in Ethiopia, Harar's economic significance dwindled after 1902, and Dire Dawa was founded to service the Franco–Ethiopian railway connecting Addis Ababa to Djibouti. Now the second-largest city in Ethiopia, Dire Dawa has experienced a recent economic boom as a result of the secession of Eritrea and subsequent border war, which greatly increased the port volume through Djibouti. Since 1995, Harar and Dire Dawa have both been recognised among the country's three federal city-states (along with Addis Ababa).

Harar and the far east highlights

Historic Harar

The old town, known locally as Jugal, extends over 60ha and is enclosed by the 5m-high wall that defined its full extent from the 1560s until the end of the Italian occupation. By contrast, the newer part of town, outside the city walls, is predominantly Christian, though the traditional Oromo

Harar Hyena Men

RAINBOW TOURS

A two-day extension on any itinerary in the Harar area is unanimously enjoyed by our clients. Remarkably different to the popular historical circuit, Islamic Harar offers colourful markets and good birdwatching as well as one of the strangest and most memorable wildlife experiences to be had anywhere in the world. Witness here the bizarre hyena-feeding rituals (page 224) – an unforgettable occasion for our team and clients alike.

al-Jami Mosque is one of the 90 mosques found in Harar (ss)

are also much in evidence. Despite its prominent role in past Muslim–Christian–Oromo conflicts, Harar today possesses a mood of religious and cultural tolerance, with compulsive *khat*-chewing dominating public life and – surprisingly – a concentration of bars within the old city walls that come close to matching public mosques one-for-one.

Five traditional gates lie along the 3.5km wall, but the normal first point of entry is the **Harar Gate**, a motor-friendly Haile Selassie-era addition that faces west, opening to the Dire Dawa road. The only pedestrian gate connecting the old and new towns is **Showa Gate**, which adjoins the Christian Market opposite the bus station. The other four gates, running in anticlockwise order from the Showa Gate, are Buda, Sanga, Erer and Fallana.

It is most convenient to enter the old town via the Harar or Showa gates, but neither has an impact comparable to arriving at **Buda Gate**. From here, a labyrinth of cobbled alleys flanked by traditional whitewashed stone houses winds uphill to the central square **Feres Megala** (literally 'Horse Market', though these days Khat Magala or Peugeot Megala would be more apt), the obvious place to start any walking tour. Overlooking the square, **Gerazmatch House** was built by Egyptians in the 1870s and later used as a warehouse by Rimbaud, while the **church of Medhane Alem** was built in 1890 on the site of a mosque constructed by the unpopular Egyptians.

The road that runs east from the square to **Erer Gate** passes the domed 16th-century **Tomb of Emir Nur**, a 19th-century **Catholic mission**, the **al-Jami Mosque** (founded in 1216 and with at least one minaret

Eating out

Make sure you venture out and sample some of the fare at local eateries. For a great steak, go to one of the 'raw meat houses'. When they're not fasting, many Ethiopians enjoy freshly killed raw beef. Whilst we don't recommend this, you can choose your cut of meat and then have it grilled to taste. Try this with some *awaze* (an Ethiopian hot sauce,) *injera* (Ethiopian bread) and a cold local beer – you'll find you make friends quickly.

dating to the 1760s), and the **Harar Museum and Cultural Centre** (⊙ 09.00–12.00, 14.00–17.00 Mon–Fri) with its complete replica of an old Harari house. Erer Gate, where Richard Burton entered Harar, is now the site of a colourful **Oromo *khat* market**. About 200m south of **Sanga Gate**, immediately inside the city wall, the **Tomb of Sheikh Abadir**, the religious leader who reputedly introduced Islam to Harar, is a popular substitute for Islamic Ethiopians who can't afford the pilgrimage to Mecca.

The narrow lane leading east from the main square is called **Mekina Girgir** ('Machine Road') in reference to the sewing machines of the tailors who work there. A left turn from here leads to **Ras Mekonnen's Palace**, a late 19th-century building where the future Emperor Haile Selassie reputedly spent much of his childhood. Next door, the vaguely oriental double-storey building known as **Rimbaud's House** is notable for its frescoed ceiling and views over town, but it was probably built in 1908, years after Rimbaud's death. It now functions as a museum, with ground-floor displays about the poet, and a collection of compelling turn-of-the-20th-century photographs of Harar on the first floor.

The tomb of Emir Nur (SS)

Rimbaud's House (AC)

Hyena Men of Harar

One of Harar's most enduringly popular attractions is its resident hyena men, so-called because they make their living from feeding wild hyenas every night on the outskirts of town. This odd custom probably started in the 1950s, but it is loosely rooted in a much older annual ceremony called Ashura, which takes place on 7 Muhharam (normally 9 July), and dates back to a famine many centuries ago, when the people of Harar decided to feed the hyenas porridge to prevent them from attacking livestock. Today, the feeding starts at 19.00 daily, usually at one of two sites outside the walled city: the shrine of Aw Anser Ahmed (between Erer and Sanga gates) or the Christian slaughterhouse (outside Fallana Gate). The ritual is that the hyena man starts calling the hyenas by name, then, after ten minutes or so, the animals appear from the shadows. Timid at first, the hyenas are soon eating bones passed to them by hand, and the hyena man teases them and even passes them bones from his mouth.

Eastern landscapes

Ethiopian Quadrants PLC
To the four corners of the country

Travelling east to Awash from Addis you drop 1.5km in altitude and, even for the amateur geologist, the landscapes provide a series of fascinating spectacles. Find here fresh lava flows, volcanic cones, fissures, hotsprings and blister cones, all with the dormant Fantale volcano as a backdrop. If you continue to Harar, from the Afar lowlands you ascend again, skirting the Arba Gugu Mountains. A great road trip, which can be done in a day.

Dire Dawa

Although it lacks Harar's sense of antiquity, Dire Dawa is a pleasant city to explore on foot. The (normally dry) Dachata River divides it into two distinct quarters. West of the watercourse, **French-designed Kezira**, a rare African product of active town planning, consists of a neat grid of tree-lined avenues that emanate from the central square in front of the old railway station (a must-see for students of colonial architecture). The old **Muslim quarter of Megala**, by contrast, is more organic in shape and mood, with all alleys apparently leading to the colourful bustle of the central market, which is busiest in the morning and often attended by rural Oromo and Afar traders in traditional garb.

Babile and surrounds

Straddling the Jijiga road about 30km east of Harar, the small town of Babile gives its name not only to a popular brand of bottled sparkling water (actually bottled at a factory in Harar) but also to the 7,000km² Babile Elephant Sanctuary. It hosts a busy general **market** on Saturdays, and an important **camel market** on Mondays and Thursdays, but the main point of local interest is the so-called **Valley of Marvels**. This is a desolate landscape of red earth, low acacia scrub, forbidding cacti and tall chimney-like termite mounds overlooked by a sequence of gravity-defying balancing rock formations, most especially **Dakata Rock**, which appears to be just one puff away from collapse, and lies a few kilometres further east along the Jijiga road.

    Babile Elephant Sanctuary supports around 150 wide-ranging elephants, assigned by some authorities to a unique subspecies *Loxodonta africana orleansi*. The best times of year to seek out the elephants is from mid-November to early March (when they congregate in Fedis District, an hour's drive south of Harar) or June and September (when they haunt the Upper Erer Valley southeast of Harar). Either way, you'll need a 4x4, and must pick up a mandatory game scout (without whose assistance you would be unlikely to locate any elephants) at the park office in Babile town. The sanctuary also provides refuge to the black-maned Abyssinian lion, various antelope, Hamadryas baboon and a selection of dry-country birds, including Salvadori's serin.

Mount Kundudo

Situated near Fugnan Bira (also known as Gursum) about 20km northeast of Harar as the crow flies, Mount Kundudo – whose beauty was extolled by Burton when he followed its base *en route* to Harar in 1855 – is a striking 2,900m-tall *amba* comprising a limestone base and a basaltic cap. Known for its beautiful scenery, including the spectacular **Immis Falls**, and as the site of one of only three feral horse populations in Africa, Kundudo is the centrepiece of a proposed conservation area being lobbied for by the Italian ecologist Marco Viganó (see ⓦ www.etio. webs.com). There are several old Islamic shrines in the area, including a tall **stone tower** dedicated to Sheikh Adem, and recent expeditions have discovered several **rock art sites**, as well as the country's most important and beautiful **limestone cave system**. *En route*, the village of **Ejerso Gworo** is known as the birthplace of Ras Tefari Mekonnen – the future Emperor Haile Selassie – on 23 July 1892.

Mount Kundudo (LR)

Pilgrimage to Kulubi Gebriel (PB)

Kulubi

This small town on the road back towards Addis Ababa enjoys a renown disproportionate to its size thanks to the presence of **Kulubi Gebriel** hilltop church. This was built by Ras Mekonnen, father of Haile Selassie, after he stopped at what was then a rather modest shrine to St Gebriel in 1896 to pray for assistance in the looming military confrontation with Italy, whose invasive force was duly defeated by an Ethiopian army at Adwa. When Ras Mekonnen returned to Harar, he ordered a magnificent domed sandstone church to be built at Kulubi in honour of the saint. Since then, Kulubi Gebriel has become the target of a fantastic biannual pilgrimage, usually on 26 July and 28 December, often attracting more than 100,000 worshippers from all over the country.

The northern Rift Valley

One of the least visited but most alluring parts of Ethiopia, the northern Rift Valley is an arid low-lying region inhabited by the semi-nomadic Afar, who traditionally make a living as pastoralists or by excavating salt blocks from a series of vast saline pans deposited many millions of years ago, when the entire region was submerged by a southern extension of the Red Sea. The northern Rift hasn't always been as arid as it is today: five million years ago it supported a lush cover of grassland and forest, as well as some of our earliest ancestors, leading to the recent discovery of some of the most important known hominid fossils in the region. The region's most accessible attraction is **Awash National Park**, which is now more notable for its scenery and birdlife than as a conventional destination. For more adventurous travellers with the budget to throw at a bespoke expedition, an altogether more alluring destination is the starkly beautiful **Danakil Depression**, officially the hottest place on earth, and also one of the most volcanically active.

The northern Rift Valley highlights

Awash National Park
Established in 1966, this 756km² national park is situated in the Rift Valley 200km east of Addis Ababa, where it is bisected by the main road

Visiting Eastern Ethiopia

UNESCO-listed Harar is the obvious draw here, with its amazing history and unique culture not found elsewhere in Ethiopia. The region has some very interesting, albeit lesser-known, destinations including many different sites with prehistoric rock art and the Babile Elephant Sanctuary. For those interested in colourful festivals, visiting the church of Kulubi Gebriel for St Gebriel's Saint Day celebration in July and December is highly recommended.

to Dire Dawa and Harar for a distance of almost 20km. Scenic highlights include the magnificent **Awash Gorge** on the park's southern boundary, the **waterfall** where the Awash River spills into the gorge, and the palm-fringed **Filwoha Hot Springs** on the northern boundary. Overlooking it all is the imperious ragged crown of **Mount Fantelle**, a 2,007m-high dormant volcano responsible for the bleak 200-year-old lava flows around the 40km² **Lake Beseka** on the park's western border.

Although 80 mammal species have been recorded in Awash, poaching has been rife in recent years and game viewing is erratic,

Goat herding in an Afar village near Afambo (EL)

Practicalities

Awash National Park, which is bisected by the main Dire Dawa road, can only be explored in a private vehicle, ideally a **4x4**. However, the well-equipped villages of **Metahara** and **Awash Saba**, on the park's western and eastern borders, are readily accessible from Addis Ababa or Adama, and offer good access to Lake Beseka and the Awash Gorge respectively.

Elsewhere, the excellent surfaced road connecting Addis Ababa to the seaports of Assab (Eritrea) and Djibouti via the northern Awash Valley is one of the best anywhere in the country and is a busy trucking route, but public transport is limited once it branches north from the main road to Dire Dawa. The thinly populated Afar region and Danakil Depression can only realistically be explored over a week or so on a **tailored 4x4 tour**, with an experienced specialist operator, and it is not advisable to head far off-road without a back-up vehicle and knowledgeable guide or GPS.

Accommodation

Moderate
Bilen Lodge north of Awash National Park ⓦ www.village-ethiopia.net

Budget
Awash Hotel Metahara ⓣ 091 122 1992
Awash Meridian Hotel Awash Saba ⓣ 022 224 0051
Buffet D'Aouache Awash Saba ⓣ 022 224 0008
Kereyou Lodge Awash National Park ⓦ www.ras-hotels.com
Lem Hotel Assaita ⓣ 033 555 0050

particularly where vulnerable large predators such as lion and leopard are concerned. The most visible large mammals are **Beisa oryx**, **Soemmerring's gazelle** and **Salt's dik-dik**, all of which might be seen from the surfaced public road through the park. Elsewhere, there are **lesser** and **greater kudu**, **Defassa waterbuck**, **desert warthog**, and **vervet** and **guereza monkeys**. The ranges of the **Hamadryas** and **Anubis baboons** converge on the park, and hybrids are frequently observed along the river east of the waterfall.

Awash is one of Ethiopia's **premier birding destinations**, with a checklist of 450 species including Abyssinian roller, seven species of bustard and the gorgeous carmine bee-eater. For dedicated tickers, the primary attraction is the presence of the **yellow-throated seedeater** and **sombre rock chat** on the slopes of Fantelle, as well as the undescribed **Ethiopian cliff swallow** in the Awash Gorge. Other good birding spots include the riparian forest fringing the Awash River close to the waterfall, and the shores of Lake Beseka, which host an interesting selection of water-associated species.

Yangudi Rassa National Park

Proposed in 1977 but never officially gazetted, this 5,000km² national park, to the east of the village of Gewane, comprises the dormant 1,383m-high volcano called **Mount Yangudi** together with the surrounding **Rassa Plains**. It harbours Ethiopia's only extant population of the **African wild ass**, a critically endangered species ancestral to the domestic donkey, but the odds of seeing a wild ass in transit are extremely slim. Other large mammal species include **Beisa oryx**, **Soemmerring's** and **dorcas gazelle**, **gerenuk** and possibly **Grevy's zebra**, but – like the ass – they are thinly distributed and unlikely to be observed by casual visitors. A good selection of **dry-country birds** includes **Arabian bustard** and **Somali ostrich**, and the park lies along an important migration passage.

Assaita and surrounds

The former administrative capital of Afar and largest town in the region, **Assaita** is situated some 50km south of the Assab road on a rise overlooking a stretch of the Awash River lined with palms and cultivation. First impressions as you enter this fantastically hot and dusty backwater, passing through a jumble of rundown administrative

The main square in Assaita (EL)

In conversation with...

Which experience would Rainbow Tours recommend for a first time visitor to Ethiopia?

That depends on your interests, really. For culture, we'd propose seeing at least two of the sites on the popular historical circuit. First and foremost would be Lalibela. We find people enjoy Gondar for its castles and also because it is the access town to the Simien Mountains. If you like colourful events, go in mid January for Timkat or in September for Meskal. If your interest is natural history, the most impressive location is Bale Mountains National Park with its juniper woods, Afro-alpine moorlands and high concentration of endemic birds and mammals.

What kind of involvement do your tours and lodges have with local communities?

This varies across the country but an exemplary lodge is the remote Simien Lodge, the only good quality accommodation servicing the Simien Mountains National Park and Debark region. The owner, Nick Crane, has done an enormous amount for impoverished communities with employees almost all from the local area. The lodge was designed and is managed following guidelines aimed at preventing global warming. Impressively, during one recent rainy season, the lodge assisted with the planting of 7,000 trees. Wherever possible we do try to select owner-run accommodation. An excellent and highly rated example is the Rowda Waberi Cultural Guest House in Harar, owned by a local family. Guests can enjoy the experience of staying in a typical Harari home and the hospitality here is top notch.

Do you cover any areas particularly good for wildlife and what might be seen there?

Indeed, we do. One of the foremost wildlife hotspots would have to be Bale Mountains National Park, to the south of the Rift Valley. At the park your chances of seeing endemic mammals such as mountain nyala and Menelik's bushbuck are good in the juniper and hagenia woods around Dinsho.

Much higher up, on the Sanetti Plateau, is the stronghold for most of the remaining 500-odd Ethiopian wolves. They are diurnal and often allow a close approach. Their chief prey, the giant mole-rat, is another endemic mammal. Further north in the Simien Mountains wildlife is more sparse and less diverse but two flagship species are found here: the 'bleeding-heart' or gelada monkey, and the critically endangered Walia ibex. The geladas are the only primates which graze and often congregate in large troops. It is possible to

take a drive up to Chennek, to seek the ibexes on sheer rock faces there. Ethiopia is a fantastic destination for birders, with some 30 species being endemic to Ethiopia and neighbouring Eritrea. Almost anywhere in the country, birding is rewarding, and even along the historical circuit you could tick off new endemics at each stop.

Please could you share your top tips for travel in Ethiopia with us?

Try to view a trip to Ethiopia as an educational/learning experience rather than just a holiday. It is essential to go there with an open mind, and to be aware that the tourism infrastructure – although very slowly improving in that a handful of good quality lodges and hotels have opened fairly recently – remains modest at best. Some roads are in reasonable shape, while others are rutted and in need of repair. Temperatures vary considerably, particularly in the highlands where during the day you might experience blazing sunshine, but just after nightfall it can quickly plummet to below freezing so pack accordingly. Taking insect repellent to the churches and cathedrals – even those in Addis – is worthwhile because of fleas in the carpets. Guides are generally very personable and can provide you with a wealth of information.

Rainbow Tours have been providing expert advice and tailor-made tours to Ethiopia for over a decade. Focusing on comfortable adventure, Rainbow's trips are aimed at allowing travellers to experience the best of the country's highlights in the time they have available, led by experienced guides. We spoke with Derek Schuurman of the company.

℡ 0207 666 1250 Ⓔ info@rainbowtours.co.uk
Ⓦ www.rainbowtours.co.uk

buildings and offices, are less than promising. Once you're settled in, however, Assaita is not without interest: overwhelmingly Muslim and defiantly rustic, the town centre has an atmosphere and architectural mood quite unlike anywhere else in Ethiopia, and it is an excellent place for contacts with **Afar people**, particularly on Tuesday when the main **market** is held.

The end of the road as far as public transport is concerned, Assaita is the only possible springboard for exploring the upper reaches of the **Awash River**, which empties into a chain of half-a-dozen shallow lakes, of which the largest, and last, is **Lake Abbe** on the border with Djibouti. The deep blue lakes, fringed by lush salt-tolerant vegetation and surrounded by high mountains, support dense populations of **hippos** and **crocodiles**, and also form one of the most important **water-bird sites** in Ethiopia, attracting large flocks of Palaearctic migrants during the European winter.

East of Assaita, the surfaced Assab road passes through some fascinating scenery, dominated by ancient lava flows and bizarre volcanic outcrops, before reaching the small town of **Dichioto**. This is the one stretch of the Assab road where you're likely to see much **wildlife** – for instance, Soemmerring's gazelle, Hamadryas baboon and Somali ostrich – and it also passes a few small lakes where **Afar pastoralists** bring their camels to water. Dichioto, an odd settlement of brightly painted corrugated-iron buildings with large balconies, is the last Ethiopian town before the Djibouti border, and a popular stopover with truck drivers, giving it an unexpectedly shiftless, seedy atmosphere. But it is worth continuing past Dichioto into the **Eli Dar Depression**, which is the most accessible of several salt lakes in Afar, reached by a spectacular descent of evocatively barren rocky slopes with the lake shimmering off-white below.

Danakil Depression

The Danakil (or Dallol) Depression, which straddles the Eritrean border to the north of Assaita and the east of the Tigraian Highlands, is officially the hottest place on earth, with an average temperature of 34–35°C. Much of this vast and practically unpopulated region lies below sea level, dipping to a frazzled nadir of -116m at Dallol, near Lake Asale, the lowest spot of terra firma on the African continent. One of the driest and most tectonically active areas on the planet, the Danakil is an area of singular geological fascination: a strange lunar landscape studded with more than 30 active or dormant volcanoes, malodorous sulphur-caked hot springs, solidified black lava flows and vast salt-encrusted basins.

(EL)

The Afar

The oldest of Ethiopia's ethnic groups, the Afar (or Danakil) have occupied their inhospitably arid homeland to the east of the Ethiopian Highlands for thousands of years. Until the 20th century, Afar country effectively served as Ethiopia's mint, producing the *amoles* (salt bars) that have served as currency in the highlands since Axumite times. These salt bars still form a major item of trade for the Afar people, who transport them by camelback along ancient caravan routes connecting the remote salt pans of the Danakil to Mekele and elsewhere in Tigrai. Traditionally, the Afar are nomadic pastoralists, living in light, flimsy houses made of palm fronds and matting, which they transport from one location to the next. Recent decades have seen a trend towards urbanisation around Assaita, as well as an increased dependence on agriculture. Nevertheless, the nomadic lifestyle is still widely practised and visitors will often see Afar men – taller and darker than most Ethiopians, with wild Afro-styled hair and a light cotton toga, which is draped over one shoulder – driving their precious camel herds along the roadside.

The most regularly visited volcano in the Danakil is **Erta Ale**, the most active volcano in Africa, which has been in a state of continuous eruption since 1967, with nested craters that have hosted a permanent lava lake for at least 120 years. One of the most alluring and physically challenging off-the-beaten-track goals in Ethiopia, Erta Ale can be ascended by foot or on camelback along a shadeless three to four hour track from the village of El Dom – ideally at around 03.00 so that your arrival at the peak coincides with the sunrise.

Danakil travel warning

In January 2012, a group of foreign tourists was attacked by gunmen approximately 30km from the Ethiopian–Eritrean border, near the site of the Erta Ale Volcano. The attack resulted in the death of five tourists. Two others were injured and four people, including two tourists, a local driver and a police escort, were kidnapped. This region is a high-risk area and has been the subject of Foreign Office warnings for a number of years. In 2007, a group including British Embassy staff from Addis Ababa was taken hostage in the region and released a week later, and in 2004 a French tourist disappeared without a trace. Before arranging any visit to Danakil or the Afar region, we urge you to contact your embassy for up-to-date information or to enquire the issue with the tourist office in Addis Ababa.

The 100km² **Lake Afrera**, 30km southeast of Erta Ale, is a highly saline body of water fed by thermal springs that rise on its eastern shores. It lies at an altitude of 103m below sea level, and the solitary island in the southern half of the lake (which goes by the rather apt name of Deset) is listed as the lowest-lying in the world. A stunning apparition, its emerald-green waters are overshadowed by the looming black basalt of mounts Borale and Afrera, dormant volcanoes that respectively rise to 812m and 1,295m above its eastern and southern shores. Afrera is also known as Lake Giulietti, in honour of Italian explorer Giuseppe

Erte Ale is the most active volcano in Africa. (V/S)

Maria Giulietti, whose pioneering 1881 expedition to the Danakil was curtailed when his entire party was slaughtered by Afar tribesmen.

Further north, the abandoned phosphate-mining encampment of **Dallol** is the lowest point of the depression and is set amid a surreal multi-hued field of sulphurous **hot springs** studded with steaming conical vents, strange ripple-like rock formations, and sprinkled with a rather adhesive coarse orange deposit that looks rather like dyed icing sugar. Try to get here in the early morning, when the light is fantastic and the temperature not too unbearable. **Lake Asale**, some 13km from Dallol, is an important centre of **salt-mining activity**, with literally hundreds of Afar cameleers chipping at the salty crust to extract neat 30x40cm rectangular tablets.

Southern Rift Valley   241

Lake Ziway   241
Lake Langano and Abijatta-Shala National Park   243
Shashemene and surrounds   244
Hawassa   245
Dilla   247
Yabello and surrounds   248
Arba Minch, Nechisar and Chencha   248

Bale Mountains and surrounds   251

Adaba-Dodola Integrated Forest
   Management Project   251
Bale Mountains National Park   253
Goba and Robe   254
Sof Omar Caves   258
The Goba-Yabello road   259

South Omo   260

Karat-Konso   261
Weita, Key Afer and Koko   265
Arbore and Lake Chew Bahir   265
Hamer country: Turmi and Dimeka   267
Omorate   267
Murelle   268
Mago National Park   268
Jinka   270

10 Southern Ethiopia

Very different in character to the more heavily touristed north, the south of Ethiopia is better known for its natural attractions than its archaeological and historical sites. Geographically, it is dominated by the mid-altitude southern Rift Valley, where a string of six beautiful lakes, partially protected within the Abijatta-Shala and Nechisar national parks, is home to a wonderful diversity of birds and a more limited selection of mammals. To the east of this, the Bale Mountains, protected within an eponymous national park, support extensive forests as well as the world's largest expanse of Afro-alpine moorland, providing sanctuary to the endangered Ethiopian wolf and mountain nyala, and offering some fantastic opportunities for of-the-beaten-track rambling. The south is also no slouch on the cultural front: archaeological treasures include the Manchiti rock engravings, while the legendary South Omo region is home to a dozen different animist tribes whose traditional lifestyle and striking body adornments scarcely acknowledge that the 20th century ever happened.

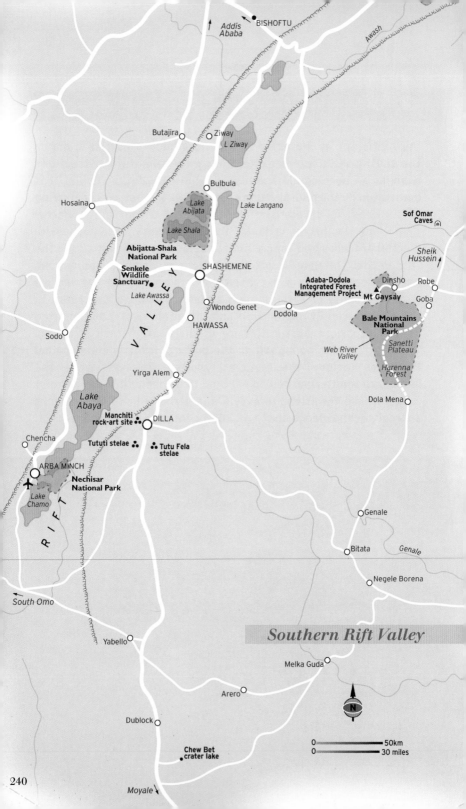

BISHOFTU

Addis Ababa

Awash

Butajira

Ziway

L Ziway

Bulbula

Lake Abijata

Lake Langano

Hosaina

Lake Shala

Abijatta-Shala National Park

Senkele Wildlife Sanctuary

SHASHEMENE

Sof Omar Caves

Sheik Hussein

Dinsho

Robe

Adaba-Dodola Integrated Forest Management Project

Mt Gaysay

Goba

Lake Awassa

Wondo Genet

Dodola

Bale Mountains National Park

V A L L E Y

HAWASSA

Sanetti Plateau

Sodo

Web River Valley

Harenna Forest

Yirga Alem

Lake Abaya

Dola Mena

Manchiti rock-art site

DILLA

Chencha

Tututi stelae

Tutu Fela stelae

ARBA MINCH

Nechisar National Park

Genale

Lake Chamo

Bitata

Genale

R I F T

Negele Borena

South Omo

Yabello

Southern Rift Valley

Melka Guda

Arero

N

Dublock

Dublock

0   50km

0   30 miles

Chew Bet crater lake

Moyale

Southern Rift Valley

Relatively hot and low-lying, the southern half of the Rift Valley is perhaps the most archetypically African part of Ethiopia, supporting a characteristic cover of scrubby acacia woodland and inhabited by the like of the Oromo and Borena, who – unlike their northern and eastern compatriots – are either traditional animists or relatively recent converts to Islam or Christianity. Generally drier than highland Ethiopia, the southern Rift is an important agricultural region, and several of its larger towns lie alongside one or other of the six lakes that form its main tourist focus. It also supports a rare ornithological wealth, from the stunning flamingo and pelican flocks associated with the lakes, to the more esoteric presence of some of the country's most localised endemics, especially around Yabello. Cultural highlights include the Borena singing wells at Dublock, and the broodingly mysterious stelae fields in the forested highlands around Dilla.

Southern Rift Valley highlights

Lake Ziway

Also known as Lake Dambal, this shallow 430km² body lies about 160km south of Addis Ababa, where its western shore is readily accessible from the small but well-equipped town of the same name. Ringed by steep volcanic hills, Ziway is fed by two major rivers, and it supports an abundance of tilapias that not only feed its rich birdlife but provide a good source of protein to the townspeople. Excellent **birdwatching** can be undertaken from town, where a raised causeway and jetty fringed by papyrus marsh might easily yield 50-plus species over a couple of hours – from a variety of waterfowl, pelicans and storks to the localised lesser moorhen and lesser jacana. Look out too for the black egret, also known as the 'umbrella bird' due to its habit of fishing with its wings raised to form a canopy.

Lake Ziway supports a fair number of **hippos**, which are occasionally visible from the jetty, but more likely to

The black egret or 'umbrella bird' (IY/FLPA)

Practicalities

There are no longer any **flights** serving towns in the southern Rift Valley, so it can only be explored **by road**. The main roads in the region are surfaced and can be covered in any vehicle, but a 4x4 may be required to visit sites of

Accommodation

Upmarket
Aregash Lodge Yirga Alem; 30km south of Dilla Ⓦ www.aregashlodge.com
Hawassa Lakeside Hotels Hawassa Ⓦ www.wabeshebellehotels.com.et
Bishangari Lodge Langano Ⓦ www.bishangari.com
Sabana Lodge Langano Ⓦ www.sabanalangano.com. See advert, page 271.
Swayne's Hotel Arba Minch Ⓦ www.swayneshotel.com
Wabe Shebelle Hotel Wondo Genet Ⓦ www.wabeshebellehotels.com.et
Wenney Eco-Lodge Langano Ⓦ www.wenneyecolodge.com

Moderate
Bekele Molla Hotel Arba Minch Ⓦ www.bekelemollahotels.com
Bekele Molla Hotel Langano Ⓦ www.bekelemollahotels.com
Lakeside Motel Hawassa Ⓣ 046 221 0337/4449
Lily of the Valley Hotel Shashemene Ⓔ lilyofthevalleyhotel@yahoo.com
Wabe Shebelle Resort Hotel Langano Ⓦ www.wabeshebellehotels.com.et

Budget
Arba Minch Hotel Arba Minch Ⓣ 046 881 0206

be seen by taking a boat to one of their more regular haunts. Another worthwhile boat excursion is to the **island of Tullo Guddo** (an Oromo name meaning 'Large Mountain'), which rises about 300m above the lake surface and is clearly visible from the mainland. The island is the site of the **Monastery of Maryam Tsion**, which was reputedly founded during the 9th century by refugee priests from Axum, who brought with them the Ark of the Covenant to keep it safe from Queen Yodit, and stowed it there for 70 years. This tradition is backed up by similarity of the local Zay tongue to Tigrigna, and by the ancient Ge'ez manuscripts, most famously a 14th-century Sinkesar containing vivid illustrations of 19 popular saints, that are stored among the church's treasures.

interest that lie off the main road – for instance Abijatta-Shala, the west shore of Langano, Nechisar, Chencha, and the archaeological sites around Dilla. There are **internet** and **banking facilities** in larger towns such as Hawassa, Arba Minch, Dilla and Ziway.

Bekele Molla Hotel Ziway Ⓦ www.bekelemollahotels.com
Gebre Kristos Hotel Hawassa Ⓣ 046 220 2780-1
Lalibela Pension Dilla Ⓣ 046 331 2300
New Bekele Molla Hotel Shashemene Ⓦ www.bekelemollahotels.com
Tourist Hotel Ziway Ⓣ 046 441 3994
Yabello Motel Yabello Ⓣ 046 446 0789

Eating out

Most towns have a few decent restaurants. In **Ziway**, the **Tourist Hotel** serves excellent fish cutlets and has a good vegetarian selection. All the lodges on **Langano** serve adequate to good Western food, while the **New Bekele Molla** is a reliable bet in **Shashemene**, though the town also has a good selection of local eateries. **Hawassa** is also well served, the standout being the **Dolce Vita Restaurant**, which dishes up some of the best Italian food in Ethiopia. The **Rendezvous Bar and Restaurant** is the best place to eat in **Dilla**. **Arba Minch** is famed for its fish cutlets: the **Soma Restaurant** probably takes top honours in terms of quality and value, but the **Bekele Molla Hotel** has the advantage of a spectacular view.

Lake Langano and Abijatta-Shala National Park

The 305km² **Lake Langano**, situated on the east side of the main road to Hawassa, almost 200km from Addis Ababa, is very well developed for tourism, though the upmarket and mid-range lodges along its shore cater primarily to weekenders from the capital, meaning that it tends to be far more relaxed on weekday nights. The main attraction is that the water is reportedly safe for swimming, with bilharzia supposedly being absent. The resorts also generally offer a variety of watersports at a price, as well as boat trips in search of hippos and crocodiles.

On the west side of the main road, opposite Langano, the 887km² **Abijatta-Shala National Park** protects the two lakes for which it is named. Separated by a 3km-wide sliver of hilly land, these two could

Lake Shala hot spring (AZ)

not be more different in character. The 410km² **Lake Shala**, nestled within a volcanic caldera that collapsed 3.5 million years ago, is up to 266m in parts, and its surface is studded with volcanically formed islands. By contrast, the more northerly **Lake Abijatta** is a brackish 200km² pan, nowhere more than 14m deep, and surrounded by tightly cropped grass flats exposed by a recent drop in its water level. Much of the national park was settled and cultivated during the last years of the Derg, and large mammals are scarce: a few Grant's gazelle live in virtual captivity at the ostrich farm next to the main entrance gate, and Anubis baboon, greater kudu, black-backed jackal and spotted hyena might also be present. The **birdlife**, however, is fantastic, with up to 300,000 flamingos congregating on Abijatta at the end of the rains, along with many thousands of migrant waders. Also of interest on the northeast corner of Lake Shala is a steamy **hot spring** whose reputed healing powers attract large numbers of local bathers.

Shashemene and surrounds

The most important travel crossroads in southern Ethiopia, Shashemene stands 250km south of Addis Ababa at the junction of the roads running south towards the Kenyan border, southwest to Arba Minch, and east to Bale National Park. It has little going for it other than its logistical convenience, and it is the one town in Ethiopia that consistently draws negative feedback from travellers due to the high level of verbal abuse that is its trademark, as well as a reputation for (non-violent) crime. The town's one attraction is the **Black Lion Museum**, which documents the religious and cultural roots of the Jamaica Rastafarian community, founded here by a group of Jamaican devotees of Haile Selassie during the later years of the emperor's reign.

About 20km southeast of Shashemene, Wondo Genet is the site of a popular **hot-springs resort** founded during the Haile Selassie era in a setting of lushly forested hills. The resort gardens support Anubis baboon, colobus monkey and grivet monkey, while the juniper-covered slopes behind are home to raucous flocks of silvery-cheeked hornbill, the beautiful Narina trogon and white-cheeked turaco, along with a host of forest birds. Another worthwhile goal in the vicinity of Shashemene, situated to the south of the Arba Minch road, is the 58km² **Senkele Wildlife Sanctuary**, which supports the world's largest extant population of the formerly widespread Swayne's hartebeest, along with the greater kudu, oribi, waterbuck, warthog and common jackal.

Hawassa

The capital of the snappily entitled Southern Nations, Nationalities and Peoples' Region, Hawassa is the largest town in the Ethiopian Rift Valley, supporting a population of 140,000, and its compact but attractive centre has an unusually modern character. In addition to being something of a route crossroads, situated only 25km south of Shashemene, it is a very pleasant place to spend a night or two, with a scenic location on the eastern shore of **Lake Hawassa**, a 90km² freshwater body set in an ancient volcanic caldera. The dense scrub and fig woodland along

Tips on birding in the south

Even if you're not a birding enthusiast, prepare to be stunned when you travel to the south. Over 800 spectacular species can be viewed throughout Ethiopia, but for the novice birder, the numerous and beautiful birds in the south are easier to spot and appreciate than elsewhere in the country. Ask your guide to stop at any of the Rift Valley lakes along the main roads or any other birding site. You'll be grateful if you pack a small pair of binoculars for your trip.

In conversation with ...
Abeba Tours Ethiopia

What kind of involvement do your tours have with local Ethiopian communities?

We firmly believe that tourism should support the local communities and are constantly researching new ways to get involved with community-based projects. We have partnered with a few worthwhile organisations to give our guests the opportunity to make donations or to volunteer. Most recently, we have joined the Ethiopia Travelers Philanthropy Program, which has created innovative ways for guests to leave a positive impact during their travels.

Can you describe an example itinerary that gives a good range of experiences in Ethiopia?

We have an amazing 28-day programme that visits the north, east and south, and which really allows the visitor to experience the diversity of Ethiopia's history and culture. For people with less time, we recommend an intinerary with fewer destinations. Remember – travel in Ethiopia can be slow; distances are long and roads are full of... life. Take your time, enjoy the journey and remember to save something for your next visit.

What are your top tips for visiting and travelling to the Omo Valley?

Remember that you are visiting villages where people genuinely live; they are not set up for tourists but are actual homes. Recognise that each tribe has adapted to tourism in its own way, indicative of their own personalities and culture. To be respectful, always ask before taking someone's photo and agree a price before clicking the shutter. While we understand the desire to have photographic souvenirs, we encourage guests to put their cameras away, if only briefly, and to appreciate these amazing people and try to see life from their perspective.

Abeba Tours Ethiopia was started in 2007 by an Ethiopian-American couple with a passion for travel and a deep love for Ethiopia. They are committed to designing each tour programme with great care and expertise to ensure a unique and rewarding experience for every visitor to Ethiopia. We spoke to Tania O'Connor of the company.

ⓣ 011 515 9530/31 ⓔ info@abebatoursethiopia.com
ⓦ www.abebatoursethiopia.com

246

the lakeshore supports an astonishing variety of birds, as well as semi-habituated troops of colobus and grivet monkey, and it can be explored along an elevated dyke (built to prevent flooding when the water rises) that doubles as a walking trail, running for a couple of kilometres south and north of the town centre. Also worth a visit is the open **central market**, which draws colourful Oromo villagers from all around on Mondays and Thursdays.

Dilla

Situated 90km south of Hawassa, Dilla is an important agricultural business centre, known for the production of high-quality coffee beans. It is set amid verdant fertile hills, where indigenous forest patches are interspersed with rustic homesteads and small enset (false banana) plantations. It is also the base for exploring some of the most intriguing archaeological sites in southern Ethiopia. The most accessible of these, situated about 8km from the town centre, is the **Manchiti rock art site**, a 3,000-year-old engraving of around 50 stylised cattle moving herd-like along a vertical rock face. About 20km out of town, the **Tutu Fela stelae field** comprises 300 densely concentrated medieval stelae whose phallic shape is reinforced by the presence of clear circumcision marks near the top. Further south, the more dispersed **Tututi stelae field** consists of 1,200 mostly collapsed stelae, including one that measures 7.55m from base to top, the tallest stele known from southern Ethiopia.

Tutu Fela stelae field (AZ)

Yabello and surrounds

Situated midway along the 400km strip of asphalt that runs southward from Dilla to the Kenyan border town of Moyale, Yabello is situated at the junction with the recently upgraded eastern route towards Konso and South Omo, and a rougher road running northeast to Negele Borena. It is a rather humdrum town except on Saturday, when its **weekly market** is attended by Borena pastoralists from miles around. An essential fixture on **birding** itineraries, Yabello is home to two of Africa's most range-restricted species, white-tailed swallow and Stresemann's bush crow, respectively described in 1938 and 1942, and both restricted to the arid acacia scrub within a 100km or so of Yabello. The area is also home to a selection of dry-country mammals, including the diminutive dik-dik and long-necked gerenuk. About 65km south of Yabello, the village of **Dublock** is the site of two so-called '**singing wells**', a name that refers to the Borena tradition of forming a chanting human chain to haul buckets of water from the well to its lip. Another 35km southeast of Dublock, the saline lake known as **Chew Bet** ('Salt House') is an inky-black apparition with a starkly beautiful setting at the base of a 200m-deep crater.

Saline lake, Chew Bet (EL)

Arba Minch, Nechisar and Chencha

One of the country's most attractively sited towns, **Arba Minch** (literally 'Forty Springs') stands at the base of a mountainous stretch of the Rift Valley escarpment overlooking lakes Chamo and Abaya. In addition to being the most popular gateway to the South Omo region, this unassuming town lies at the entrance to the 514km² **Nechisar National Park**, which protects parts of the two aforementioned lakes, the mountainous **Egzer Dilday** ('Bridge of God') that divides them, a lush groundwater forest close to town, and the white-grass **Nechisar Plains** on the opposite shore. The groundwater forest, which can be explored on foot, is the site of the **hot-water springs** for which the town

Beehive-like dwelling of the
Dorze people (EL)

Lake Chamo falls within the boundaries of the Nechisar National Park (SS)

is named and it also supports plenty of monkeys, birds and other forest wildlife. The best area for game viewing, accessible by 4x4 only, is the open Nechisar Plain, which large numbers of plains zebra, along with Grant's gazelle, Swayne's hartebeest and greater kudu, and is also the only known locale for the nocturnal Nechisar nightjar, the first live specimen of which was seen here as recently as 2009.

The **Arba Minch Crocodile Farm**, 6km out of town near Lake Abaya, keeps around 8,000 crocodiles (with an age range of one to six years) hatched from eggs taken from the lake, though a proportion are regularly reintroduced to keep the natural population healthy. Far more impressive, but only accessible by boat, is Lake Chamo's so-called **Crocodile Market**, a stretch of shore where hundreds of these large reptiles naturally congregate in the sun.

A very different attraction in the Arba Minch area is **Chencha**, a small town that lies at an altitude of 2,900m in the Guge Hills, 37km north of Arba Minch by road, and reached by a dramatic series of switchbacks that climbs 1,600m over 22km. Chencha is home to the **Dorze people**, renowned cotton weavers whose tall beehive-shaped dwellings are among the most distinctive traditional structures to be seen anywhere in Africa, constructed from organic material on a moveable scaffold of bamboo sticks, and measuring up to 6m tall (comparable to a two-storey building). One hut will generally serve a married couple for a lifetime – should the base start to rot or become infested by termites, the entire structure can be lifted up and relocated.

Bale Mountains and surrounds

The highlight, in every sense, of the moist green uplands southeast of the Rift Valley is Bale Mountains National Park, which protects the upper reaches of the eponymous range, including the country's second-highest peak, the 4,377m Tullo Demtu. Bale is the best place to see a broad cross-section of Ethiopia's **endemic mammal** and **bird species**, including the alluring Ethiopian wolf, and its upper reaches can be crossed using the only road in Africa to cross the 4,000m contour, making it accessible to relatively sedentary tour groups. Bale is also one of two prime **hiking** attractions in this region, the other being the recently developed hiking and trekking circuit near the small towns of Adaba and Dodola. Other important attractions in the vicinity include the sacred **Sof Omar Caves**, carved by the Web River in the lowlands east of Bale, and – especially for ornithologists – the remote road that runs from Bale to Yabello via Negele Borena, offering an opportunity to tick several endemic birds with a highly localised distribution.

Bale Mountains and surrounds highlights

Adaba-Dodola Integrated Forest Management Project

Based out of the otherwise unprepossessing highland town of Dodola, set at an altitude of 2,400m a few kilometres past the junction of the roads from Asela and Shashemene, this elaborate network of mountain huts, tented camps and walking trails offers some of the best **hiking** and **horseback trekking** in the country. The project was established in 1998 with the support of the German non-profit group GTZ, and the

---

Amazing Ethiopia

Southern Ethiopia is famed for its colourful markets and seldom-visited tribal villages. We recommend that you visit at least one market during your stay here, perhaps either Dimeka or Key Afer. These markets are not significant for the products on sale but rather as an opportunity to see grand gatherings of local tribes, from the Hamer to the Karo people. This is a wonderful opportunity to witness the unique nature of each individual culture up close.

scenic trails range from a 30-minute walk out of town to the attractive Lensho Waterfall, to a week-long hike through slopes lined with juniper

Practicalities

The main regional transport hub is the former regional capital **Goba**. There are no longer any scheduled **flights** here from Addis Ababa, which means that the only option is to travel **by road**, a trip that can be undertaken in one very long day, using one of two routes, either through the Arsi Highlands via the substantial but little-touristed town of Asela, or through the Rift Valley via Shashemene. The better route is via the Rift Valley, since it is surfaced as far as Shashemene and (assuming you are able to give it longer than a day) it can be broken up with overnight stops at the Rift Valley lakes or Wondo Genet.

These two routes to Goba converge close to **Dodola**, the base for treks into the **Adaba-Dodola Integrated Forest Management Project**. The road then passes through **Dinsho** (site of the Bale Mountains National Park headquarters) and Robe (at the junction town for Sof Omar) before it arrives at Goba. **Hikes** and **treks** into all parts of Bale Mountains National Park, including the Sanetti Plateau (the main haunt of Bale's Ethiopian wolves), must be arranged at the park headquarters at Dinsho. These range from one to five days in duration, the most popular option being a three-day horseback trek or hike to the Sanetti Plateau, which allows you plenty of time to explore the alpine moorland and all but guarantees a sighting of Ethiopian wolf. However, if you want to visit the **Sanetti Plateau** by road, vehicle access is not from Dinsho, but in fact lies another hour past Goba along the road towards Dola Mena.

Banking and **internet facilities** are very limited in this part of the country, even in Goba.

Accommodation

Moderate

Bekele Molla Hotel (Robe) ⓦ www.bekelemollahotels.com
Wabe Shebelle Hotel (Goba) ⓦ www.wabeshebellehotels.com.et

Budget

Bale Mountain Hotel (Dodola) ① 022 660 0016
Changeti Camp (near Dodola) ① 022 666 0700
Dinsho Lodge (Dinsho HQ, Bale Mountain National Park)
Yilma Amossa Hotel (Goba) ① 022 661 0482

and other coniferous forests trees, including a few giants thought to be more than 500 years old. The forests protect a similar composition of birds to that found at Dinsho, including plenty of endemics, alongside vervet and colobus monkeys and relict populations of Ethiopian wolf, mountain nyala and Menelik's bushbuck. Treks and hikes must be arranged at the Eco-Tourism Guides Association Office in Dodola (Ⓦ www.baletrek.com).

Bale Mountains National Park (AZ)

Bale Mountains National Park

Extending for 2,200km² across the upper reaches of the Bale Mountains, this scenic national park is most notable perhaps for the wild windswept scenery of the misty, heather-strewn **Sanetti Plateau**, a vast tract of Afro-alpine moorland set almost entirely above the 4,000m contour. Formed by volcanic activity around 10 million years ago, these chilly highlands supported glacial activity until as recently as 2,000 years ago, and they still receive the occasional snowfall and feed more than 40 streams, most of which eventually converge with the Juba or Wabe Shebelle rivers *en route* to the Somali coastline. In addition to the Afro-alpine moorland, the slope of Bale protect some the country's largest stands of coniferous juniper-hagenia forest, interspersed with open grassy meadows and swampy valleys, while lush broadleaved Afro-montane forest swathes the southern footslopes below the Harenna escarpment. Unusually for Africa's taller mountains, Bale is accessible by road or horseback as well as to hikers. Despite this, it remains sufficiently out of the way that very few travellers make it there by comparison with, say, the Simiens.

Scenery aside, Bale protects a very diverse fauna, including more endemic vertebrate species than any other site in Ethiopia, and breeding populations of several Palaearctic birds found nowhere else in Africa. The two main tourist foci are the **Dinsho Park Headquarters**, which are bypassed by the main road between Addis Ababa and Goba, and the **Sanetti Plateau**, which lies about 45 minutes south of Goba along a high-altitude all-weather road originally built by the Derg to provide an alternative emergency access route to the south. Dinsho is the easiest point of access using public transport, and the surrounding forest is the best place in Ethiopia to see mountain nyala and Menelik's bushbuck, alongside several endemic birds associated with forest habitats. Sanetti, by contrast, is the best place to see the charismatic Ethiopian wolf, along with Palaearctic refugees such as the golden eagle and chough, and localised water birds ranging from the wattled crane and blue-winged goose to ruddy shelduck and spot-throated plover.

Goba and Robe

Set 13km apart along the road between Dinsho and the Sanetti Plateau, Goba and Robe are the region's largest towns, but neither exactly distinguishes itself in any other respect. **Robe**, which you'll reach first coming from the direction of Dinsho, has adequate facilities, straggling for a couple of kilometres along a eucalyptus-lined main road, but it comes across as unusually subdued and nondescript, though the hectic Thursday **market** is worth a look. **Goba**, the capital of Bale region, is more open and spacious, set at an altitude of 2,500m on the chilly slopes below the Sanetti Plateau. Either town makes a useful base for exploring the Bale region, but unless you are genuinely masochistic, best sleep (and eat) at the hotels listed above – the alternatives are uniformly dire!

Exploration of Bale Mountains

Surprisingly, given its accessibility today, the Bale range was one of the last parts of Africa to attract serious scientific explorations. The earliest-recorded visitor to the Sanetti Plateau was the German naturalist Carl van Erlanger, who traversed it in 1899, discovering the giant mole-rat in the process. Oddly, however, van Erlanger didn't encounter either of the large mammals for which the range is now renowned. The mountain nyala – Africa's most recently discovered large ungulate species – was first described in 1910 based on a specimen shot by Major Buxton in the Arsi area two years earlier, while the Ethiopian wolf, as its Latin name *Canis simensis* suggests, was then largely associated with the Simien Mountains in northern Ethiopia.

No known scientific expedition to the upper slopes of Bale was documented between 1899 and the late 1950s, which is when the Finnish geographer Helmer Smels made several visits to the area, and discovered that the mountains hosted a previously unsuspected population of the rare Ethiopian wolf. It was the British naturalist Leslie Brown, upon visiting Bale in 1963, who first recognised that it might actually be the wolf's main stronghold, and who also discovered it hosted large numbers of mountain nyala, and proposed that the area be set aside as a national park. And while the Sanetti Plateau and northern slopes are now well documented in scientific terms, the vast broadleaved Harenna Forest on the southern slopes received no scientific attention whatsoever until the early 1990s, since when it has yielded half-a-dozen new and presumably endemic species of small mammal, reptile and amphibian.

Mountain nyala, Bale Mountains
National Park (SS)

Around Bale

The following are the five key sites for hiking and wildlife viewing in Bale National Park:

Dinsho Park Headquarters

Set in a fragrant stand of juniper forest, the area immediately around Dinsho can be explored along a short but highly productive walking trail which leads through an area that protects the world's densest population of mountain nyala. It's not unusual to come across four or five herds of this handsome antelope on one walk, and other mammals you can expect to see here include Menelik's bushbuck, warthog, reedbuck and possibly colobus monkeys. Birdwatching is superb, with the endemic white-cheeked turaco, black-winged lovebird, white-backed black tit, Abyssinian catbird, Abyssinian slaty flycatcher, thick-billed raven and white-collared pigeon all present. An unusual plant of the Dinsho area is the white-flowered Abyssinian rose, the only flowering rose that is indigenous to Africa.

Gaysay extension

This northerly extension, traversed by the main road between Dodola and Dinsho, protects the eminently climbable 3,543m Mount Gaysay, and is home to large concentrations of mountain nyala and Menelik's bushbuck. At least one pack of Ethiopian wolf has a territory centred on Gaysay, and marshy areas support birds more normally associated with the Sanetti Plateau, most visibly Rouget's rail, which is very common.

Web River Valley

Set at an elevation of roughly 3,500m, about 10km southwest of Dinsho, the Web Valley supports a moorland inhabited by abundant small rodents, making it ideal Ethiopian wolf territory, several packs of which are resident and easily seen. The rough 11km track between Dinsho and the Web Valley involves crossing a natural rock bridge over the Danka River where rock hyrax are frequently observed. There is an attractive waterfall at the confluence of the Web and Wolla rivers.

Sanetti Plateau

The world's largest expanse of Afro-alpine moorland, some 45 minutes' drive south of Goba, but 1,300m higher in altitude, the Sanetti Plateau supports the most substantial extant population of Ethiopian wolf, which are seen singly or in pairs by most visitors, sniffing out small rodents before they scurry to the safety of their burrows. Other characteristic mammals are klipspringer, Abyssinian hare and the endemic giant mole-rat. It supports an ethereal mix of clumped grey heather, lichen-covered rocks, and weird stands of giant lobelia, which grow up to 3m high and whose corky bark and waxen leaves readily withstand extreme sub-zero temperatures. On the ascent road from Goba, look out for alpine chat, black-headed siskin, moorland and chestnut

Abyssinian hare (JK)

francolin, and Rouget's rail. The plateau's plentiful tarns are good for the blue-winged goose, wattled ibis and spot-throated plover. The plateau also supports sub-Saharan Africa's only breeding populations of ruddy shelduck, golden eagle and the crow-like chough.

Harenna Forest

At the southern end of the Sanetti Plateau, the Harenna escarpment affords an astounding view over the forest almost 2,000m below. The road then switchbacks exhilaratingly to the base of the escarpment, where the green heather suddenly transforms to a Grimm Brothers' forest of low gnarled trees laden with moss and swathed in old-man's beard. Before 1983, when this road was cut, this area was virtually unknown to science: but recent expeditions have found several previously undescribed vertebrate species, and many others still doubtless await discovery. A wealth of birds includes the endemic white-backed black tit, Abyssinian catbird, Abyssinian woodpecker, Ethiopian oriole, yellow-fronted parrot and the taxonomically uncertain brown saw-wing swallow. Mammals likely to be seen from the main road include olive baboon, guereza monkey, bushbuck and bushpig. The forest is also home to the recently discovered but seldom seen Bale monkey.

Harenna Forest (AZ)

Sof Omar Caves (AZ)

Sof Omar Caves

This vast network of limestone caverns, reputedly the largest in Africa, lies 100km – about four hours' bumpy drive – east of the Bale range at an elevation of 1,300m. It has been carved by the Web River, which descends from the Bale highlands to the flat, arid plains that stretch towards the Somali border. Following the course of the clear aquamarine Web River underground for some 16km, the caves are reached through a vast portal, which leads into the Chamber of Columns, a cathedral-like hall supported by limestone pillars that stand up to 20m tall. A 1.7km trail leads from the entrance through several other chambers, taking about an hour to walk and crossing the river seven times. The caves are named after Sheikh Sof Omar, a 12th-century Muslim leader who used them as a refuge, and they remain an important site of pilgrimage for Ethiopian Muslims. The area is also regularly visited by **birdwatchers** as one of two sites where it's reasonably easy to see the endemic Salvadori's serin. Note that the area around Sof Omar is prone to outbreaks of local faction fighting, so best enquire about security at Bale before heading out this way.

The Goba-Yabello road

Popular with dedicated **birding** tours, this long and rough route through some of Ethiopia's most spectacular and remote scenery offers the opportunity to see several avian endemics unrecorded elsewhere, but you need the best part of a week to cover it. The most scenic stretch is the initial 110km, which traverses the wildlife-rich Sanetti Plateau and Harenna Forest (see box, *Around Bale*, page 256) en

Wattled crane (AZ)

route to the dusty and anti-climatic town of **Dola Mena**. From here, it is 180km to **Negele Borena**, passing through Genale, where the riparian forest along the banks of the eponymous river is renowned as a reliable site for the mysterious and very beautiful **Prince Raspoli's turaco**. Negele Borena itself is something of a frontier town, a cultural boiling pot that is predominantly Oromo but also has strong Somali and Borena influences, making it quite unlike anywhere else in Ethiopia.

From Negele Borena, follow the Bogol Manyo road 15km southeast to the junction for the Yabello road. This intersection is the best place to look for the **Sidamo lark**, a taxonomically controversial endemic first collected in 1968. About 10km southwest of the junction, the Yabello road skirts the Mankubsa-Welenso Forest, an unusually low-lying patch of open-canopy juniper woodland where Prince Raspoli's turaco and **Salvadori's serin** occur sparsely. After another 100km, immediately past Melka Guda, the Dawa River Bridge is a reliable place to pick up two species whose ranges are otherwise restricted to Somalia: **white-winged turtle dove** and **Juba weaver**. Some 60km past Melka Guda, Arero lies close to the most southerly forest in Ethiopia, another good site for Prince Ruspoli's turaco and **Salvadori's seedeater**, both of which are fairly common. Past Arero, a wide variety of dry-country species includes **Stresemann's bush crow** and **white-tailed swallow**, endemics whose ranges are confined to the vicinity of Yabello.

Prince Ruspoli's turaco (HTCRI)

259

South Omo

Nothing in highland Ethiopia prepares one for South Omo. Nor, for that matter, does much else in modern Africa. Descending from the green, urbane highlands into the low-lying plains of South Omo feels like a journey not merely through space, but also through time, into something close to an Africa untouched by outside influences. Four of Africa's major linguistic groups are represented here, with the so-called Omotic-speakers being unique to the region. The most renowned of the region's many animist tribes are the Mursi, famed for their practice of inserting large clay plates behind the lower lips of their women, while other cultural groups such as the Hamer, Karo and Ari practice adornments such as body scarring and body painting, and the hairstyles associated with the region are simply outrageous. It seems facile to label South Omo as a living museum. Yet in many senses, that is exactly what it is – and while travel in this remote corner of Ethiopia tends to

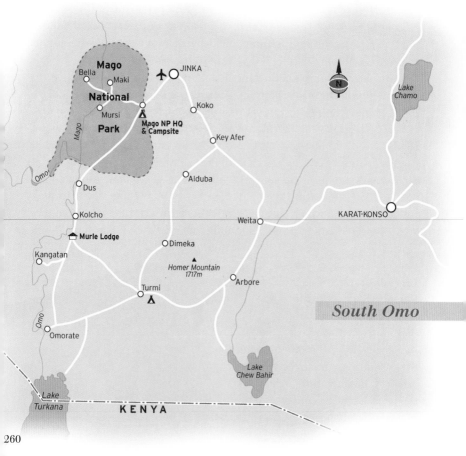

run a lot less smoothly than in the highlands, it is a truly educational once-in-a-lifetime experience. See *Chapter 1, People* and culture, page 29 for more information on the people of South Omo.

South Omo highlights

Karat-Konso

Set at an altitude of 1,650m on the banks of the seasonal Segen River, tiny Karat-Konso, the funnel through which all road traffic into South Omo must pass, is dominated by a traffic roundabout of comically vast dimensions, surrounded by a sprawl of dusty lanes lined with scruffy, low-rise buildings. It is also the principal town of the unique **Konso**

Boys from the Karo tribe take in the South Omo views. (EL)

Practicalities

Travel in South Omo is limited by seasonal factors, thanks to the poor roads and treacherous black cotton soil typical of the region. Travel anywhere south of the main road between Karat-Konso and Jinka is strongly advised against during April and May, when the big rains usually fall. March or June can be problematic, and the short rains, generally in October, can also put a temporary hold on travel sometimes.

Jinka, though little more than an overgrown village in any other context, is the principal town of South Omo. It used to be an important staging post for fly-in trips to the region, but this has changed since Ethiopian Airlines cancelled its thrice-weekly scheduled flights there. **Organised tours** now generally drive to South Omo from Addis Ababa, a round trip to which you should allocate at least eight days, but ideally ten to 12, or fly to Arba Minch and travel by road from there, which would crop two to three days from the duration.

Either way, the **gateway town** to South Omo by road is **Karat-Konso**, which lies at the intersection of the only three access routes to the region. The best and most popular of these routes, tying in with itineraries that include **Nechisar National Park**, is the regularly graded 85km mixed asphalt and gravel road from Arba Minch, which takes up to three hours, with little to distract *en route*. A well-established alternative is the 105km road from Yabello, a decent gravel route that takes about three hours in normal conditions, but may require 4x4 after rain. Finally, there is the 175km all-weather dirt road from Fiseha Genet, which branches southwest from the main road between Addis Ababa and Moyale some 55km south of Dilla.

South Omo is an utterly fascinating place to visit, but do be warned that travel there sometimes feels more like hard work than fun. Conditions are basic, even by Ethiopian standards. The climate is hot and dusty, roads are poor,

Accommodation

Upmarket
Kanta Lodge (Karat-Konso) Ⓦ www.hesstravelethiopia.com
Murelle Explorer's Lodge (Murelle) Ⓦ www.ethiopianriftvalleysafaris.com

Moderate
Evangadi Lodge (Turmi) Ⓦ www.evangadilodge.com
Jinka Resort (Jinka) Ⓦ www.sites.google.com/site/jinkaresort
Turmi Lodge (Turmi) Ⓦ www.splendor.com.et

accommodation is mostly on the rudimentary side, food is at best indifferent, and facilities such as air conditioning are non-existent. In addition, tourism, though small scale, has nurtured a vociferous commercial element that can seriously detract from what would otherwise be a fascinating experience, and generate an uncomfortable sense of voyeurism (see box, *Photography*, page 267).

All private vehicles are stopped at the Weita Bridge, on the road between Karat-Konso and Jinka, and risk being turned back if a written **letter of authority** is not produced. If you are on an organised tour, the company should have this in their possession.

Banking and **internet facilities** are non-existent in this part of the country.

Market in Jinka (EL)

Budget
Goh Hotel (Jinka) ℡ 046 775 1033
Nasa Hotel (Key Afer) ℡ 046 775 6449
Strawberry Fields Eco-Lodge (Karat-Konso) ⓦ www.permalodge.org. See advert page 270.

people, who live in an isolated region of basalt hills flanked by the semi-desert Borena lowlands to the east and South Omo to the west. Mixed agriculturists, the Konso make the most of the hard, rocky slopes that characterise their relatively infertile homeland through a combination of rock terracing, crop rotation and hard work, with the most important crop – sorghum – being harvested twice annually.

A distinctive feature of Konso country is its **fortified hilltop villages**, labyrinthine and congested but readily defensible settlements enclosed by tall walls and accessible only via a few steep footpaths.

The closest traditional village to Karat-Konso is **Dekatu**, a self-standing walled settlement of 21 subcommunities set on the outskirts of the modern town. **Mecheke**, set on a hill 13km from Karat-Konso, is very photogenic and a lot more used to tourists, who are likely to be greeted by youngsters playing the *kehaita* (a local musical instrument). Judging by the number of generation poles, Mecheke is at least 400 years old, and it also has four groups of *waga* statues, some more than 150 years old. Smaller and less atmospheric than Mecheke, **Gesergiyo** is of interest primarily for an adjacent formation of sand pinnacles –

Konso communities

Every village is divided into several subcommunities, each centred upon a tall *mora* (communal house), where men, boys and girls (but not grown women) can relax and make important communal decisions. Konso society is structured around generation sets, inducted every 18 years when a new *Olahita* (generation pole) is erected in the ceremonial square (you can tell roughly how old any given village is by counting the number of poles). The Konso are also famous for the carved wooden statues, known as *waga*, that are erected at the graves of important men, and come complete with enlarged teeth made from animal bones – the latter creating a rather leery expression reinforced by the impressively proportioned penis the deceased typically clasps firmly in his hand.

A generation pole can be used to mark the age of a village – a new one is erected every 18 years. (EL)

A busy market in Key Afer (AZ)

sculpted by occasional water flow in a normally dry gorge – that bears a superficial resemblance to a row of skyscrapers, hence its nickname 'New York', a name that has stuck.

Weita, Key Afer and Koko

The scenic 205km road running west from Karat-Konso to Jinka, currently being upgraded to asphalt, passes through three villages of interest. First up, some 75km west of Karat-Konso, a few minutes' drive past a bridge across the eponymous river, is the rather impermanent looking village of **Weita**. Set in Tsemai territory, it is best visited on Sunday, when the busy **market** is also attended by Ari and Bana people. Much larger and more cosmopolitan, some 42km northwest of Weita, is **Key Afer**, which is dominated by the Ari but also hosts plenty of Bana and Hamer people, especially on Thursday, when its multi-cultural **market** is as colourful as any in the region. Finally, situated roughly halfway along the 40km stretch of road between Key Afer and Jinka, **Koko** is a small but attractive Ari village noted for its **Monday market**.

Arbore and Lake Chew Bahir

A 120km road runs southwest from Weita to the popular junction village of Turmi, passing through flat arid acacia scrub inhabited by the Tsemai in the north and the closely related Arbore in the south. This harsh landscape, thinly populated by pairs of Guenther's dik-dik and home to a variety of colourful dry-country birds, is dominated by the austere

Children from the Bana tribe in Key Afer (EL)

Hamer Mountains, which rise to a height of 1,707m on the western horizon. The only urban punctuation *en route*, known as **Arbore** after the predominant people there, is among the most rustic towns in the region, with the police station being perhaps the only building not constructed along traditional lines. The town lies at the convergence of several tribal boundaries, and it is also inhabited by Hamer and Borena people, who add a cosmopolitan South Omo flavour to the worthwhile **Saturday market**.

Arbore territory runs as far south as the Kenyan border and **Lake Chew Bahir**, a vast but little-visited saline sump whose existence remained little more than a rumour until Count Teleki arrived on its shore in April 1888. Teleki christened it Lake Stefanie (after the consort of his Hungarian sponsor Prince Rudolf) but the older name Chew Bahir – literally 'Ocean of Salt' – seems more apt. The lake is noted for its substantial fluctuations in water level and expanse: in the 1960s, it comprised 2,000km² of open water, but before and since it has more often been a rank swamp set in an otherwise dry basin. It is nominally protected within the vast **Chew Bahir Wildlife Reserve**, which supports low numbers of ungulates such as Grevy's zebra, greater and lesser kudu, gerenuk and Grant's gazelle, as well as lion, spotted hyena and various small carnivores. The permanent swamp at the **Gelana Delai River mouth** is inhabited by many thousands of flamingos, and a miscellany of storks, waterfowl and waders.

Hamer country: Turmi and Dimeka

With their characteristic high cheekbones, thick copper necklaces and elaborate costumes of beads, cowries and leather, the Hamer rank among the most readily identifiable of the South Omo. Their main towns are Turmi and Dimeka, which host compelling and colourful **weekly markets** on Monday and Saturday respectively, and will also reward anybody who settles into them for a few days. **Turmi** is the more important transport hub, lying at the pivot of the three main roads that run southwards from the road between Karat-Konso and Jinka road. In addition to the Monday market, a couple of smaller traditional Hamer villages lie within walking distance of Turmi, while the Kaske River, a short drive out of town, is rattling with monkeys and woodland birds. **Dimeka**, which lies 20km north of Turmi and 55km south of Key Afer along the road connecting these two towns, is larger and more built-up than Turmi, and less traditional, so only make the side trip on market day.

Omorate

Also known as Kalem, Omorate lies on the sweltering eastern bank of the Omo River at the terminus of a 72km road running west from Turmi. An archetypal tropical backwater, it is unexpectedly large, not at

Photography in South Omo

It is customary to pay to take photographs of people in South Omo, though the going rate varies from one person and one village to the next. For straight portraits, a one-off fee is asked, but be warned that the subject may count how many times you click the shutter and increment the fee accordingly – in other words, somebody who asks for birr 5 will demand birr 25 if you click the shutter five times – so if you want to spend some time photographing one particular person, it's best to explain this and agree a higher rate in advance.

Unfortunately, the 'pay-to-snap' mentality in South Omo has recently mutated into the rather presumptuous expectation that tourists should be willing pay to photograph any local who asks. This can sometimes create an unpleasant atmosphere: every person you walk past seems to yell '*faranji*', 'photo', 'birr' or a variation thereof, and some become quite hostile if you don't accede to their demand. Sadly, photography has come to dominate relations between travellers and the people of South Omo to the extent that any less voyeuristic form of interaction seems to be all but impossible. One way around this is to simply pack away your camera, and buy a few postcards instead.

all traditional in mood, and has suffered from economic stagnation ever since a grand agricultural scheme initiated with North Korean funds in the Mengistu era faltered to a standstill. It also functions as a minor border town, with pick-up trucks from goodness-knows-where in Kenya regularly appearing on the west bank of the Omo to unload mysterious parcels onto the small river ferry. The main cultural attractions are the **Dasanech villages** on the west bank, which can be visited using the self-same ferry. The road from Turmi is also pretty good for wildlife, with Guenther's dik-dik, gerenuk and plentiful birds in evidence.

Murelle

Set on the eastern bank of the Omo River, 55km north of Omorate and a similar distance northwest of Turmi, Murelle is the site of the most upmarket lodge in South Omo, a somewhat relative accolade but one that ensures it forms a popular base for people who opt to charter a flight into the region. It lies in a shady riverine grove fringing the Omo River, home to colobus monkeys and a profusion of birds, and the surrounding acacia scrub hosts fair numbers of antelope such as Guenther's dik-dik, gerenuk, Grant's gazelle and tiang, as well as the delightful bat-eared fox. It is also the best base for visits to **Kangatan**, which is the only accessible habitation of the Bumi, set above the

Mago National Park is known more for its Mursi villages than its wildlife. (M/A)

Get up-close to nature

PARADISE ETHIOPIA TRAVEL

Owing to our love of nature, we believe we can offer the best route through this land of incredible bio-diversity. Our trekking, cycling and horseriding trips in the Bale Mountains and the Omo Valley bring you closer to the fauna, flora and people of this unique region. Our special birdwatching, flori-culture, butterfly-watching

and coffee tours are unrivalled while our trips to seldom-visited villages and cultures allow you to visit markets and witness traditional ceremonies.

western bank of the Omo. The photogenic village of **Kolcho** is likewise accessible from Omorate; set in magnificent sand cliff overlooking a large sweep in the Omo River, the Karo inhabitants of Kolcho will gladly display their traditional face painting to visitors.

Mago National Park

Proclaimed in the 1960s, this 2,162km² park is bisected by the Mago River, which flows into the Omo on the park's southern boundary. It shares 5km of boundary with Omo National Park, but while these protected areas effectively form one ecological unit, crossing between them has been practically impossible since all bridges were swept away by flooding in 1997. Mago is the closest thing in Ethiopia to the renowned savanna reserves of east Africa, and its potential as a tourist attraction – marketed in combination with the fascinating cultures of South Omo – is immense. However, as things stand, most tourists to Mago are not there for the wildlife, but to visit one of several Mursi villages, which are famed for the lip plate worn by the women (see page 32).

In terms of wildlife, the likes of buffalo, elephant, lion, leopard, Grevy's zebra and reticulated giraffe are still present in Mago, but numbers are low and sightings are infrequent. More common are antelope such as Defassa waterbuck, gerenuk, tiang, bushbuck, Lelwel hartebeest, greater and lesser kudu and Guenther's dik-dik. Olive baboon are frequently seen, while the common savanna-dwelling patas and vervet monkeys are supplemented along the river by guereza, blue and DeBrazza's monkey – the last an isolated population of a species associated with the west African rainforest. More than 300 bird species have been recorded, with typical dry-country specials boosted by more localised birds such as Egyptian plover, Pel's fishing owl, black-rumped waxbill and dusky babbler. The park headquarters lie 115km drive from Murelle, a trip that takes around six hours, and they are connected to Jinka by a steep 40km-long road that takes two hours to cover in the dry season, and might be impassable after heavy rain.

Jinka

The administrative capital of the South Omo zone, end-of-the-road Jinka exists in virtual isolation from the rest of Ethiopia. Jinka has a rather quaint atmosphere that combines urban and rural attributes in equal proportion – and which of the two appears to the fore will depend largely on whether you've bussed or flown in directly from Addis Ababa or Arba Minch, or bumped and skidded uphill from the sultry backwaters of South Omo. It is a likeable enough town, with a large **Saturday market** that attracts traders from all over South Omo. Its only formal tourist attraction, perched on a hill overlooking the town centre, is the **South Omo Research Centre & Museum** (⊘ 08.00– 18.00 daily; ⓦ www.uni-mainz.de/Organisationen/SORC), an excellent anthropological museum that provides a useful overview of the various cultures of South Omo, including a selection of ethnographic movies.

271

Appendix 1

Language

Amharigna

Amharigna (pronounced *Amharinya*) is a semitic language derived from Ge'ez, the ancient Axumite language still used by the Ethiopian Orthodox Church. It's the first language of the Amhara people of north-central Ethiopia, and the *lingua franca* of the rest of the country. For visitors, it is possible to get by in English in most tourist areas, but it is very useful to know a few words of Amharigna, and most Ethiopians appreciate your linguistic efforts. For anybody serious about learning the language, *Amharic for Foreigners* by Semere Woldegabir is readily available in Addis Ababa, and Lonely Planet's *Amharic* phrasebook is also useful.

Amharigna, like most other African languages, is pronounced phonetically – the town name Bore is not pronounced like boar, but *Bor-ay*. It is worth noting that there is often no simple English transcription of Amharigna words, as evidenced by such extremes of spelling as Woldio/Weldiya, Mekele/Maqale, Zikwala/Zouqala and even Addis Ababa/Adees Abeba.

The magic word

A word that every visitor should know, *ishee* more or less means 'OK', but can be used in a variety of circumstances: as an alternative to the myriad ways of saying 'hello' or 'goodbye', to signal agreement, to reassure people, etc. This is not just a foreigners' short cut – conversations between Ethiopians often apparently consist of nothing more than two people bouncing *ishee*s backwards and forwards.

Greetings and farewells

Useful all-purpose greetings are *tadias* and *tenayistillign*, which basically mean 'hello, how are you?' In many parts of the country, the Arabic greeting *selam* – literally 'peace' – is in common use. To ask how somebody is, ask *dehnaneh?* to a male and *dehnanesh?* to a female. The correct response, always, is *dehena*, (pronounced more like *dena*) or *dehnanegn* – 'I am well'. Tens of other greetings exist, depending on the time of day and the sex and number of people you are speaking to, but there is little need for visitors to learn them. There are just as many ways of saying 'goodbye' or 'farewell' – *chau* (adopted from and pronounced like the Italian *ciao*) is fine in most circumstances, and often preceded with an *ishee*.

Some essentials

The first barrier to be crossed in linguistically unfamiliar surroundings is how to ask a few **basic questions** and to understand the **answers**. The answers first: *awo* means 'yes' and *aydelem* means 'no'. In casual use, these are often shortened to *aw* (pronounced like the 'ou' in our) and *ay* (pronounced like eye). Some Ethiopians replace their *aw* with a startling inhalation of breath.

In general travel queries, you'll often use and hear the words *aleh* ('there is') and *yellem* ('there is not'). To find out if a place serves coffee (*buna*), you would ask *buna aleh?* The response should be *aleh* or *yellem.*

Once you have established that what you want is in the *aleh* state, you can ask for it by saying *ifelegalehu* ('I want'). More often, Ethiopians will just say what they want and how many – *and buna* (one coffee) or *hulet birra* (two beers). It is not customary to accompany your request with a please, but you should always say *ameseghinalehu* ('thank you'), the response to which is usually *minimaydelem* ('you're welcome'). If you don't want something, then say *alfelagem* or simply shake your head.

In Amharigna, the word *no* means something roughly equivalent to 'is'. In Amharigna conversations, Ethiopians often interject a *no* much as we might say 'true' or 'really'. Needless to say, this can cause confusion if you say 'no' to somebody unfamiliar with English – they may well assume you are saying 'yes'.

The word for 'where' is *yet*, from which derive the questions *yetno?* ('where is?'), *wedetno?* ('to where?') and *keyetno?* ('from where?'). The word for 'what' is *min*, which gives you *mindeno?* ('what is it?'), *lemin?* ('why?'), *minaleh?* ('what is there?') and *indet?* ('how?'). *Meche?* means 'when?', which gives you *mecheno?* ('when is it?'), *man?* means 'who?' and *sintno?* means 'how much?'.

Some useful Amharigna words

again	*indegena*	banana	*muz*
and	*na*	beautiful	*konjo*
at	*be*	bed	*alga*
bad	*metfo*	beef	*yebere siga*

beer	*birra*	I	*ine*
big	*tilik*	in	*wust*
bus	*awtobus*	insect	*tebay*
but	*gin*	island	*desiet*
cart	*gari*	key	*kulf*
cent (or just		lake	*hayk*
money)	*santeem*	little	*tinish*
chicken	*doro*	luggage	*gwaz* or *shanta*
church	*bet kristyan*	me	*inay*
clean	*nitsuh*	meat	*siga*
coffee	*buna*	milk	*wotet*
cold	*kezkaza*	money	*genzeb*
come (female)	*ney*	morning	*tiwat*
come (male)	*na*	motor vehicle	*mekeena*
correct	*lik*	mountain	*terara*
cost	*waga*	Mr	*Ato*
country/area	*ager*	Mrs	*Weyzero*
cow	*lam*	Miss	*Weyzerit*
dirty	*koshasha*	much	*bizu*
donkey	*ahiya*	mutton	*yebeg siga*
egg	*inkulal*	near	*atageb* or *kirb*
enough	*beki*	newspaper	*gazeta*
Ethiopian	*Habesha*	nice	*tiru*
	or *Ityopyawi*	night	*lelit*
excuse (me)	*yikirta*	now	*ahun*
far	*ruk*	of	*ye*
fast	*fetan*	or	*weyim*
first	*andegna* or	orange	*birtukan*
fish	*asa*	peace	*selam*
food	*migib*	petrol	*benzeen*
foreigner	*faranji*	pig	*asama*
glass	*birchiko*	problem	*chigger*
go	*hid*	quickly	*tolo*
good	*tiru*	region	*bota*
he	*issu*	restaurant	*migib bet*
help	*irdugn*	river	*wenz*
here	*izih*	road	*menged*
horse	*feres*	room	*kifil*
hospital	*hakim bet*	salt	*chew*
hour	*sa'at*	sea	*bahir*
house (or any		she	*iswa*
building)	*bet*	shop	*suk*

short	*achir*	there	*iza*
shower	*showa* or	they	*innessu*
	metatebia bet	ticket	*karnee* or *ticket*
sleep	*inkilf*	today	*zare*
slowly	*kes*	toilet	*shintbet*
small	*tinish*	tomorrow	*nege*
sorry	*aznallehu*	very	*betam*
stop	*akum*	warm	*muk*
sugar	*sukwar*	water	*wuha*
tall	*rejim*	yesterday	*tilant*
tea	*shai*	you (female)	*anchee*
thank you	*ameseghinalehu*	you (male)	*ante*

Numbers

1	*and*	20	*haya*
2	*hulet*	25	*haya amist* (*hamist*)
3	*sost*	30	*selasa*
4	*arat*	40	*arba*
5	*amist*	50	*hamsa*
6	*sidist*	60	*silsa*
7	*sabat*	70	*seba*
8	*simint*	80	*semagnya*
9	*zetegn*	90	*zetena*
10	*asir*	100	*meto*
11	*asra and*	200	*hulet meto*
12	*asra hulet*	1,000	*shee*
		1,000,000	*meelyon*

Days of the week

Monday	*Segno*	Friday	*Arb*
Tuesday	*Maksegno*	Saturday	*Kidame*
Wednesday	*Irob*	Sunday	*Ihud*
Thursday	*Hamus*		

Festivals

New Year	*Inkutatash*	Easter	*Fasika*
Christmas	*Gena*		

Appendix 2

Selected further reading

Outside of the country, bookshops seldom stock many books about Ethiopia, but most of the volumes listed below are available through online sellers such as ⓦ www.amazon.com, ⓦ www.amazon.co.uk or ⓦ www.abebooks.co.uk. The Red Sea Press, one of the most prolific publishers about Ethiopia, has online ordering facilities at ⓦ www. africanworld.com, and Shama Publishers, with its ever-expanding selection of tantalising titles, should soon have similar facilities at ⓦ www.shamabooks.com. Within Ethiopia, the best places to buy local-interest books are Bookworld and the Africans Bookshop in Addis Ababa.

General

Batistoni, M and Chiari, P C *Old Tracks in the New Flower: A Historical Guide to Addis Ababa* Arada Books, 2004. A fascinating record of the early days of Ethiopia's capital, with illustrations and descriptions of several old buildings.

Beckwith, C and Fisher, A *Africa Ark* Harry N Abrams, 1990. One of the finest (and costliest) photographic books ever produced about Africa, this covers Ethiopia's traditional cultures, from South Omo to Tigrai, with text by Graham Hancock.

Golzábez, J and Cebrián, D *Touching Ethiopia* Shama Books, 2004. This sumptuous 400-page tome can't decide whether it wants to be a coffee-table book or something more authoritative, but succeeds on both counts.

Hancock, Graham *The Sign and the Seal* Heinemann, 1992. This account of the Ark of the Covenant's alleged arrival in Ethiopia is as popular with tourists as it is reviled by academics – an entertaining work, but its wilder assertions are difficult to verify.

Munro-Hay, Stuart *Ethiopia: The Unknown Land* IB Tauris, 2002. Site-by-site overview of the most popular antiquities, a superb companion to readers seeking detailed scholarly background information.

Nomachi, Kazyoshi *Bless Ethiopia* Odyssey Publications, 1998. A photographically creative work capturing typical ecclesiastical scenes from unusual and striking angles.

Pankhurst, Richard and Gerard, Denis *Ethiopia Photographed* Kegan Paul, 1997. A must for monochrome junkies, consisting of a wealth of photographs taken from 1867 to 1936, contextualised by Richard Pankhurst.

Travel accounts

Graham, John *Ethiopia off the Beaten Trail* Shama Books, 2001. This collection of informative and occasionally irreverent essays reflects its author's delight in exploring Ethiopia's less-travelled corners.

Henze, Paul *Ethiopian Journeys* Shama Books, 2001. Classic travel account of Ethiopia during the last years of the imperial era.

Kaplan, Robert *Surrender or Starve: Travels in Ethiopia, Sudan, Somalia and Eritrea* Vintage, 2003. A chilling journalistic travelogue detailing the political factors that hugely exacerbated drought-related famines in the Horn of Africa during the 1980s.

Pakenham, Thomas *The Mountains of Rasselas* Seven Dials, 1999. A vivid account of the author's failed attempt to reach the remote Ethiopian mountaintop where princes were imprisoned in the Gondarine period.

Rushby, Kevin *Eating the Flowers of Paradise* Flamingo, 1999. A fascinating book about the culture of *khat* consumption, half of which is set in Ethiopia.

Thesiger, Wilfred *The Life of my Choice* Harper Collins, 1987. Childhood reminiscences of growing up in Abyssinia, Haile Selassie's coronation, the liberation campaign in 1941, treks in the south of the country and a six-month journey through the Danakil in 1933.

Waugh, Evelyn *Remote People* Penguin, 1931. Witty travelogue detailing parts of Haile Selassie's coronation, plus travels in Djibouti and an account of the railway to Awash.

History and background

Bredin, Niles *The Pale Abyssinian* Flamingo, 2001. Highly readable biography of the explorer James Bruce.

Buxton, David *The Abyssinians* Thames and Hudson, 1970. A good general introduction to just about every aspect of Ethiopian history and culture, albeit slightly dated.

Henze, Paul *Eritrea's War* Shama Books, 2001. Written by a recognised expert on Ethiopian politics, this describes the recent border war between Ethiopia and Eritrea.

Henze, Paul *Layers of Time: A History of Ethiopia* Hurst, 2000. Highly approachable one-volume history, particularly good on modern events up to the fall of the Derg.

Kapuscinski, Richard *The Emperor* Random House, 1983. An impressionistic and compelling account of Haile Selassie's last days, transcribed from interviews with his servants and confidants.

Marcus, Harold *A History of Ethiopia* University of California Press, 1994. A very readable general history, summarising all the initiate needs to know over a flowing and erudite 220 pages.

Mezlekia, Nega *Notes from the Hyena's Belly: An Ethiopian Boyhood* Picador, 2002. A fascinating account of a boy's life in Jijiga and the coming of the Derg.

Pankhurst, Richard *The Ethiopians (People of Africa)* Blackwell Publishers, 2001.   .is reissued title by the doyen of modern Ethiopian historical writing provides an excellent introduction to Ethiopia's varied cultures and social history.

Plant, Ruth *Architecture of the Tigre* Ravens Education & Development Services, 1985. Hardback copies can be purchased from the author's granddaughter, Jasmine Petty, at a cost of £20+pp (© jasminepetty@ googlemail.com).

Tibebu, Teshale *The Making of Modern Ethiopia 1896–1974* Red Sea Press, 1995. An excellent and original overview of modern Ethiopia and its ancient cultural roots.

Zewde, Bahru *A History of Modern Ethiopia 1855–1974* James Currey, 1991. Pitched at the general reader, this book is accurate and well written, and available cheaply in most bookshops in Addis Ababa.

Art and music

Falceto, Francis *Abyssinie Swing: A Pictorial History of Modern Ethiopian Music* Shama Books, 2001. Irresistible document of the emergence of the jazz-tinged music scene that blossomed in the dying years of the imperial era, complete with monochrome photographs spanning 1868–1973.

Heldman, Marilyn et al *African Zion: The Sacred Art of Ethiopia* Yale University Press, 1994. Expensive but lavishly illustrated book covering the art of highland Ethiopia from the 4th to the 18th century.

Natural history

Ash, J and Atkins, J *Birds of Ethiopia & Eritrea* Christopher Helm, 2009. Hardcover bird atlas mapping the distribution of 872 Ethiopian and Eritrean species, with more detailed background information than any field guide.

Behrens, K, Barnes, K and Boix, C *Birding Ethiopia* Lynx, 2010. The ideal complement to a field guide or bird atlas, this is a perfect hands-on starting point for anybody planning a birding trip to Ethiopia.

Kingdon, Jonathan *The Kingdon Field Guide to African Mammals* Academic Press, 1997. The most detailed, thorough and up to date of several titles covering the mammals of the region, transcending all expectations of a standard field guide.

Last, Jill *Endemic Mammals of Ethiopia* Ethiopian Tourist Commission, 1982. Includes detailed descriptions of Ethiopia's seven endemic mammal species and races. A worthwhile purchase!

Redman, N, Stevenson, T and Fanshawe, J *Helm Field Guide to the Birds of The Horn Of Africa* Christopher Helm, 2009. The first dedicated field guide to a vast region dominated by Ethiopia, this is the one book that all birders to Ethiopia absolutely need.

Spottiswoode, C, Gabremichael, M and Francis, J *Where to Watch Birds in Ethiopia* Christopher Helm, 2010. An excellent complement to the same publisher's field guide and bird atlas, with detailed coverage and GPS readings for 50 key sites.

Index

Entries in *italic* indicate maps

Abba Garima Monastery 166
Abijatta-Shala National Park
  243–4
Abreha and Atsbeha 9
Abreha we Atsbeha 175
Abuna Abraham Debre Tsion 181
Abuna Gebre Mikael 180
Abuna Yemata Guh 180
Ad Hankara 165
Adaba-Dodola Integrated Forest
  Management Project 251–3
Adadi Maryam 126–7
Adama 124
Addis Ababa 106–18, *108*
  accommodation 110–11
  airport 110
  Arat Kilo 117–18
  city centre 112–15
  eating out 111
  Entoto Maryam 118
  history 109–12
  Institute of Ethiopian Studies
    118
  Kidane Mihret 116
  Kiddist Maryam 116
  Kiddist Selassie 116–17
  Mercato 116
  National Museum of Ethiopia
    118
  Piazza 115–16
  practicalities 110
  safety 109
  short trips from 120–9
  Siddist Kilo 117–18
  walking tour 112–15

Addis Ababa and surrounds 74,
  106–29, *120*
Adi Chewa Arbuta Insesa 176
Adigrat 173
Adwa 166
Afar people 235
Ahmed Gragn 12–13
Aliyu Amba 211
Ambo 128
Amharigna 272–5
Ankober 210–11
antelope 50–4
aquatic habitats 45–6
Arba Minch 248–50
Arbore 265–6
Arero 259
Ari 29
Ark of the Covenant 8, 25–7
Asheton Maryam Monastery 201
ass, African wild 55
Assaita 231–5
Aster Aweke 27
ATMs 95
Awash National Park 79,
  228–31
Awassa *see Hawassa*
Axum 75, 156–66
Axum Museum 160
Axum stelae field 161–2, *160*
Axumite Empire 8–9

Babile 225–6
Babile Elephant Sanctuary 226
Background information 3–33
Bahir Dar 132–43, *136*

Bale Mountains National Park 79, 253–4, 255
Bale Mountains and surrounds 251–9
banks 93–4
Bati 208
Battle of Adwa 16
Bet Abba Libanos (Lalibela) 198
Bet Danaghel (Lalibela) 196
Bet Debre Sina (Lalibela) 196
Bet Emanuel (Lalibela) 198
Bet Gebriel-Rafael (Lalibela) 198
Bet Giyorgis (Lalibela) 198–9
Bet Golgotha (Lalibela) 197
Bet Maryam (Lalibela) 196
Bet Medhane Alem (Lalibela) 196
Bet Mercurios (Lalibela) 198
Bet Meskel (Lalibela) 196
Biblical Ethiopia 6
Bilbilla 196–200
binoculars 85–6
birds 58–62
Bishoftu 78, 120–2
Bizunesh Bekele 26
Black Lion Museum 245
Blue Nile Falls 77, 142–3
Bole International Airport 110
Bumi 31
business hours 104

calendar 105
Chele Anka Waterfall 182
Chelekot 182
Chencha 250
Chew Bet 248
climate 37–40
climatic zones 38–9
clothing 82, 84–6
Coptic Church 25
credit cards 95
crocodile 56

cultural etiquette 105–6
culture 25–33

Daga Istafanos 140
Dallol 237
Danakil Depression 77, 234
Danquaz 149
Dasanech 31
Debark 150
Debre Birhan 210
Debre Birhan Selassie 149
Debre Damo Monastery 72, 173–4
Debre Libanos 124–5
Debre Liqanos Monastery 164
Debre Maryam Korkor 180
Debre Zeyit *see* Bishoftu
Dek Island 140
Dekatu 264
Derg, the 20–1
desert 41–2
Dessie 203–4
Dichioto 234
Dilla 247
Dimeka 267
Dinsho 254, 256
Dire Dawa 225
disabled travellers 82–3
Dodola 252
Dongar 165
Donkey Sanctuary 123
drinks 97–9
Dublock 248

Eastern Ethiopia 214–36, *216*
Eastern Tigrai 169–85, *169*
economy 23–4
Eli Dar Depression 234–5
email 101
Emperor Haile Selassie 17–19
Emperor Menelik II 15–6
Emperor Tewodros II 14–15

Emperor Yohannis IV 15
Empress Zawditu 16
entrance fees 87
Eritrea War 21–2
Erta Ale 234
Ethiopian Orthodox Church 25
Ethiopiques (CDs) 26
Eyesus Hintsa Church 183

Fasil Ghebbi 147
Fasilidas's Pool 148
flights to Ethiopia 80
food 95–7
foreign exchange 94
forest 43–4
further reading 276–9

Gaysay 256
Gebriel Tsilalmao 176
Gefersa Reservoir 128
gelada monkey 50
geography 26–46
Gesergiyo 264–5
Gheralta churches 71, 178, 180–1
Gigi 27
Gish Abay 143
Gishen Debre Kerbe Monastery 205
Goba 79, 252, 254, 259
Gobedra Lioness 165
Gondar 75, 144–9, 146
Gondar and the Simiens 144–53
Gondarine era 13–14
Gorgora 152–3
Guassa Plateau 208–10
Guder Falls 128
Gudit stelae field 165

habitats 41–6
Hamer 30
Hamer country 267

handicrafts 100, 101
Harar 72, 216–24, 220
Harar and the far east 216–27
Harenna Forest 257
Hawassa 245–7
Hawzien 178
Hayk 203–4
health 81–2, 90–5
hippopotamus 55
history 5–23
human evolution 5–6
Hyena Men of Harar 221, 224

ibex, Walia 54
internet 101
Italian occupation 17–18
itineraries 65–79

Jinka 262, 270

Kaleb and Gebre Meskel tombs 164
Karat-Konso 73, 261–4
Karo 31–2
Kebre Negest 8
Key Afer 265
khat 99
Kibran Gebriel 140
King Basen's Tomb 163
King Ezana 9
King Ezana's Park 163
King Gebre Meskel 9
King Kaleb 9
King Menelik I 7–8
King Solomon 7
King Yakuno Amlak 10, 11
Koko 265
Konso see Karat-Konso
Kosoye viewpoint 152
Kulubi 227
Kuskuam 148

Lake Abaya 248–50
Lake Abbe 234
Lake Abijatta 244
Lake Afrera 237
Lake Asale 237
Lake Chamo 248–50
Lake Chew Bahir 265–6
Lake Hawassa 245–7
Lake Hayk 203
Lake Langano 243
Lake Shala 244
Lake Tana monasteries 71, 138–42
Lake Tana Region 130–53, *132*
Lake Ziway 241–2
Lalibela 70, 187–201, *192*
Lalibela and the Northeast Highlands 184–210
language 272–5
lizards 57
Lucy (*Australopithecus afarensis* skeleton) 5
luggage 84–5

Mago National Park 269–70
Mahmoud Ahmed 26
Mai Shum 162–3
Makdala Hill 205–8
Manchiti rock art site 247
Maryam Tsion Church 162
Maryam Tsion Monastery 242
Mecheke 264
Medhane Alem Adi Kasho 176
medieval Ethiopia 9–11
Mekele 178–82
Meles Zenawi, President 21, 22
Melka Guda 259
Melka Kunture 126
Menegasha Forest 129
Mengistu Haile Maryam 19–21
Menz 208–10

modern Ethiopia 21–3
money 86–7, 93–4
monkeys 49, 50
Mount Abuna Yosef 201
Mount Kundudo 226
Mount Wenchi 128
Mount Zikwala 122–4
mountain habitats 46
Murelle 268
Mursi 32–3
music 26–7
Muslim–Christian War 11–13

Nakuta La'ab Monastery 200
Narga Selassie 140
Natural World 34–61
Nazret *see* Adama
Nechisar National Park 248–50
Negash 177
Negele Borena 259
Northeast Highlands 202–10, *186*
Northern Rift Valley 228–36
Nyala, mountain 53

Omorate 267–8
On the Ground 88–104
Organisation of African Unity 18

Panteleon Monastery 165
people 25–33
Periplus of the Erythraean Sea 8
photography 85–6, 267
Planning a Trip 62–86
predators 47
prehistory 5–6
primates 49, 50
public holidays 65

Queen Makeda 7
Queen of Sheba *see* Queen Makeda

Queen of Sheba's pool *see* Mai
  Shum
Queen Yodit 10, 11

religion 25–8
reptiles 56–7
Rift Valley lakes 79, 241–50
Robe 254

Sanetti Plateau 254, 256–7
savanna 42–3
Selassie Chapel (Lalibela) 197
semi-desert 41–2
Senkele Wildlife Sanctuary 245
Shashemene 244–5
shopping 99–100
Simien Mountains National Park
  76, 150–2
snakes 56, 93
Sof Omar Caves 258
Solomonic Dynasty 10
South Omo 29–33, 73, 260–70, *260*
Southern Ethiopia 239–70
Southern Rift Valley 241–50, *240*

Tana Chirkos 140
Teka Tesfai 176
telephone 100–1
television 100
TESFA 201
Tigrai 154–83, *156*
time 104–5
tipping 94
Tis Abay *see* Blue Nile Falls
Tiya stelae field 76, 127
Top 20 attractions 70–9
tortoise 57
tour operators 67–9
tourist information 80
traditional history 7–8
Tsemai 29

Tullo Guddo 242
Turmi 267
Tutu Fela stelae field 247
Tututi stelae field 247

Ura Kidane Mihret 140

Valley of Marvels 226
vegetation 41–6
visa 80

warthog 55
Web River Valley 256
Weita 265
when to visit 64–5
wildlife 46–61, 92–3
wolf, Ethiopian 48
Wolleka 149
women travellers 82
Wondo Genet 245
Wukro 174, 177
Wukro Chirkos 177

Yabello 79, 248, 259
Yangudi Rassa National Park 231
Yeha 76, 166–7
Yemrehanna Kristos 200
Yohannis Maikudi 181

Zagwe Dynasty 11
zebra 55
Zege Peninsula 140

Index

Index of advertisers

Ankober Palace Lodge 129
Heritage Plaza Hotel 237
Jerusalem Hotel 211
LAL Hotels & Tours 212
Lalibela Hudad Ecolodge 213
Sabana Beach Resort 271
Simien Lodge 153
Strawberry Fields 270

Index of featured tour operators

Abeba Tours Ethiopia 68, 229, 246
Amazing Ethiopia 68, 251
Awaze Tours 68, 137, 168, 189, 194–5, 223, 245
BJ Tours & Trekking 69, 139
Ethiopian Quadrants 69, 167, 175, 225
Paradise Ethiopia Travel 69, 151, 206–7, 268
Rainbow Tours 65, 69, 150, 205, 221, 232–3 254

First published June 2012
Bradt Travel Guides Ltd
IDC House, The Vale, Chalfont St Peter, Bucks SL9 9RZ, England
www.bradtguides.com
Published in the USA by The Globe Pequot Press Inc,
PO Box 480, Guilford, Connecticut 06437-0480

Text copyright © 2012 Philip Briggs
Maps copyright © 2012 Bradt Travel Guides Ltd
Photographs copyright © 2012 Individual photographers (see below)
Project Manager: Anna Moores

ISBN: 978 1 84162 434 1

British Library Cataloguing in Publication Data
A catalogue record for this book is available from the British Library

Photographs Alamy: Thomas Cockrem (TC/A), dbimages (DBI/A), Interfoto (I/A),
marka (M/A), PhotoStock-Israel (PS-I/A), Paul Strawson (PS/A); Patrick Bayens (PB);
Davide Comelli (DC); Alan Coogan (AC); Corbis: Chrisophe Boisvieux/Hemis (CB/
H/C), Gavin Hellier/Robert Harding World Imagery (GH/RHWI/C), John Hicks (JH/C),
Atlantide Phototravel (AP/C), Patrick Robert/Sygma (PR/S/C), Radu Sigheti/X00255/
Reuters (RS/X/R/C), Hugh Sitton (HS/C), George Steinmetz (GS/C); Yvon De Bruin
(YDB); Daniel Crapper (DCr); Dreamstime: Galyna Andrushko (GA/DT), Edwardje
(E/DT), Dirk Sigmund (DS/DT); FLPA: Neil Bowman (NB/FLPA), Patricio Robles
Gil/Minden Pictures (PRG/MP/FLPA), Michael Hollings (MH/FLPA), Imagebroker (I/
FLPA), Ignacio Yufera (IY/FLPA); Harlem Tours and Car Rental Information (HTCRI);
Ka Fai Kan (KFK); Jeff Kerby (JK); Eric Lafforgue (EL); Ros Pan (RP); Laura Rodolfi
(LR); Phil Reece (PR); Shutterstock: Galyna Andrushko (GA/S), JM Travel Photography
(JMTP/S), Trevor Kittelty (TK/S), Vulkanette (V/S); Henrik Stabell (HS); Superstock
(SS); Paulina Tervo www.awraamba.com (PT); Miguel Valverde (MV); Ariadne Van
Zandbergen (AZ); Wikipedia Commons (WC)

Front cover (Top, left to right) Danakil Depression (AZ); Child from the Erbore tribe
(EL); Gelada monkey, Simien Mountains (AZ); (bottom) Priest standing in entrance of
Abuna Yemata Guh rock-hewn church (AZ)
Back cover Golden-breasted starling (AZ); Mural in the Debre Sina Maryam Church
(AZ)
Title page Ethiopian wolf (AZ); Awash River with Afar settlement in the distance (AZ);
Painting in the Narga Selassie Monastery, Lake Tana (AZ)

Part & chapter openers
Page 1: Child from the Erbore Tribe (EL); Page 2: Stele in the Axum stelae field (DS/
DT); Page 3: Mural in the Debre Sina Maryam Church, Gorgora (AZ); Page 34: Little
egret, Laka Awassa (AZ); Page 35: Gelada monkeys (IY/FLPA); Page 63: Trekking in the
Simien Mountains (SS); Page 89: Hot springs in the Danakil Depression (AP/C); Page
106: Lion of Judah statue (AZ); Page 107: Kiddist Selassie Cathedral (SS); Page 130:
Fasil Ghebbi Fortress, Gondar (SS); Page 131: Lake Tana (MH/FLPA); Page 154: Mural
in the Abuna Yemata Guh Church (CB/H/C); Page 155: Man walking past cracked stele
in Axum (HS/C); Page 184: Gathering at the Bati market (AP/C); Page 185: Lalibela
church (GA/S); Page 214: Young Afar girl (EL); Page 215: Danakil Depression, 116m
below sea level (AZ); Page 238: Wooden grave markers, Konso (AZ); Page 239: Couple
from the Karo tribe (EL)

Maps David McCutcheon

Typeset from the author's disc by Artinfusion (www.artinfusion.co.uk)
Production managed by Jellyfish Print Solutions; printed in India